THE A TO Z OF DIGITAL PHOTOGRAPHY

By

DMITRIY BUSLOVICH

Please visit our website for the additional video content and
to connect with fellow photographers

www.digitalphotographycentral.com

United States

TABLE OF CONTENTS

PRACTICALITIES AND CONTINGENCIES   **324**

INTRODUCTION

Probably billions of people take pictures with some kind of camera regularly. It's such a common and ubiquitous activity/hobby that you can lose sight of what makes it and you, as a photographer, so special. Why would you want to learn more about it and become proficient with a camera?

1. It Lasts a Lifetime

You may shoot pictures with a smartphone, a compact camera or an entry-level DSLR or you may be an experienced professional making a living with multiple cameras, lens and other equipment. Whatever your level of photography you can pursue your passion and enjoy the experience from the first day you're able to hold a camera in your hands and throughout the remainder of your life.

What should excite you is that your perspective, your skills and the subject matter that attract you are likely to change as you age. In fact, you should purposely plan to revisit locations and environments you've previously photographed every 10 years or so because they will have changed as well as how you perceive them. With new skills and more experience, you're sure to discover angles and lighting conditions you couldn't recognize as a beginner.

2. A Life of Creativity

Being involved in a creative process has proven to be important to your mental health and acuity, especially at an older age. Few activities provide such a creative opportunity as photography. There are always new concepts and techniques to learn and equipment to use; and, although it is challenging, photography as a creative outlet doesn't require as much natural talent, education and practice as a musician, painter, sculptor or illustrator. You can be unable to create in any of these disciplines, but still experience the wonder of creativity as a photographer.

3. Technical Prowess

You may never learn or know as much as a professional about photography equipment, but to enjoy and to create with a camera, lens and other photo gear does require that you acquire some technical prowess. You may be all thumbs under the hood of a car, fixing a faucet or using woodworking tools, but as a photographer, you are a technician and will be considered such by many others. People with little interest in photography, other than to look at pretty pictures, will be astounded at your abilities to operate a digital camera successfully, determine a correct exposure manually, use lighting for more dramatic images and edit and manipulate images with photo software.

4. A Globetrotter

Although there is plenty to photograph in your backyard, in your neighborhood and city and throughout a "typical" day in your life, photography will always compel you to visit exotic, unfamiliar and spectacular places across the globe. Great creativity often springs from the challenge of photographing people and places you never seen. Plus, it's an opportunity to be more knowledgeable about geography, history, culture and nature.

5. A Vision Beyond

As you gain more experience with your camera, allow your creativity to flow free and learn from your mistakes, your photographic vision will evolve. Every day, mundane places and objects will slowly reveal other levels of existence and possibilities for exciting photos. It doesn't have to be your vision alone. By recognizing the new and interesting in the world around you, you'll be able to share it with others who don't have your visionary acumen.

6. The Right Kind of Popularity

As a photographer, especially one who has learned how to take above-average pictures, your popularity will increase; but it will be the right kind of popularity. People want to be with those who are creative and can show them new ways to see the world. You can brighten someone's day that has been otherwise dull. You can provide family members and/or friends with pictures that becomes part of their heritage, both to remind them of previous generations that have passed and to leave behind a record of their lives for future generations to revisit and marvel at the changes since. With social media, it's now very easy to enlarge your circle of picture lovers to encompass the entire globe as well as sharing tips and techniques with other photographers. You will also be contributing to reducing the barriers between people and cultures and promoting diversity as one of human's most positive attributes.

7. Reaching goals

Photography is a very goal-oriented activity, but you can accomplish much without your photos gracing the cover of National Geographic or becoming one of the world's most sought fashion photographers. The size of a goal reached is less important than your commitment to reaching it. This experience easily translates to other parts of your life: accomplishing a photographic goal teaches you how to accomplish others.

In addition, the entire process of advancing from very little knowledge about photography techniques and how to use the equipment to creating images that match your visions and thrills others is another accomplishment that can only boost your spirit.

8. An Open Road

Many people have filled their hands with their first camera thinking the only purpose was to take some common pictures during a family event or vacation. Something magical happens to some beginners, however. They discover a previously unknown passion for photography that leads to more creative results than they ever thought possible or even a complete change of career to a full-time professional. Photography doesn't just open your mind, but can open your life to incredible possibilities.

9. A Member of a Special Club

Photographers may be members of the biggest club in the world since there are probably billions of them. There are no specific dues, hazing ceremonies or secret handshakes. All it takes is a camera in your hands and a passion to record the passing parade of the world.

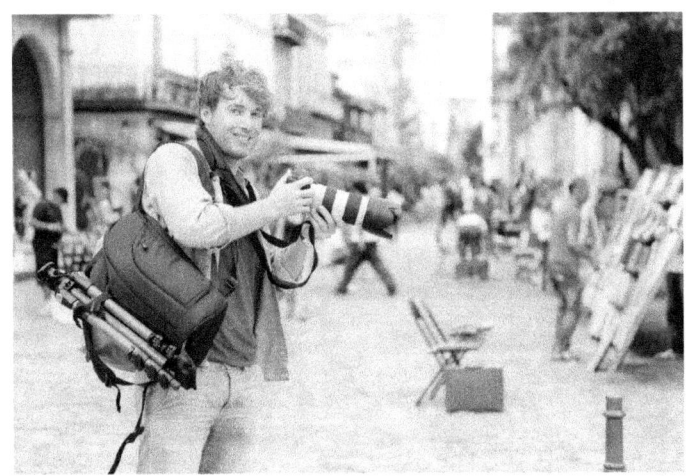

GETTING STARTED WITH DIGITAL PHOTOGRAPHY

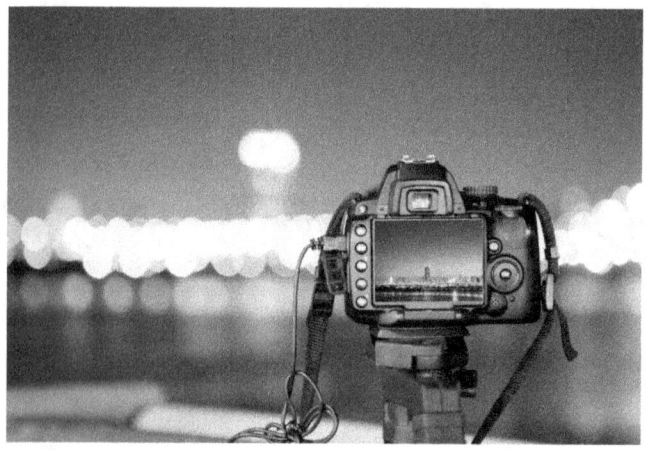

You are here because you're serious about becoming a better photographer and are excited about putting in the work that is required to improve your skills and create the best photos possible. Otherwise, you would save your money and take a vacation with your smartphone camera.

Whether digital photography will be a casual or serious hobby or you aspire to the possibility of becoming a professional, there are practical steps to choosing and buying your first digital camera. Understandably, many first-time DSLR buyers are attracted to a camera's clean, modern lines and the high-tech capabilities "under the hood". You can prove you are serious about becoming a DSLR photographer right from the beginning if you take a more mature approach. These three steps will ensure you'll spend your money wisely and choose the camera that matches your photography goals.

1. Ask yourself which types of subject matter interest you the most. Your answers may be landscape, wildlife, nature, portraits, sports/action, etc. If you're not sure, then study some of the images of the various types. Read about famous, successful photographers in each genre to understand better how they find, compose and capture their images.

2. Once you've selected the type (or types) of photography you want to shoot, then research what is the right lens (or lenses) required for each type. Many of those same successful photographers you study will explain which lenses they use. Then, buy the lens first.

3. Now, you're ready to select a DSLR camera that is compatible with the right lens. Not only will this help narrow the choices of cameras, but also make it clear how much you must spend to shoot the kind of subject matter that interests you. You might discover that it exceeds what you thought you would have to spend for a DSLR and lens. If that is the case, then you may have to be patient and save some money or still choose the right camera/lens combination, but lower-priced models. If price is still an obstacle, then don't overlook the option of buying a manufacturer- reconditioned camera. You can use it as a learning tool, and then it can become your backup camera once you buy a new one or resell it to the used camera vendor. Also, take a look at the section where we discuss the best way to buy used equipment as well.

DSLR CAMERA AND LENS COMBINATIONS FOR SPECIFIC PHOTOGRAPHY

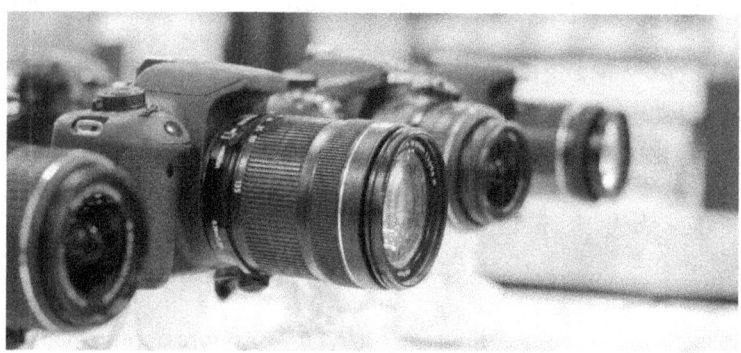

- **General photography** – If you haven't decided on a kind of photography that interests you the most, then it may be wise to start with basic DSLR camera/lens combination to gain some experience. Shooting a variety of photography subjects may then reveal a favorite that would require a specific camera/lens combination.

  In the Canon family, good choices are the EOS Rebel series of cameras. You can buy any of these DSLR camera models with a standard 18–55mm lens.

  Among your Nikon choices are the D3XXX and D5XXX cameras. All of these DSLRs are also available with Nikon's standard 18–55mm lens.

  Sony's general photography equipment include the A-series mirrorless cameras.

- **Landscape photography** – If your photographic interest is capturing both the spectacular and the subtleties of natural and city landscapes, then any of the DSLRs listed above will certainly serve you well;

however, you may want a different lens. Some of these include a 24–70mm, 18–135mm, 24–105mm, 28–135mm or 18–200mm. The reasons for these types of lenses will be explained in more detail in the landscape photography section.

- **Portrait photography** – To shoot pleasing portraits of people in casual settings and not a studio like a professional, many of the same cameras for general DSLR photography and the landscape photography lenses above are also good choices. Again, they portrait photography section will reveal why these are the best lenses to use.

- **Wildlife, sports and action photography** – Typically, there will be a big distance between you and wildlife, sports and action subjects, so you need telephoto lenses to bring the image closer. These include 55–250mm, 70-200mm and 70–300mm.

What are you going to be photographing? Look around you. What do you see? What are your passions, your hobbies? What have you taken pictures of in the past and enjoyed it? Nature, people, sports, architecture, food? Or all of the above? Are there certain things that you want to get out of photography? Do you want to make money from it? Are you into social media and just want to share your photography and wish it were better? Do you live in the city or in the country? Do you travel? Do you like landscapes or seascapes? Answering all these questions may be difficult but different equipment is required for different conditions.

The good news is, most of the cameras available today are quite capable of encompassing all of the subjects, with the proper lenses and accessories, and most of which can be bought for a reasonable price. When you get into the more expensive equipment with more bells and whistles, naturally price goes higher. Now you're entering the professional realm. This book provides not just a single stepping stone but many stepping stones for you to enjoy photography either as a career or a hobby. It opens up many roads that lead in many different areas unless you choose to focus on one area of photography.

Photography is a wide-open field of study, and you're not going to just learn how to take great pictures, you're going to develop a working knowledge of the world around you. You will see things in a different way. The dynamics of this world, it's form and function, are fascinating to us all. They become even more fascinating when we learn to realize that there is more to this world than meets the eye. Your eye not the eye of your camera. Although similarities abound, it is the differences that you are going to learn from. Welcome to the world of photography, learn and enjoy.

DOING YOUR HOMEWORK

Think of your camera as a highly advanced technological device, the same as your computer, smartphone or a tablet. Just as with these, you can't realize the maximum benefits of your camera without learning about and practicing all its major features, functions and capabilities.

One of the simplest ways to learn all you need to know about your camera is to do what too many new DSLR photographers fail to do: read the manual! It's been organized and written to take the least amount of time to understand how your camera works. Your camera manual is also your #1 reference, so by working through it the first time, it will be much easier to find the right sections when you do start shooting with it and need reminders.

Don't stop with the manual, however. Access additional resources, in the form of a book, video or online content to expand your knowledge. Videos are especially useful learning tools since the presenter will not only explain your camera's capabilities, but also show you where they are and how to use them. Assuming you've chosen a DSLR from one of the Big 3 manufacturers (Canon, Nikon or Sony), look for the free camera seminars that these companies conduct at local camera stores regularly.

No doubt, all of this homework will take some time and you might be chomping at the bit to start shooting with your new DSLR, but focusing on learning about your camera before shooting with it will pay long-term dividends and ensure your first images will be better.

The next three sections are critical and will address the topic that probably confuses more new DSLR photographers than any other: understanding the three parts of exposure: aperture, ISO and shutter speed.

TAKING CONTROL OF EXPOSURE: APERTURE

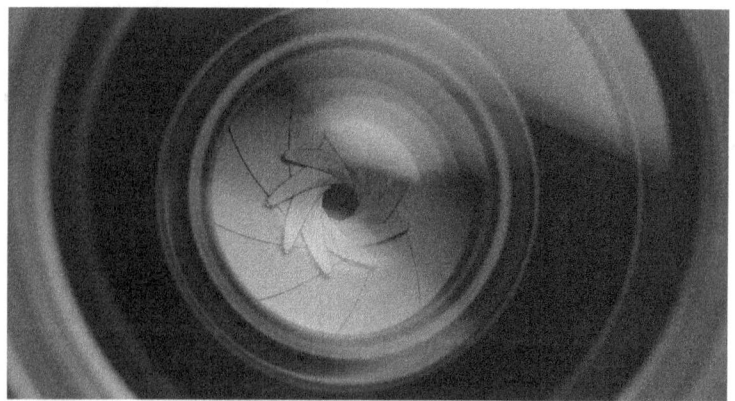

One of the primary advantages of DSLR photography is that you have the opportunity to take more control of the picture-making process than you had with a smartphone or a compact camera. Sure, it was easy and convenient to shoot with these devices because you only had to frame an image how you wanted it and push a button.

Choosing to upgrade to a DSLR camera is somewhat like choosing to go to college. You were required to attend grades 5–12, but because college is a choice, you are much more responsible for earning a degree. The same goes for DSLR photography: you must assume significantly more responsibility for the quality of your images versus those that were created automatically by a camera phone or compact camera.

"Graduating" to a DSLR camera requires that you commit more time to learning how to use it and that means there is a long list of "courses" you must take. First on the list is Exposure 101; and the three parts of the course are aperture, shutter speed and ISO. The challenge you will face, as millions of new DSLR photographers have faced before you, is to understand how these three parts work together.

- Aperture is the size of the opening of the camera's iris, which controls how much light enters the lens and camera.

- Shutter speed indicates how fast or slow the camera's shutter opens, and then closes.

- ISO is a measurement of how sensitive the camera's sensor is to the light striking it.

Each is dependent on the other, but aperture and shutter speed have a closer relationship than ISO to the other two, although ISO is still very important. Once you have a firm grasp of their relationship, you'll be able to create the unique images that only now exist in your head. (Shutter speed and ISO will be explained in detail in separate sections.)

Aperture is a good place to start because you use an aperture mechanism thousands of times every day: the iris in your eyes. This opening becomes smaller when you are outside on a sunny day, for example, especially if you're on a beach. Not only is bright sunlight entering your eyes directly, but also reflecting off the sand. Conversely, if you're outside on a moonless night far from the bright lights of the city, the opening of each iris will be its largest to allow as much of the dim light as possible to enter your eyes.

The lens of virtually every camera works essentially the same: Inside is an iris, or diaphragm, that consists of a number of overlapping leaves to create a round opening similar to the iris in your eye. Since DSLR cameras have an automatic exposure mode like a camera phone or compact camera, the camera will read the light entering the lens and automatically open or close the diaphragm according to how much light is required for a good exposure.

What makes DSLR photography so exciting and more creative is that your camera will also operate in a manual exposure mode, which means you must choose and set the iris opening. The various openings of the lens diaphragm are often known as "stops," or f-stops, since each is a position on a scale. You'll find this scale on the f-stop ring on the lens. A mathematical formula is used to calculate the opening for each f-stop, based on the focal length of the lens.

Generally, the f-stop scale on a lens could include any of the following stops: f/1.4, f/1.8, f/2, f/2.8, f/3.5, f/4, f/5.6, f/8, f/11, f/16 and f/22. The f-stop scale for any specific lens depends on its focal length. Because mathematics is almost always logical, a result of the formula is that the next f/stop number on the scale is one-half of the opening of the previous f/stop number. This can seem a bit complicated and counterintuitive because the number 1.4 is not half of 1.8. Obviously, the opposite is also true: f/1.4 is twice the opening of f/1.8, which means when you set your lens to the f/1.4 stop, you are allowing twice as much as light to enter the lens than at f/1.8.

Aperture, therefore, is your first point of exposure control. You choose the f-stop and the amount of light that enters the lens and camera. Of course, this begs the question, "Why would I want to control the amount of light entering the lens and camera?" When it comes to the iris in your eye, your brain decides how large or small to make the opening based on the amount of light striking the optic nerve at the back of your eye. With your DSLR camera (in manual exposure mode), you must become the brain of the camera and decide which f-stop, or lens opening, is appropriate, based on how much light is present in the scene or reflecting off the object or subject you want to photograph.

Just as the iris in your eye works, you would want to choose a small f/stop number on a lens (f/1.4, f/1.8, f/2.0, etc.), or a larger opening, when the light level is low and a large f/stop number (f/8, f/11 or f/22) when you are shooting where the light is bright. For example, if you are photographing a street party or event at night with some lights, you need f/1.4 or any of the other small f/stop numbers, so more of the available light can enter the lens. Conversely, if you're on vacation at the beach on a very sunny day, then you need a large f/stop number, because there is so much light, you don't need very much of it to result in a proper exposure.

Shutter speed will be our next topic and it will include more about its relationship to aperture and why you must be always thinking of the two together.

TAKING CONTROL OF EXPOSURE:
SHUTTER SPEED

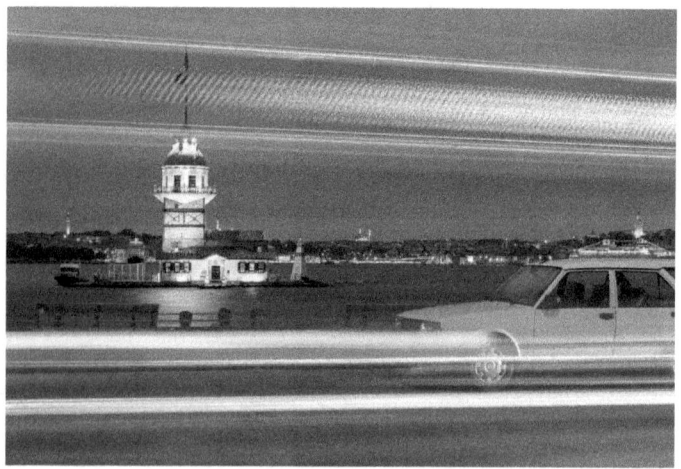

Of the three exposure components – aperture, shutter speed and ISO – aperture and shutter speed are like dancing partners. Each must be synchronized with the other, moving in balance and harmony. When you can see their performance as a whole, you will be able to direct the dance and use its creativity to produce above-average images and eventually capture the unique vision you see in your head.

The shutter is a mechanical system that is located just in front of your DSLR camera's sensor, which puts it between the iris, or diaphragm, in the lens and the sensor. As described in the companion Aperture section, the size of the iris opening regulates how much light is directed through the lens toward the sensor. Before the light reaches the sensor, the speed at which the shutter "curtains" open and then close also regulates the amount of light striking the sensor.

Other than water and oxygen, light is the most important natural phenomenon critical to life, as we know it. We mostly associate light with that which is generated by the sun, and sunlight triggers the process called photosynthesis, which results in the growth of plant life and the foods it provides. Light, as you might know, is represented by a spectrum that relates to color and its temperature, and without going into details of the science here, humans can only see part of that spectrum. Of course, to create and view photographic representations of life, a camera must be sensitive to the same part of the spectrum.

Because Earth resides it what is called the Goldilocks Zone, the light we experience from the sun is warm, comfortable and generally safe, so we often forget how powerful it is. Even though we live where the light "is just right," it's still powerful. Combine that power with the sensitivity to light that is built into a camera sensor and very little light must be reflected off the scene or subject you are photographing and into a lens, and then strike the sensor.

Even though it is reflected light and only some of the rays enter the lens, the amount of time required to reproduce the scene or subject as a digital image on the sensor is generally a very small fraction of a second. The primary purpose of the shutter is to allow the light to strike the sensor for those instant moments of time. For example, on a bright, sunny day with many reflective surfaces in a scene, such as water, sand and/or a flat, green field, the shutter may open and close in 1/500th, or even 1/1000th of a second. In addition, even the shutters in beginner DSLR cameras can operate as fast as 1,4000th of a second.

This means the shutter in your DSLR camera is quite a delicate, but very durable mechanism. Without explaining the details of a shutter's operation, it consists of two curtains and the mechanical controls to open and close them at quite incredibly fast speeds. In addition, shutters must also have a long life and, in general, most can operate 100,000 times; some professional models as many as 200,000 times.

Just as the aperture ring with its f-stops is found around the lens of the camera, the shutter speed dial, often on the top plate of the camera body, is where you select shutter speeds. This is another good reason to read/study your camera's manual, so you know where the dial is located and to learn what the various markings represent. A good rule of thumb is that 1/30th of a second or slower (1/15th, 1/10th, etc.) is a slow shutter speed. Just as a bright, sunny day requires a very fast shutter speed, such as 1/500th of a second or faster, it should make sense that a slow shutter speed is needed when the light level is low, such as shooting indoors, or during early morning or late evening hours.

It's also true that if you try to take a photograph holding your camera in your hands and at a slow shutter speed, then the picture is likely to be blurry and not its sharpest. Experienced DSLR photographers under the right conditions may be able to produce a sharp image at 1/30th of a second, but as a beginner you won't. When the light is so low that you must choose 1/30th of a second or slower, you'll need a tripod to keep your camera steady and a shutter release cable or remote shutter release. Pushing the shutter release button on the camera at these slower speeds will likely cause the camera to move ever so slightly, but more than enough to make it impossible to capture a sharp image. When shooting at those fast shutter speeds, 1/500th or faster, you can hand hold your camera and produce sharp images. Even sports photographers with very long and heavy telephoto lenses can capture sharp images when photographing outdoor sports or action because they need very fast shutter speeds for the bright light and/or to stop the action of an athlete or racecar in motion.

The relationship of one shutter speed is quite straightforward and seemingly counterintuitive like f/stops. For example, 1/250th of a second is half as slow as 1/500th, or 1/500th is twice as fast as 1/250th or four times faster than 1/125th.

UNDERSTANDING THE CHOREOGRAPHY OF THE APERTURE-SHUTTER SPEED DANCE

Remember, your ultimate goal is to determine and set the correct exposure for whatever scene or subject you are shooting; and understanding the coordinated dance of aperture and shutter speed helps you choose the correct exposure. The often-confusing concept of this dance for beginner DSLR photographers is that there can be multiple aperture-shutter speed dance partners on the floor, with each partner different, but their combinations identical.

For example, you're shooting during the brightest period of a sunny day, generally at noon or the early afternoon. Because the light is so bright, you want a rather small iris opening, or aperture, in the lens and a fast, even very fast, shutter speed. A possible correct exposure under these conditions could be f/16 at 1/500th of a second. Remember, a large f-stop number, 16 in this case, is a very small opening. Hold on tight because f/11 at 1/1000th of a second could also be a correct exposure. Because you've selected an aperture opening that is twice as large, f/11 compared to f/16, you must compensate by choosing a shutter speed that is twice as fast, 1/1000th compared to 1/500th. Theoretically, this also means that an aperture of f/8 and a shutter speed of 1/2000th would also be a correct exposure, or f/5.6 and 1/3000th. Now, in practical terms, some of these combinations are not the best for reasons that will be explained later in the book.

You can conduct a little test by shooting the same scene (a bright, sunny one is probably best) at a number of these aperture-shutter combinations, and then compare them on a computer screen. The exposures should all be essentially identical.

The final part of the exposure equation is ISO, which does affect the correct exposure too, but not as much as aperture and shutter speed; however, that is our next subject.

TAKING CONTROL OF EXPOSURE: ISO

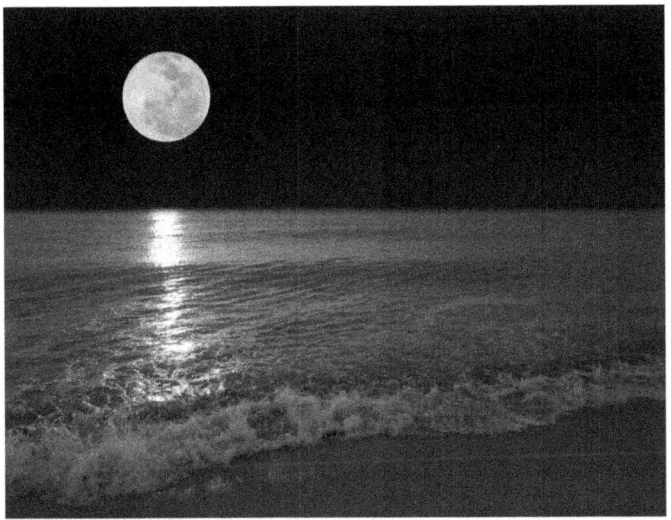

At its core, photography works by capturing the light reflected from objects or subjects; so a photograph is actually a picture of light, a representation of the real world painted with light. The concepts of aperture and shutter speed, as two parts of the exposure formula, are relatively easy to understand, as they control the amount of light that enters the lens (aperture) and then the light that is allowed to enter the camera (the shutter) and strike the sensor. The iris, or diaphragm, in the lens and the shutter, with its moving curtains, in the camera serve as mechanical light gateways.

They don't interact with the light, but regulate how much passes through their gates.

The sensor, however, is where the magic happens. Its interaction with light results in a digital image (the equivalent of a film negative) being captured. This interaction can also be controlled by the third component of the exposure formula, or ISO. First, ISO is an acronym for International Standards Organization. It established a standard measurement of the sensitivity of a digital camera's sensor to light, or the speed with which it responds to light, so it would be the same for all digital cameras manufactured throughout the world. When all photography was film-based, ASA was the equivalent measurement, and is the acronym for the American Standards Association, the body that established the ASA standard.

As the previous sections explained, aperture is measured in f-stops and shutter speed in fractions of a second. In neither case is there a "perfect" or even an "average" aperture or shutter speed; however, the ISO scale has a starting point, expressed as ISO 100. For most of the photos you take, you can set your camera to ISO 100 and leave it there. This was the common standard that the international body selected because the science behind it revealed that a photograph shot at the ISO 100 setting produced a smooth-looking image with no easily visible digital noise.

Digital noise is the same as the graininess that is visible in some photos shot on film. Either is produced when a higher ISO number is selected because at those higher settings the sensor becomes more sensitive to the light, which results in an image with visible noise. In digital photography, noise is often first noticed in any shadows in the image in the form of multi-colored dots. When film photographers shoot at a higher ISO setting, they often refer to it as "pushing" the film, or pushing it to respond to light at a faster speed.

THE MATHEMATICS OF ISO

Some digital cameras have ISO settings less than 100, typically 50, but this is usually a setting that is only useful for professional photographers. Many entry-level DSLRs, such as the Canon EOS Rebel series, have a range of ISO settings from 100 to 6,400, for example, that operate automatically; however, you can manually set ISO to 12,800, and even 25,600. Just as there was a mathematical relationship for aperture and shutter speed value, there is one for ISO too. Each setting point is twice the previous number, so the typical ISO settings are 100, 200, 400, 800, 1,600, 3,200, 6,400, etc. At ISO 200, for example, only half as much light is required to register an image on the sensor that has an equivalent exposure as an image shot at ISO 100. At ISO 400, the sensor is only one-fourth as sensitive to light as at ISO 100, etc.

The mathematics involved extends to the relationship of ISO and shutter speed, much the same as the relationship of aperture and shutter speed. As explained in the shutter speed section, there can be more than one aperture-shutter speed combination that will be a correct exposure – f/16 at $1/500^{th}$ a second is the same as f/11 at $1/1000^{th}$ of a second. Similarly, there are multiple ISO-shutter speed combinations that will result in a correct exposure WHEN THE APERTURE, OR F-STOP, IS THE SAME. An ISO setting of 100 and a shutter speed of $1/125^{th}$ of a second is the same as an ISO setting of 200 and a shutter speed of $1/250^{th}$ of a second. An ISO of 200 means only half as much light is required to produce a similarly exposed image as ISO 100, so the shutter speed must double, from 1/125th to 1/250th, so the curtains open and close faster, allowing less light to strike the sensor.

CHOOSING AN ISO TO MATCH LIGHTING CONDITIONS

As a beginner DSLR photographer, you can set the ISO on your camera to the "normal" of 100 for most of the photos you'll shoot. On a bright, sunny day shooting outdoors, you want to restrict the amount of light striking the sensor because there is so much of it. Of course, you can control the light with your aperture, or f-stop setting, and the speed at which the shutter operates, but ISO will also help.

One of the most important skills a DSLR photographer can learn is to be always conscious of the current light level. Eventually, that bright, sunny day will become late afternoon, sunset and then twilight, which, of course, means there is less light available to strike the sensor and produce an exposure that results in an acceptable image. This is also what happens when you move inside a building, even on a bright, sunny day, but especially at night when you are totally dependent on the artificial lighting of the interior space, be it your living room, a reception hall or a basketball arena.

It's when you find yourself shooting under low levels of light that you MAY need a higher ISO setting to "push" the speed at which the sensor responds to light. "May" is the operative word here, as, of course, you can choose an aperture-shutter speed combination that will also allow you to capture a correctly exposed photo; however, there are limits to what you can do with just aperture and shutter speed.

For example, if the light is so low that you are forced to use a shutter speed 1/30th of a second or slower, then you will probably not be able to hand hold your camera without producing blurry images. If your composition is a beautiful sunset on the ocean or an outdoor scene during twilight (after the sun has disappeared, but there is still some light leaking over the horizon), then you'll probably want to use a tripod. You'll be able to shoot at a slow shutter speed and not need a higher ISO setting, which could cause your beautiful sunset to have visible digital noise.

There may be occasions when you are shooting indoors, such as parties, weddings, receptions, etc., and it isn't appropriate or you're not allowed to use a flash. (The light from a flash unit has its own effect on aperture, shutter speed and ISO, but that explanation is in the one of the future topics.) A tripod doesn't work well in such situations either, so to use a shutter speed fast enough to hand hold your camera, you will likely have to choose a higher ISO setting.

Another example is the challenge facing sports photographers when shooting indoor sports in a large hall or arena, such as basketball. They must use a faster shutter speed not only because the light is low, but also because they want to freeze the action of the quickly moving players, so their images are sharp. Sports photographers may have to shoot at ISO 800 or even higher, so they can use that faster shutter speed. They must be willing to accept some digital noise to capture the images their editors are expecting.

There are a number of other shooting situations or compositional goals that require a thorough understanding of and an ability to choose the right ISO setting, in combination with aperture and shutter speed.

MASTERING DEPTH OF FIELD

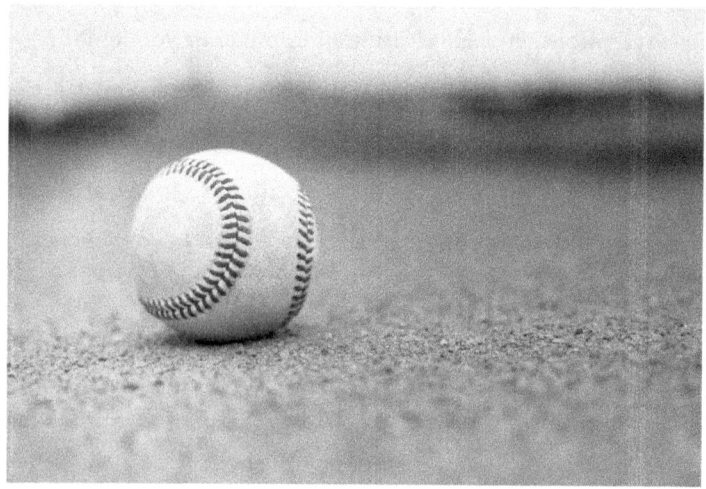

The physical laws of this universe dictate that we exist in a three-dimensional world: height, width and depth (or for you mathematically inclined, the X, Y and Z axes). These laws seem to be suspended for photography because the images your camera captures are two-dimensional representations of our three-dimensional environment. Depth is missing – well, sort of – our brains are able to "recreate" the third dimension, or depth, when we view a photo although it's not actually there.

The concept of depth of field is relatively easy to understand: there are objects in the foreground of a photo, the mid-ground and the background.

Each resides in a different plane or layer of the image. You decide which object or subject in which plane or layer will be in focus by choosing a specific f/stop or aperture. The trickier part of depth of field is that some portion of the space in front of and behind the in-focus object or subject will also be in focus. How much of that depth appears in focus depends on a number of factors, one of the most important the aperture setting you choose for the lens.

Before explaining the relationship of aperture and other factors to depth of field, it's important to understand its origins. Prior to the Renaissance of the 14th, 15th and 16th centuries, stone carvings, drawings and paintings depicted all objects or subjects as being the same size. During the Renaissance, however, painters "discovered" the concept of perspective, which in its simplest terms means that the more distance between you (or your point of view) and any objects and subjects the smaller they appear. Perspective also refers to a diminishing point on the horizon to which all lines appear to gather. The classic example is standing astride railroad tracks and, although they are parallel where you are standing, they appear to move closer and closer the farther you look into the distance until they appear at just one point on the horizon.

CONTROLLING DEPTH OF FIELD WITH APERTURE

What you learned in the previous section about aperture is about to become useful because the aperture you choose directly affects the depth of field in your photos. Without boring you with the mathematics, the "rule" is that there is less depth of field at the widest lens openings, or f/1.4, f/1.8, f/2.0, etc. and more depth of field at the narrowest lens openings, f/8, f/11, f/16, etc. With this knowledge, you're able to control how much of the total depth of your image appears to be in focus – and this is important for specific kinds of photography. Experimentation is the best method to learn and understand depth of field and its relationship to aperture.

- **Portraits** – In this example, you want to shoot a pleasing, but casual portrait of a friend (or significant other) outside with a background that is mostly trees and their branches and green leaves. To give the photo as much three dimensionality as possible and separate the portrait subject from the background, you would want to select an aperture setting that causes the background not to be in focus. You'll learn through practice that the smallest f/stops (largest openings) will probably create too narrow of a depth of field; so narrow, in fact, that your subject may not be totally in focus. Using bigger f/stops (smallest openings) will increase the depth of field and likely bring the trees in the background more into focus than you would want.

Another concept at work here is what is called "bokeh". It simply refers to the quality of the out-of-focus blur of the background. A nice, pleasing blur is your goal, especially for portraits because it will improve the three-dimensionality of the photo and make it appear your subject is projected well in front of the background.

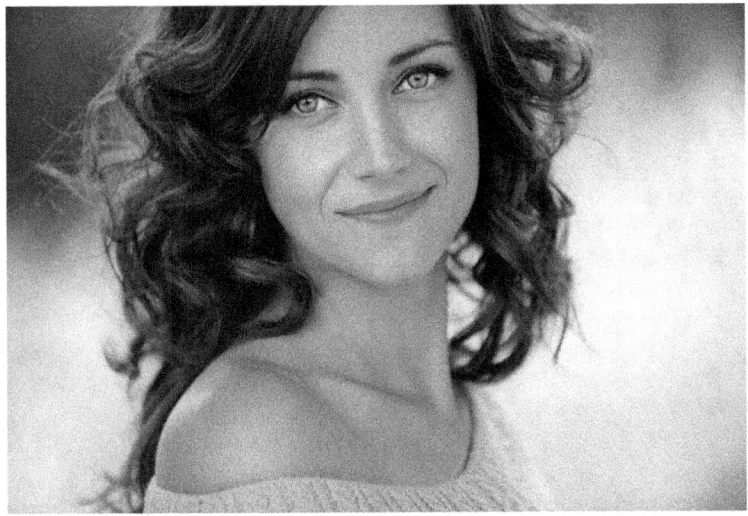

- **Landscapes** – If you study the best landscape photos, then you may notice that there is often a smaller point-of-interest in the foreground – a rock formation, a small tree or bush, a bed of wildflowers or a small water feature. In contrast, the remainder of the photo may be a grand landscape, with a river or large lake or an expanse of desert in the mid-ground and a mountain range or spectacular sky as the background. Landscape photographers will often shoot with a wide-angle focal length to include all these elements in the photo and place the camera at a low angle to see the smaller point-of-interest in the foreground. Most importantly, they will choose a high-number f/stop to create as much depth of field as possible because they want the foreground, mid-ground and background all to appear to be in focus.

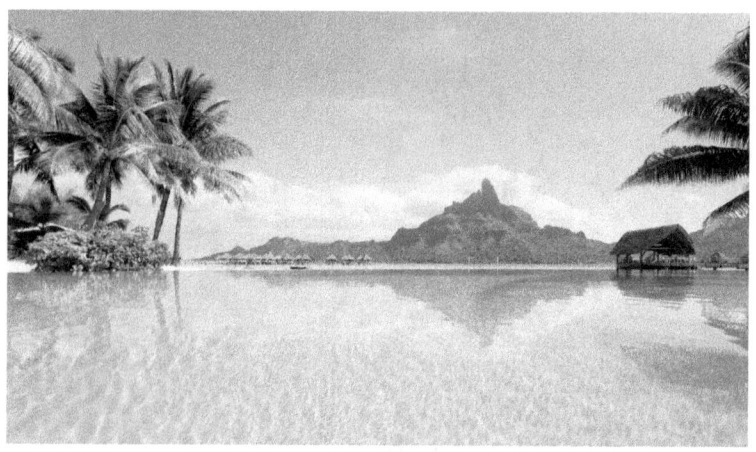

- **Sports and Action** – As mentioned in the Aperture section, sports and action photographers, especially when shooting outside, need a very fast shutter speed (1/500th, 1/1000th, 1/2000th, etc.) because typically there is so much light illuminating a playing field or racetrack. Plus, a fast shutter speed is required to freeze the movement of the athlete or racecar or racehorse. The strong sunlight also means the photographer must use a small aperture opening (large f-stop number), which creates a deeper depth of field. The challenge is to use the aperture that provides enough depth of field, but not too much because the photographer of a football game, for example, doesn't want the player in the foreground or mid-ground to be lost against a colorful background of fans in the seats. An aperture-shutter speed combination of f/16 at 1/500th of a second may result in too much depth of field, so f/11 or f/8 may be needed, which would change the shutter speed to 1/1000th or 1/2000th. That's OK because the photographer wants a fast shutter speed to freeze any action.

As mentioned in the ISO section, sports photographers shooting inside arenas for basketball and hockey, for example, must often choose a higher ISO setting than the "norm" of 100 because they need a faster shutter speed to freeze movement or action. These photographers may also select a wider aperture opening (smaller f-stop) because the light is low; however, they also want to control the depth of field. Their best f-stop may be f/5.6 or f/8, so the background is out of focus, but this will likely mean a higher ISO setting is required.

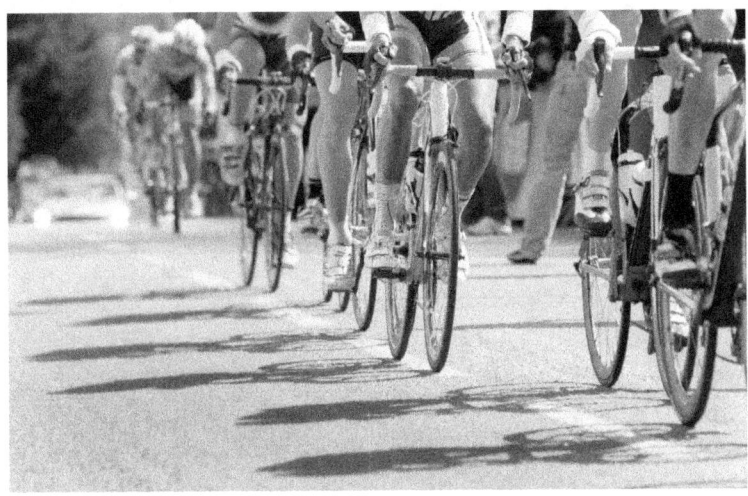

An excellent learning exercise is to shoot a series of photos of these different types of photography at a variety of aperture, shutter speed and ISO settings, and then compare them on a computer screen.

LEARNING HOW TO READ LIGHT

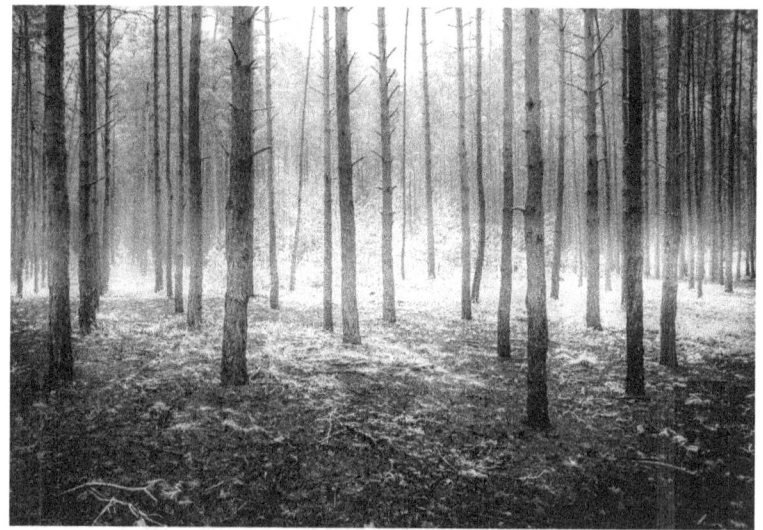

Nothing is more important to producing excellent photographs than determining and selecting the correct exposure values – aperture, shutter speed and ISO – for each image. Previous sections explained each of these three components of a photographic exposure, but this one focuses on how you read the light to know what the correct exposure is.

Virtually all digital cameras have a built-in light metering system. As light travels through the lens, it first strikes the mirror and reflects the light to a second sensor in your camera, the metering sensor. It reads the light and automatically selects the right exposure, so the light that eventually strikes the imaging sensor creates a properly exposed digital image.

Most metering sensors operate in one of four modes. They may have slightly different names, depending on the camera brand, but function essentially the same. For example, in Canon EOS DSLRs, the four metering modes are spot, partial, center-weighted and evaluative.

- **Spot metering** – As the name implies, the spot metering mode only reads the light at the very center of the image frame, or approximately 1 to 2 percent of the entire photo. If you're a beginner photographer, then you are less likely to use the spot-metering mode. Professionals and serious amateurs use it for portraits and macro photography, so the primary object/subject is precisely exposed.

- **Partial metering** – This mode is essentially the same as spot metering, except the partial metering mode reads the light from a bigger "spot," approximately 6 to 10 percent of the exact center of the image frame. Again, portrait and macro photographers are more likely to use the partial metering mode.

- **Center-weighted metering** – This is the "standard" metering mode, as it reads the light across the entire image area, with an emphasis on the object or subject in the middle of the frame. As a beginner, hobbyist or enthusiast DSLR photographer, you can set your camera to center-weighted metering and leave it there for all the casual or general photos you   take.

Evaluative metering – This metering mode also reads the light in the entire area of the image, but recognizes the point of focus wherever it might be in the frame and adjusts for proper exposure at that spot.

Professional photographers are more likely to use evaluative metering because the most important object or subject in a composition may not be in or near the center of the frame.

THE SCIENCE OF 18% GRAY

The goal of your camera's metering system is to produce at 18% gray tone of the scene, object or subject you're photographing. The 18% gray tone represents the average light in most photographs. It was determined with a mathematical formula that is unnecessary to explain here, but it's based on the average light reflected from new, clean snow, which is approximately 95% of all the light, and an undisturbed sooty surface, from which only 3% to 4% of the light is reflected. This average is 18%.

It's important to understand that the light meter in your camera doesn't distinguish the surface of one object or subject in your photo from another. Whether it's skin tone, light or dark, or a green leaf or red door, the meter will select an exposure that produces an 18% gray tone.

The metering system in your DSLR camera will be quite accurate for those casual and general photos, but it struggles whenever it is confronted with the extremes of light: a bright sunset, a person with the sun behind him or her, low light inside or outside at night or a person of color.

MANUAL LIGHT METERING

As your photography skills advance and you are ready for new challenges where the light levels may be very bright or low and dark, you'll want to learn how to use two manual metering systems.

The first is the photographic gray card, with a surface that accurately reflects an 18% gray tone. For example, you are composing an outdoor portrait of a person in a partially shaded area. You'll need an assistant to hold the card where you plan to position your portrait subject and at the same angle to the primary light source that will illuminate the subject. Point your camera at the card from the same position you will shoot the portrait, so the meter can read the light and select an exposure you know will be extremely precise.

The other light-reading tool is a separate, or hand-held, light meter. It works differently than the meter in your camera, although a separate meter will be as accurate as an 18% gray card. Instead of a reading of the light reflecting off the object or subject, as your DSLR camera does, the separate light meter reads the incident light, which is the light striking the object or subject. When you use a separate light meter, you point it at the source of the light illuminating the subject, not at the subject, which would read the reflective light.

"LOOK MA, NO METER!"

At this point, you are probably ecstatic that this light meter business is almost totally automatic. If that is so, then you need a mindset checkup. When you entered the world of DSLR photography, you made a commitment to improve your skills, take better pictures and never stop learning. Of all the advice the greatest living photographers offer, most often the first is "Never stop learning."

One of the most important DSLR skills you can learn is not to rely solely on what the camera is telling you; as brainy as it is, your brain is better and should be fully contributing to the process of taking better pictures.

The #1 reason to learn about exposure and how it works is so you are able to enter any environment, observe the light conditions and come very close to selecting the correct exposure without any input from your camera.

This is a sign that you are developing the eye and mind of a photographer and it is one of the qualities that separates the beginner from the serious amateur and professional.

HOW THE SHUTTER WORKS IN
YOUR DSLR CAMERA

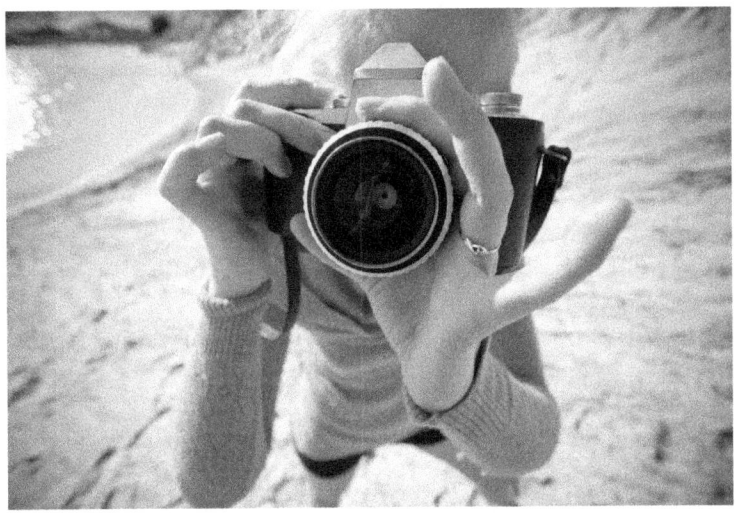

It's probably safe to say that most people are less interested in the details of how new technologies work – be they the wheel, the printing press, the light bulb, the computer and the digital camera – and more interested in how to derive as much value and benefit as possible from their use. You may not be indifferent to the science behind the light bulb, but when you need light, you expect it to illuminate your life with the flip of a switch.

Your DSLR camera is different, however, because it is an artistic tool that becomes an extension of your creativity, the visions of the world you want to capture and share with others. You can't extract more light from a light bulb by understanding the science, but you can be more creative with your camera when you understand exactly how it operates and transforms the pictures in your mind to pictures in your portfolio and/or displayed on the wall.

A previous section explained the role of shutter speed in arriving at the correct exposure for any scene or subject matter; and, on the surface, it was rather straightforward: You select and set a shutter speed, you push the shutter release button, you hear it working and there is a digital image. This one, however, will go below the surface, taking you inside the body of your camera to reveal how the shutter works and why having this knowledge could make you a better photographer.

A MECHANICAL WORKER IN A DIGITAL WORKPLACE

Without a doubt, the digital camera, with its light-sensitive sensor that digitally records an image, was a giant leap for photography. Interestingly, many parts of a digital camera are still mechanical, or analog, with moving parts, such as the shutter. You would have thought that engineers could give the sensor the capability to accept the proper amount of light for a correct exposure, so there wouldn't be the need for the same shutter mechanism that was used in film cameras.

The reason is found in the science of the digital sensor. It consists of a series of pixels on which the light is collected. If there were no mechanical shutter, each pixel would need additional electronics, or circuitry, to turn them on or off and accept the specific amount of light. Sensors with such electronics would be significantly more complex, inefficient and costly, so a mechanical shutter is used because it costs much less and can be synchronized with the operation of the digital sensor.

A HARMONIOUS RELATIONSHIP

Typically, the shutter mechanism in a DSLR looks a bit like a window frame and is located directly behind the mirror. The shutter has two curtains with multiple leaves that move vertically and at the speed you (or your camera) have selected for a correct exposure. The one limitation of any mechanical device with moving parts is how fast they can move. Having two curtains compensates for this limitation. At the fastest shutter speeds, one curtain would be unable to rise vertically and then return to the closed position. Because it would operate at a slower speed than required, the top or bottom of the sensor would be exposed to too much light, creating very unacceptable images. When you select a faster shutter speed, the two curtains move in unison, so just a small opening appears between them, precisely regulating the amount of time light strikes the sensor.

To familiarize yourself with the movement of the shutter curtains, try the following experiment, but make sure you're in a quiet place because you must listen carefully. First, set the shutter speed to one second or slower (2 seconds, 3 seconds, etc.). Second, press and release the shutter button; you should hear the mirror flip up, so the light can enter the camera body, and the clap, or snap, of the first curtain. The second curtain moves according to the shutter speed you've selected, which you will hear at the end of that interval. The mirror will then flip back into its closed position.

THE SHUTTER AND THE FLASH

Flash photography is a large topic; however, the first lesson starts here because using a flash correctly has a direct relationship to the two curtains in the shutter mechanism. Whether your DSLR camera comes with a built-in flash or you use a separate unit, it can be programmed to operate when either the first or second curtain moves. At faster shutter speeds, the flash will fire in unison with the movement of either curtain and light a scene or subject correctly. It's at slower shutter speeds and photographing a moving object that the synchronization of the flash and the curtains becomes important.

A moving object creates a blur, which can be captured when shooting at slow shutter speeds, $1/20^{th}$ of a second or slower, and using a flash. Typically, you want the blur to appear behind the object/subject since it imparts the illusion of motion. The flash unit must fire in unison with the movement of the second curtain to create this illusion, which allows the light to illuminate the object/subject at the end of the exposure period. If the flash unit fired with the movement of the first curtain, then the blur would appear in front of the moving object/subject.

This is an excellent example of why understanding the inner workings of your camera's shutter (or its many other systems) will help you be more creative. If you were photographing a racecar, a track sprinter, or a dancer on stage and you wanted to give your photos more interest and to suggest motion in a still image, then knowing how to synchronize a flash unit with the two curtains of a shutter gives you the means to elevate the quality of your photography...and isn't that the ultimate goal?

USING YOUR CAMERA'S VIEWFINDER AND LCD SCREEN TO THEIR OPTIMUM ADVANTAGE

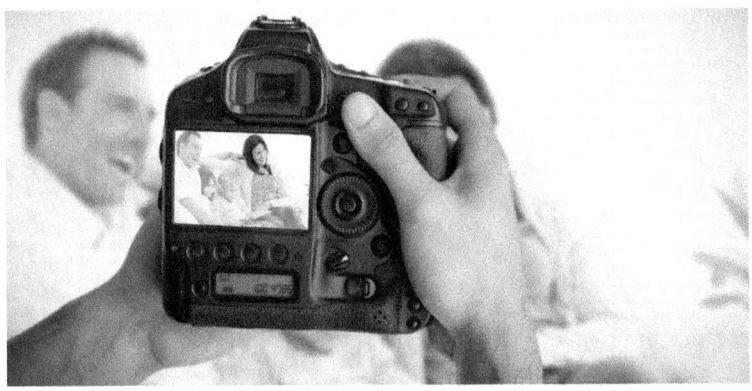

Good photographs – and certainly great photographs – begin with a vision in your head; a mind picture of how you would like to compose a photo: the angle, the lighting, the relationship of objects within the frame, etc. To create any composition and to capture your vision, your camera must obviously have a system for viewing the scene or object or subject, so you can frame it accordingly. This system is your DSLR camera's viewfinder.

Typically, the viewfinder is contained within the extension on the top center of the camera body. The light that enters the camera first strikes the primary mirror located in front of the sensor. The light is then reflected to a second mirror that is part of the viewfinder system. Unlike the first mirror,

41

which is essentially flat, the viewfinder mirror, is a pentaprism, or a five-sided prismatic device. With this type of mirror, the light rays do not become reversed, so whatever is on the left side of the scene you want to shoot appears on the left side of the image you see in the viewfinder.

If you bought at entry-level DSLR camera, then it is likely your viewfinder doesn't have a pentaprism, but a pentamirror. Professional-grade DSLRs almost always have pentaprisms because professional photographers need the brightest and highest quality view of what they are shooting. Although pentamirrors do a good job, they don't quite provide as much as brightness and quality as a pentaprism. The eyepiece for the viewfinder is located at the top back of the camera body and the view you see through it and all the various elements of the scene – lighting, angle, etc. – are exactly what your camera will record.

Remember, the view through the viewfinder is a reflected representation of what you are about to photograph, not a direct view. The LCD screen on the back of your camera, which works essentially the same as your camera phone's LCD, displays the view direct from the sensor, so it is more commonly referred to as the Live View.

For you to see a "live view" on the LCD monitor, however, the mirror must be flipped, so it doesn't block the light from striking the sensor. A future section will explain the automatic focus system on a DSLR, but it typically has two: phase-detection and contrast. The Live View on the LCD uses the contrast autofocus system with the tradeoff of it being slower than the phase-detection system, but very accurate. This can become an issue when you are using Live View to frame and follow an object or subject in motion (especially when shooting video) since the contrast autofocus system is slow.

In almost all cases, you should use the viewfinder to frame/compose any photo you want to take. The primary reason is that you can hold your camera much more securely with it to your eye than holding it at arm's length to be able to see the LCD screen. There are specific situations, however, when you want to use the LCD screen instead of the viewfinder.

- The viewfinder on many entry-level DSLRs doesn't provide a 100-percent view, often cropping the outside of the frame. For example, the viewfinders on the Canon EOS Rebel T5i and Nikon D5300 are only 95% of the view. The LCD screen, even on these lower-priced DSLRs, offers a complete, 100% view of what the camera (and its sensor) is seeing.

- The magnification of the scene in the viewfinder is often less than a 1:1 ratio, and there is no way to magnify the image larger. This can be a significant disadvantage when manual focusing the lens because it's difficult to see fine lines or to make sure a person's eyes are perfectly in focus. You can magnify the image on the LCD screen a number of times as well as magnify a specific portion of your composition to make sure your manual focus is perfect.

- Because of the LCD display's magnification capability, Live View is the best composition/framing tool for macrophotography, or close-ups of flowers, insects, etc. The depth of field of a close-up view of an object is very shallow, often a few inches or less than an inch, which is why manual focusing is almost always necessary for macrophotography. As mentioned above, precise manual focusing is much easier in Live View than through the viewfinder.

- You can also choose to superimpose a grid on the LCD screen to help with composition and to be sure that any lines in the image are straight.

- Photojournalists and sports photographers often find the Live View of the LCD screen extremely important when shooting in a crowd. These photographers can hold the camera above their heads and still see the LCD; and it provides a large-enough image even at a number of feet to see what the camera sees, thus obtaining the shot their editors expect them to bring home.

- The LCD monitor on some DSLRs is articulate. They can be swung on a hinge to one side of the camera or tilted at a number of angles. Photojournalists and sports photographers find this feature useful and an articulated LCD can also make it easier to shoot video, especially when the camera and/or the subject is moving.

A good comparison exercise is to shoot a series of the same photos looking through the viewfinder and the LCD. You should find that the viewfinder images are sharper, but you may also want to try some of the specific kinds of shooting situations that produce better results with Live View.

UNRAVELING THE MYSTERIES OF YOUR DSLR'S AUTOFOCUS SYSTEM

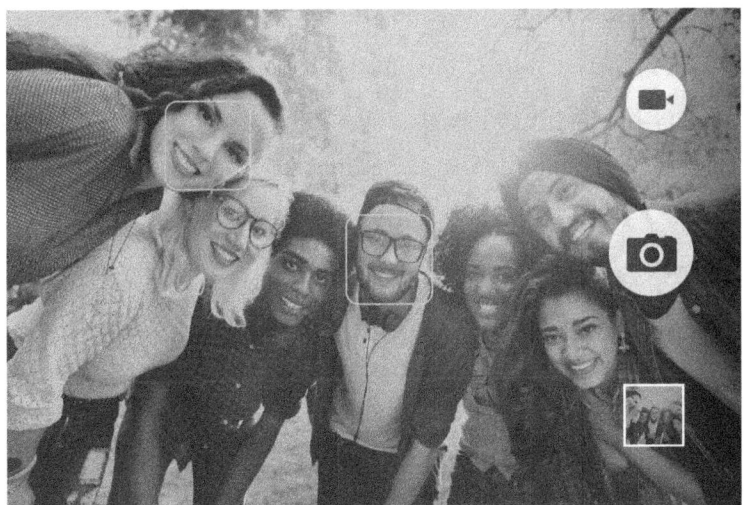

Before you graduated to a DSLR camera, it's likely you shot photographs with your smartphone and/or a compact camera; you probably still shoot some pictures with your smartphone. It was all so automatic, basically point and shoot and the camera did the work of calculating and setting exposure and focus.

As explained in the series of earlier sections about exposure, your DSLR will also calculate and set exposure. Sometimes, however, you'll want to do that task manually, first because the auto-exposure system doesn't work well in all light conditions and, second because manual exposure control enhances your creativity. The autofocus (AF) system in your DSLR works much the same: Most of the time it focuses quicker and more accurately than you can, but under certain light conditions it becomes confused, so it requires human intervention; and on occasion, manual focus is a better choice for the type of shot you are trying to capture or the composition you are trying to create.

That being said, there is a very good reason to rely on the AF system for most of your photos. Unlike older film cameras and their lenses, digital technology has given your DSLR much higher levels of resolution, which requires an AF system with equally modern technology to render the scene or subject in your photos as sharp as possible.

HOW THE AUTOFOCUS SYSTEM WORKS

A DSLR camera can have (and many do have) two types of AF systems: phase-detect and contrast-detect, with phase-detect the one most in use because it operates faster than contrast-detect. At the heart of the phase-detect AF system is a separate AF sensor. Some of the light traveling through the lens and into the body strikes this sensor. It is capable of capturing and combining two images from each side of the lens of what you are photographing. The AF sensor calculates, or detects, whether each image is front-focused or back-focused and the distance between them, and then directs the lens to refocus to sharpen the focus of the composite image. Keep in mind that all this detection, calculations and refocusing occurs incredibly fast.

An AF system, depending on the DSLR camera, has a series of focus points, or individual pixels, which are seen as a pattern in the viewfinder. In general, the number of points equates to the level of accuracy of the AF system. For example, an entry-level DSLR, such as the Canon EOS Rebel T5i has 9 points; however, the top-of-the-line Canon EOS-1D X has 61 points. This kind of focusing precision is important to a top professional, which is why he or she would pay thousands of dollars for this camera body.

Without explaining in too much detail, the pattern, or geometry, of the points also have an effect on the focusing accuracy of the camera. Some points are called cross-type; all 9 points on the Rebel T5i are of this type. This means that at any of these AF points, they detect lines in your image in both the horizontal and vertical orientation. The Rebel T5i also has one dual-cross center point. A dual-cross point detects horizontal and vertical lines in four directions (or north, south, east and west on a compass) as well as four additional directions, northeast, southeast, southwest and northwest, using the compass analogy again.

For comparison purposes, 41 of the Canon EOS-1D X 61 points are cross-type, but its AF sensor also has 5 dual diagonal points and a cross-type support center point.

WHEN AUTOFOCUS STRUGGLES

Despite all the digital technology designed into an autofocus system, it can struggle, depending on the light level, subject contrast and camera or subject motion. None of these factors have an effect independent of the others. For example, there might not be much light illuminating a subject, but if the subject has high contrast, then the AF system will typically be able to achieve precise focus. Another example is a static background and a moving subject in the foreground without much light illuminating it. An AF system is more likely to detect the background and put it in focus instead of the subject.

To adjust for subjects in motion, AF systems have a mode that continuously tracks the subject and changes focus. In Canon DSLRs, this is the AI Servo and in Nikon DSLRs, it is called continuous focusing. Rather amazingly, this mode is capable of predicting the future position of the moving subject, so it can anticipate and preset the correct focus for when the subject enters that space.

A WORD ABOUT CONTRAST-DETECT AUTOFOCUS

As mentioned above, most DSLR cameras also have a contrast-detect AF system. It is typically used with Live View on the LCD screen instead of the viewfinder, and is most useful when photographing or recording video of moving subjects. Again, without going too deep into the science, contrast-detect reads the contrast of the subject or scene at adjacent pixels on the image sensor, not the AF sensor. Like many DSLRs, the Canon EOS Rebel series has a hybrid AF system that incorporates the use of both phase-detect and contrast-detect for very quick and accurate focusing.

As with all systems in your camera, the manual is the best place to read about its specific AF system. The camera manufacturer's Website will also have additional information to help you understand how your camera's AF system works.

TAKE CONTROL OF YOUR PHOTOGRAPHY WITH APERTURE PRIORITY MODE

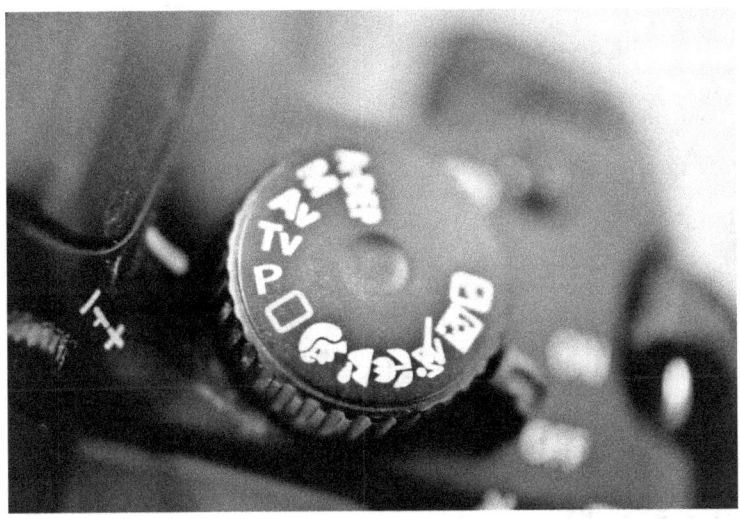

The exterior of your DSLR camera has many points of control, but maybe the most important and one you should understand the most is the mode dial typically located on the top plate of your camera. Four settings are of particular interest: M, manual; A or Av, aperture priority; S or Tv, shutter priority; and P, program mode.

Of these, aperture priority is probably the most versatile because it allows you to use depth of field as the first factor in determining an accurate exposure equation before choosing a slower shutter speed or a higher ISO sensitivity. For example, when photographing people, you typically want a moderate shallow depth of field, so the background will blur nicely, which is also known as bokeh. This helps to "lift" the person from the background, creating more three-dimensionality. For landscapes, you want more, even maximum, depth of field, so foreground objects and distant background objects or scenery are all in focus. In addition, aperture priority mode is preferred when the light levels are relatively even throughout the scene, giving you more control of shooting speed, technique and achieving the best exposure simultaneously.

To achieve that optimum exposure, you set the dial to the maximum aperture in aperture priority and the camera will select the fastest shutter speed to match the aperture. Because the widest, or maximum aperture (the smallest f/stop number), allows the most light to enter the camera, it is preferable to a slower shutter speed, which could cause a blurred image from camera shake or the motion created trying to hand hold the camera, or a higher ISO setting, which could add digital noise.

SHUTTER PRIORITY LIMITATION

If you use shutter priority mode as the first exposure control, then you may have trouble when shooting where the light is low, such as indoors. For example, you're shooting with a lens with a maximum aperture of f/4. To achieve an accurate exposure in an indoor setting, the aperture may be f/4 and shutter speed 1/30th of a second; however, if because of what you are photographing, such as movement, think a basketball game, requires a faster shutter speed of 1/125th, then there must be a compensation of 2 stops (the difference between $1/30^{th}$ and $1/125^{th}$). Either the aperture must be opened another 2 stops to f/2 or the ISO setting must be increased.

Of course, the lens isn't as fast as f/2. If you've set the ISO to auto, then it will compensate for those 2 stops, but that is not the best outcome. If the ISO has been manually set to a low sensitivity, then the camera can't adjust for the 2 additional stops it needs, resulting in an image underexposed by 2 stops. In shutter priority mode, the camera doesn't care if you need a faster f/stop that isn't available on the lens. The camera will allow the shutter speed to change until it reaches either the minimum or maximum shutter speed required.

Shutter priority mode is best for bright lighting conditions, such as outdoors under full sunlight, especially sports or action. Shutter priority will set a much smaller aperture opening (bigger f/stop number) and a fast shutter speed, 1/500 and f/11, for example, because there is so much light. The action is frozen and sharp without any blur and plenty of depth of field. In addition, this exposure combination is well within the aperture limit of the lens.

THE MANUAL ADVANTAGE

Many photography instructors advise their students and hobbyists and enthusiasts in general to learn how to shoot in manual mode. The upside is that you're required to think more about the correct exposure and most of the other camera settings. This will help you develop a more precise interpretation of light levels and other factors for every photo. The downside, however, is that you will usually spend more time making these adjustments, which could lead to missing a great shot.

The manual mode is also often preferred for flash photography; but its primary advantage over aperture priority is when a scene has very bright and very dark light levels and many levels between. This can confuse the light meter in the camera and result in an inaccurate exposure setting. With some manual experience, you can make subtle adjustments of the aperture and/or shutter speed to compensate for the unbalanced lighting and expose the image precisely.

PROGRAM MODE HAS ITS PLACE

Program mode can be very useful since it provides control of ISO, white balance and the flash and it will recommend matching settings for aperture and shutter speed. If you're photographing a party, street carnival or other fast-action or rapidly changing scene, then program mode could be your best choice. It allows you to shoot quickly when technique is not a priority, knowing you'll have the right exposure.

Ultimately, learning how to use aperture priority mode as well as shutter priority, manual and program modes requires some experimentation. No doubt, you'll make mistakes, but they are often a much better way to learn.

10 PHOTOGRAPHY CONDITIONS WHEN MANUAL FOCUS IS A BETTER CHOICE

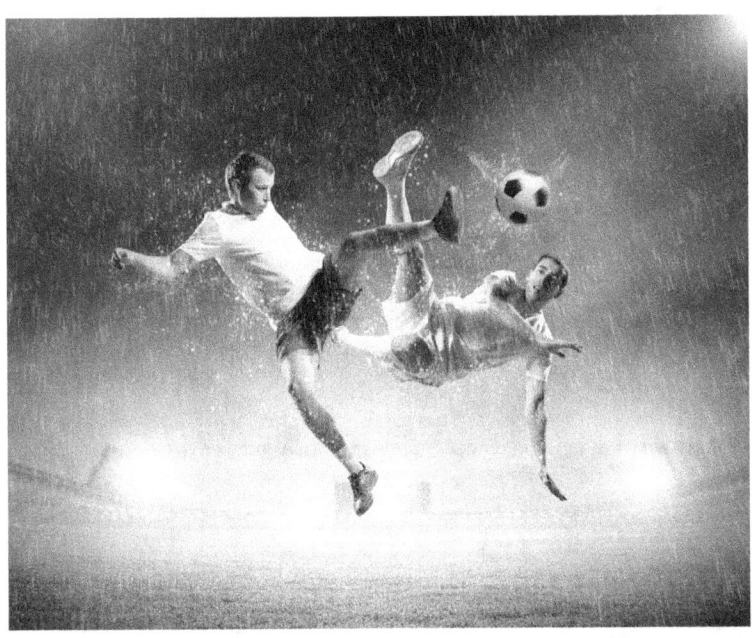

It doesn't take long for most DSLR photographers to fall in love with the autofocus system on their camera. As a new DSLR photographer, the AF will likely work just fine for most of your shooting conditions; however, as your skills advance, you'll discover more conditions and subjects that require very accurate focusing. You may love your camera's AF, but the AF doesn't always love the object of its focus, as certain situations will confuse the AF system.

Manual focus can also be a creative tool; so regardless of how much you rely on your camera's AF, it's important to become an accomplished manual-focus photographer – and it's definitely the best choice whenever the following 10 shooting conditions present themselves to you and your camera.

1.   Low Light

Your camera's AF system needs a sufficient amount of light to operate accurately and the low light of sunrise, sunset, twilight, night, cloudy days and dark interiors is often typically not enough. Manual focus is an absolute necessity for photographing of the moon, the starry sky or other astrophotography subject matter.

2.   Equal Contrast Value

Be aware of a scene, subject or composition where the contrast, or tonal, quality of most of the image is the same or within the same range. Whether most everything in the image is red (a red-headed woman wearing a red dress, holding a red ball in front of a red fire truck) or black (a black car against a night sky), the camera's AF system won't know on what to focus because of equal contrast values. Composing images with equal contrast values can be creative, but just make sure you are focusing manually.

3. Freezing movement

It's unlikely you make a living photographing fast-action sports images for *Sports Illustrated* or wild animals on the move for *National Geographic*. The pro photographers spend many thousands on the best DSLR cameras because they have the most precise AF system that are capable of following the action and freezing it with exceptional focus. You may be surprised to learn that they don't totally rely on these top-of-the-line AF systems, often using manual focus to ensure their images are sharp. As a hobbyist, enthusiast or amateur DSLR photography, the AF system in the camera you can afford is good, but not nearly as good as the models the pros use; so your camera's AF system has even more problems trying to follow a moving object and maintain focus. Under most conditions, you shouldn't even try. It's better to develop your manual-focusing skills, including this technique. Make your best guess of where your subject will move, and then pre-focus on that space and snap the shutter when it has entered the space.

4. HDR Photography

HDR, or High Dynamic Range, photography is a method to create an enhanced version of a common scene (It works best with landscapes) by shooting multiple images at different exposure values, and then combining them in post-production. As you might imagine, your camera can't move as it captures the images of the same scene, so they blend together perfectly; therefore, you must focus manually. The most overexposed and underexposed image is likely to confuse the AF. In addition, your camera must be on a tripod and you should trip the shutter with a cable release or a wireless release, which is preferable.

5. Through the Leaves

AF systems don't have much love for you when you compose an image with objects, such as leaves or a wire fence, either between you and your subject or to frame the scene. Photographing animals at the zoo is an excellent example. With your camera close to the fence, it virtually disappears from your photo, but the sensitivity of your AF system could still "read" it and focus on the fence instead. One solution is to move the lens as close to the fence as possible, select a wide aperture to create a shallow depth-of-field and position the lens so its center portion is at the center of the gap in the fencing.

6. Multiple-Image Portraits

Although not a common portrait technique, you can create some very interesting and unique photos with the use of multiple images of your subject. Turned 90 degrees in both directions to the camera, for example. Now, if you use this technique in the controlled environment of a formal portrait studio, the AF is usually capable of distinguishing the background from the subject, since it's likely the background will have a fairly equal tonal value.

As a hobbyist, enthusiast or amateur, your portraits are more likely to be shot outdoors, or even indoors, but the tonal value of the background will vary – and this can confuse the AF. Plus, it's simply a best practice to focus manually for all portraits because you want to be absolutely sure that the eyes are the focus point and they are sharp.

7. Macrophotography

Almost all macrophotography situations require the lens to be less than foot, and even mere inches from the subject, resulting in a depth-of-field that is extremely shallow. Your camera's AF system isn't particularly fond of this condition either. You may often find yourself trying to decide to focus on the end of the flower stamen or the plane of the petals, or the end of an insect's antenna or its head or "face." Manual focus is the only method to achieve such precise focusing.

8. Landscapes and Hyperfocal Distance

Briefly, hyperfocal distance is when the entire depth of a landscape image appears in focus. Remember, one of the most common types of landscape images is a small foreground object or group of objects that complements or contrasts with a wide-open mid-ground and/or background, such as a lake, the ocean or a distant mountain range. Your camera's AF system is most comfortable and more accurate when it can lock onto an object or a part of a scene in a specific focal plane. Wanting all of a landscape image in focus, therefore, requires manual focus.

9. Through glass surfaces

Much like the leaves or wire fence at the zoo in #5 above, autofocus doesn't like a confrontation with glass, especially since its surface is never perfect. There are always scratches, reflections and imperfections in the glass, any of which may become the AF system's focus point instead of your intended subject. Unless you're doing a close-up study of glass surfaces, always use manual focus when shooting through glass.

10. Fog Layers

Fog is a tricky metrological substance. Despite the message your eyes are sending to your brain that the fog is only in the distance, it's also likely to be surrounding your camera just as thickly. You're just too close to recognize it. Your camera – and its AF system – sees differently than your eyes, so the AF may try to focus on a layer of fog immediately in front of the camera, which presumably is not your subject. To capture that interesting and eerie fog photo, rely on manual focus instead.

WHITE BALANCE

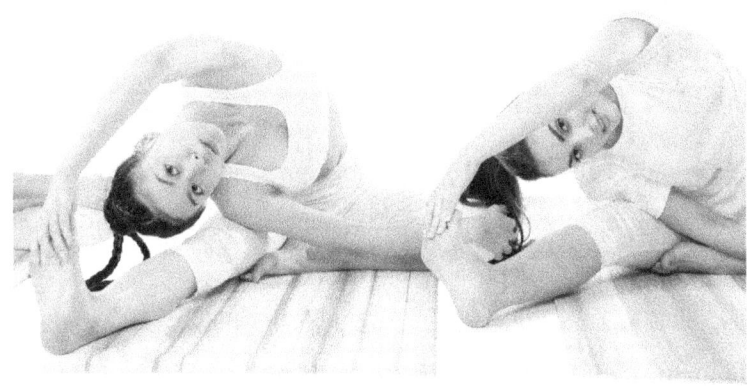

An underlying theme you may have noticed is that when you enter the world of digital photography, you are confronted with plenty of science. In fact, you may suddenly realize that your science teacher in high school was telling the truth when he said that someday you will have wished you paid more attention – the day you bought your DSLR camera was that day.

The subject of this section is white balance, which as you're about to learn has much to do with the science of light, temperature and color. In fact, they are essentially all the same, or at least from the perspective of physics. Before the science, however, there is the practical point that one of the most important goals of any photograph you shoot is that the white portions are truly white. This is why your camera has a white balance mode that works both automatically and that you can override and use manually when necessary.

When the whites are exactly white, then the colors will also be accurate. When the white balance on your DSLR is not set correctly, you may notice that the white areas have a bit of an orange, blue or yellow cast, which means the areas of color are not true either. This will be more pronounced in a large print of the image or if you look at it on a high-resolution computer monitor.

THE SCIENCE OF WHITE BALANCE

As a new or beginner digital photographer, it's important to start to recognize light: its source, its direction, its angle, etc. If you look and think carefully about light, you'll realize that various sources generated it: the sun, an incandescent light bulb (or tungsten light), a fluorescent tube and the flash unit on your camera or a separate flash unit.

The light from these sources operates at different temperatures and each temperature is represented by a specific color on the visual spectrum. If you think very hard, then you might remember your science teacher using a prism and a single light source to create the rainbow of colors of the spectrum. The extreme left side of the spectrum is deep red with bands of orange, yellow, green in the middle and blue and violet to the right side of the spectrum.

It might seem counterintuitive, but generally the light from the sun and a fluorescent tube are both blue, which is described as cool light. An incandescent light bulb and a candle are yellow, which means they are hotter than blue light, but not as hot as red light. The white balance you want your

DSLR camera to produce in your photos is the equivalent of the noonday sun, which is a balanced blend of the whole spectrum.

The scale used to measure light (or its temperature or color) is the Kelvin scale. It's a temperature scale much the same as the Fahrenheit and Celsius scales; however, the coldest point on the Kelvin scale, also known as absolute zero, is -457.67 degrees Fahrenheit and -273.15 degrees Celsius.

THE MAGIC OF THE WHITE BALANCE MODE

It may seem amazing enough that the image sensor in your DSLR camera is capable of recording a digital representation of whatever you are shooting; however, it also reads the amount of red, green and blue light of the light source illuminating the scene of subject. You might remember the color wheel from a science class (or even an art class), which shows the three basic colors, which, when combined in various percentages, create all the other colors. They also represent the entire visible spectrum.

Different sections of the sensor in your camera are sensitive to the red, green and blue light. Each not only read its matching color, but also adjusts the color, so the light is balanced.

Using the Canon EOS Rebel entry-level DSLR as an example, the "WB," or white balance, button is one of the four that surround the shutter release button on the top right of the camera body. When you press it, the white balance sub-menu then appears on the LCD screen. You'll see a number of icons that are the selection of white balance presets matched to various light sources. A light bulb is the setting for incandescent light; a narrow, vertical dash for fluorescent; the sun for sunlight; a cloud for a cloudy day; etc.

As helpful as these presets are, you can't rely on them 100 percent because the sunlight may seem strong, but the air is slightly hazy or an old light bulb doesn't produce as much light as a new bulb. Very bright or low light or uncommon light sources can also cause these presets to be inaccurate. When you're faced with these kinds of lighting conditions, then choose your camera's manual white balance setting. This will require the use of a neutral gray card. Pointing the camera (in the manual white balance mode) at the card will allow the camera to set the white balance precisely.

Excuse the repetition, but your camera's manual is where you'll find information about where you set white balance and which presets to use under different lighting conditions. It's also a good idea to experiment with white balance. For example, select your camera's daylight white balance preset and shoot the same subject or object outdoors in full sunlight, outdoors in the shade and indoors with a tungsten light, and then compare the differences.

IT'S ALL ABOUT LIGHT

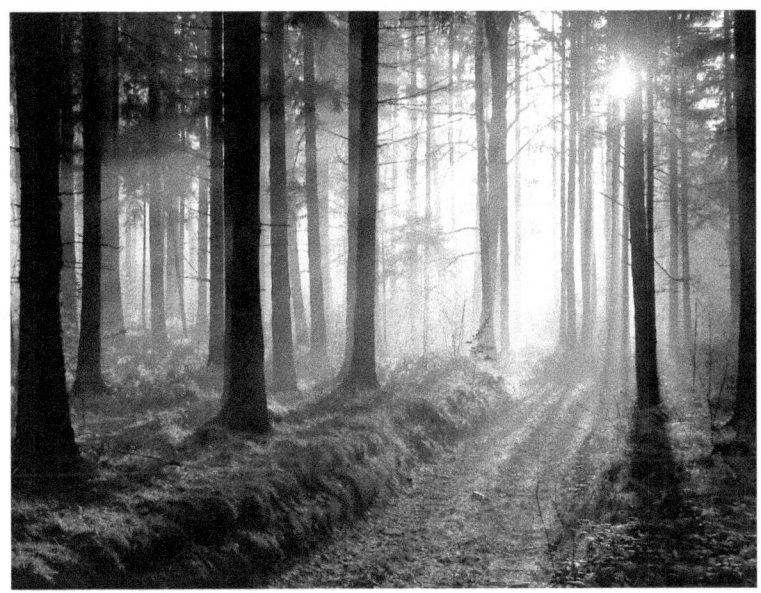

For beginner, hobbyist and enthusiast photographers, it can't be emphasized enough that photography is all about the light. The image you capture on a frame of film or a sensor is a "picture" of the light reflected from the scene you are shooting and all the objects within the scene. In a sense, a photograph is not a representation of the reality of our world, but the reality created by reflected light.

Light, therefore, is the most important photographer's tool. The lens and camera are "just" the equipment that allows you to convey the light (the lens) and capture the light within a dark box (the camera). In fact, this is the concept that led to the development of the camera and photography, known as "camera obscura".

Since light is the photographer's tool, it's incumbent on you to learn how to find and observe the direction of the light, and then use it as a compositional element. Few techniques will improve your photography more.

THE NATURAL LAWS OF LIGHT

Light may act strangely in other parts of the universe, but where us humans live, one of the laws of light is that it always travels in a straight line until it strikes a surface dense enough to cause some of the photons to bounce or reflect. Many of the photons will bounce back in the same direction as the incoming rays when the surface is smooth and/or shiny. A substance or surface that creates fewer reflections scatters more of the photons in multiple directions, so the light appears diffused or softened.

COORDINATING TWO VIEWS

With light the most-important photographer's tool, then the camera is certainly second in importance since it is the light capture box. It is critical to the advancement of your skills and the quality of your photography to understand and coordinate both the angle of view of the scene or subject you see through the viewfinder and the angle of light striking the scene or subject.

Instead of just pointing your camera at something interesting, you must also be conscious of the direction of the light and how it illuminates your composition. In many cases, you'll discover that when you take the time to recognize the direction of the light, you'll want to move the position or angle of the camera, so the light is being used to its maximum effect.

Try this experiment to help burn this concept on your brain, using a light source, a small lamp, and your eyes as the camera (after all, they both work essentially the same). While standing in front of a mirror, hold the lamp on one side of your face at both a high and low angle and repeat this on the other side. Then, position the lamp above your face and below it for the classic Halloween lighting effect.

As you move the lamp to different positions, hold it long enough to focus your attention on the light, and not on you. Then, take careful notice of the shadows and how differently your face looks at these different light angles. This ability to see the light and manipulate the scene, subject or light creatively is a powerful tool and will definitely elevate your photographic prowess.

SUNBEAMS AS COMPOSITIONAL ELEMENTS

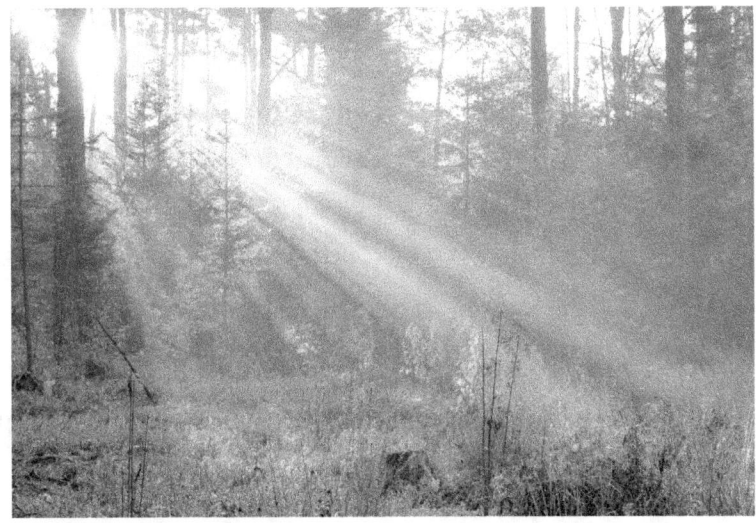

Your new understanding of the direction and reflective qualities of light can be put to practical use by planning a shoot during those magic hours of sunrise and sunset. This is when the angle of sunlight is the severest, having to penetrate more of the atmosphere, diffusing and softening the light. Sunbeams are actually invisible; it's the particles in the air that reflect the light that create the illusion of a sunbeam, such as the sharp, bright light coming through a window. (If there are too many particles, then you need to do some more dusting.) Another example is the visible sunbeams streaming through a forest canopy and strongly illuminating a small clearing.

You can add the beauty and dramatic effect of "visible" sunbeams with these tips.

1. Sunrise and sunset are the best times to add sunbeams to your photos, but only during the half-hour before and after sunrise and sunset. You must be at the location and your equipment ready to shoot, and preferably a place you've previously scouted, so you know sunbeams occur there. Once you've found a good position, scan the 360-degree view because there are often excellent photos behind you.

2. Don't be afraid to help nature. Just as you can inadvertently cause more particles to intercept the sunlight coming through a window by simply walking across the room and causing more dust particles to fly, you can also artificially add particles to a natural outdoors scene to help your camera record sunbeams. Create a few small wisps of smoke (but don't set the woods on fire) or kick or throw a small handful of dirt in the air. The lighter particles will fall very

slowly just like the dust in your house and cause the sunbeams to come to life.

3. You can also position your camera, so there is a partial obstacle between you and the direction of the light. You can also assume a camera angle that places the sun outside the frame. Fewer rays will enter the scene, which can help your camera record them.

4. Shooting in places with general low light or against a dark background will also make sunbeams visible. This is how the classic forest photo is created with beams of light penetrating the canopy. You'll want to try various exposure values, so the sunbeams are brighter than all other parts of the composition. Your exposure should have some balance, however, so the trees in the dark forest, for example, in the background can still be seen. This may require pointing your camera at different parts of the image to obtain meter readings or using a separate light meter.

5. When you're ready to capture those sunbeams, set your lens to a narrow aperture to create maximum depth of field, which is likely to require a longer shutter speed because, except for the sunbeams, the rest of the scene will be in low light.

REFLECTED LIGHT IS OFTEN MORE CREATIVE LIGHT

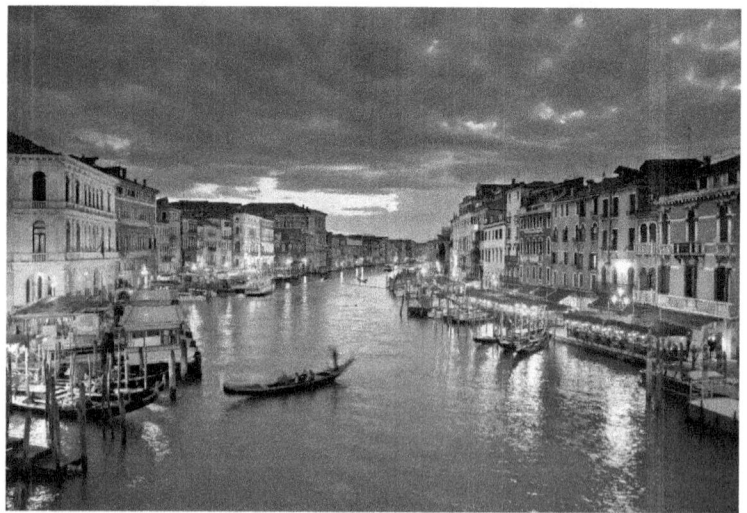

As you focus more of your attention on the light in your photographs and not just the objects and scenery, you'll come to realize that light comes in two varieties: direct and reflective. The direct rays of light have been explored earlier. Here we will reveal how reflective light can also be used to create interesting and different images.

From the perspective of an Earthbound human, all rays of light eventually reflect off one surface or another, and at different intensities.

Obviously, water, mirrors and shiny metallic surfaces are highly reflective; windows a bit less so; and darker or less dense substances and surfaces the least. The reflectiveness of all these surfaces are not necessarily consistent, as time of day, the amount of clouds in the sky and the angle of view of your camera can cause less reflection off water, for example, or more off a black, shiny hood of a car.

It's your effort to develop a true photographer's eye that will help you recognize the various reflections and their intensity and how to use them creatively. The following tips will point you in the right direction.

1. Reflections in the outdoors environment certainly occur during the brightest time of the day, but often they are too intense and become detrimental to what you want to achieve creatively. Plus, when the sunlight is at its smallest angle relative to any natural or artificial surface, more of the photons are reflecting back at the same angle, which aren't as useful photographically.

    What you want is sunlight at its maximum angle, which occurs during sunrise and sunset. Since these rays of sunlight must pass through more of the atmosphere, they become diffused, so the reflections are less harsh and more pleasing as a photographic element. The reflections during early morning and late afternoon/evening are also more "visible" because of their angle and diffusion. Since it's easiest to see them, you'll be better able to place the subjects/objects in your photos and your camera at the optimum position and angle to control reflections, so they enhance the vision you are trying to create.

2. You can certainly shoot photos utilizing reflections handholding your camera, but you should bring a tripod because many of the best images

with reflections may be in low light. You may need to use narrow apertures for more depth of field, which would require slower shutter speeds and, therefore, a tripod. Make sure to add your filter kit to your camera bag. Of course, the UV filter should already be attached to the front of the lens to protect its otherwise exposed front glass element. A polarizing filter will help you control the intensity of the reflected rays of light. An ND, or neutral density, filter is needed, so the lighter sky isn't overexposed. Minimizing its brightest a bit will help to emphasize the reflections and make them the brightest part of the image.

You may also want a photographic reflector, either store-bought or handmade with aluminum foil or similar materials attached to a piece of cardboard. With a reflector, you'll have some control as to where reflections fall in your scene. If you're shooting a portrait on the beach at sunset, then you can keep the lowering sun in the image to one side of your subject, but also reflect some of that waning light onto his or her face to reveal more details and lessen the silhouette effect.

3. Water is a versatile reflective element for photography. During an overcast day or, again, during sunrise and sunset, the reflections aren't as intense, bathing your composition in more subtle reflections. Conversely, during the brightest time of the day, reflections from water will be so strong as to illuminate objects from below. This can create an interesting backlight effect or light people's faces in a canoe, for example, in the shade of the trees along the water's edge. Maximize the smoothness of the surface of water by using a longer shutter speed. You can also use reflections in combination with various depths of field to add creative qualities to your images. Shoot at different aperture

settings to discover which works best, depending on the time of day and intensity of the light and reflections.

It isn't often apparent to inexperienced photographers that water also creates reflections below the surface, just within the first few inches or a foot, depending on the brightness of the light and clarity of the water. The best environment for this type of image is in tropical waters near the shore or a reef where the light reflects off the colorful and often shiny scales of fish and coral. Of course, you'll need an underwater camera or underwater housing specifically for your camera make and model.

4. Play with focus when using reflections in your compositions. Try positioning your camera and your subject, so you capture both him or her in focus and his or her reflection not in focus. You can also do the opposite and make the focus point the reflected object or subject and the actual object or subject not in focus. Likely you've seen this technique used with the reflection of the colorful trees of autumn on a lake's smooth surface as distinct as the "real" subject. The image could be rotated 180 degrees in either direction and it would be difficult to discern the real from the reflection.

5. It's easy to focus your search for reflections from horizontal or mostly horizontal surfaces, but don't overlook vertical surfaces. The obvious example is the low morning or afternoon sky brilliantly reflected from the windows of a skyscraper or its smooth, shiny exterior.

6. Although a smooth surface may seem the best source for reflections (and they generally are), look also for highly reflective, but uneven surfaces. Rippling water can cause reflections to dance across a subject

or scene, which can make for interesting video footage or an HDR image. Convex and concave surfaces of shiny material cause the reflections to bounce in more directions and cross paths, which could offer a number of abstract compositions for your camera.

7. It's generally difficult to use artificial light, such as a flash or constant studio light, with reflective surfaces. When they are very shiny, bouncing light from a flash could cause a hot spot in your image or could severely overexpose the image. If your creative vision or low light conditions require the use of artificial light, then you'll probably want to restrict its use to above or behind the subject.

LEARNING HOW TO READ AND SHOOT BETTER PICTURES WITH HISTOGRAMS

You look through the viewfinder of your camera and the scene or subject you want to capture looks good: the lighting, the composition, the camera angle, etc. Despite the marvelous abilities of the human eye, it is unable to determine whether the picture is accurately exposed. When you rely only on your eyes and what you see through the viewfinder, you are apt to discover that more of your photos are overexposed or underexposed than you expected.

The histogram will help you capture more properly exposed images, which is why it is one of the most important displays that you can access on your camera's menu. When using the Live View display on the LCD, you can view the scene or subject you want to shoot and its matching histogram.

A histogram is a scale with peaks and valleys that represent the tonal qualities of your picture, shown as the number of pixels for the black, gray and white tones. The peaks in the histogram are the tones with the largest number of pixels. The positions of the peaks within the histogram are also important. The pixels that equate to the bright portion of an image are on the right side and those that equate to darker pixels are on the left side. Any part of the histogram in the middle of the scale equate to gray, or mid-tones.

The histogram scale is also represented by values of 0- black at the left edge to 255- white at the right edge.

The histogram of an overexposed image typically displays the tones representing the white portion of the image at the extreme right edge of the screen, with narrow, tall spikes. You'll see a histogram that looks the opposite for an underexposed image: the peaks representing the black, gray and white tones are compressed and the black tones are located close to the left edge of the histogram with a few narrow, tall peaks.

The "optimum" histogram is shaped like a triangle, with the tallest peaks in the center of the scale and the peaks gradually reducing in size to the left and right. In reality, however, there is no "optimum" histogram, as the various kinds of photos you may shoot have different histograms, but are still correctly exposed.

For example, the portrait of a woman dressed in white against a white background with studio lighting will likely have a right-weighted histogram because there are so many white tones in the image. Shoot a silhouette of a person against the setting sun and the histogram will be skewed to the left because of so many dark tones. In these examples, more pixel spikes to the right and left are accurate representations of the tonal quality of the images; however, if you are shooting pictures that do not have a preponderance of white or black tones and the pixels are gathered at the right or left edge, then the exposure is probably incorrect. This is also the source of the term "clipping." When many pixel spikes are gathered at the right or left edge, the whitest or darkest are actually beyond the edge of the histogram, meaning that the highlights or shadows have been clipped.

ADJUSTING EXPOSURE FOR A "FALSE" HISTOGRAM

The light meter in your camera creates the histogram of whatever scene or subject you're shooting. Since the light-metering mode you will use the most reads the light across the entire frame and as mid-tone gray, it can render a "false" histogram. As with the example above of the woman dressed in white against a white background, the meter will read the bright light reflected from the white surfaces and the camera will adjust the exposure because it wants to render it as a mid-tone gray image. This, of course, results in an underexposed image. The opposite is true if the image has more dark tones. Once again, the camera wants to produce a mid-tone gray image, so it must adjust the exposure to allow more light into the camera, but the image is overexposed.

Fortunately, your DSLR camera has an exposure compensation button that allows you to make a manual adjustment of the exposure to "compensate" for the inaccurate reading of the light meter and the false histogram. For example, the Canon EOS Rebel series camera has an Av button (Aperture value) located at the top right on the back of the camera and an exposure compensation dial at the top of the front right of the body. You simply push and hold the Av button and turn the dial to the right to increase exposure or to the left to decrease exposure. You can also see the exposure compensation level on the viewfinder display and the LCD screen. On the Rebel, you can select 5 stops, or positions, to the right or left, and in 1/3-stop increments.

As an experiment, activate Live View while adjusting exposure and you can watch the histogram change in real time. You'll improve your understanding of the histogram and how small exposure compensations will affect your pictures. Becoming a good histogram interpreter is a sure sign your DSLR photography skills are advancing and you're ready to capture more complex, compelling and creative images.

HOW TO CHOOSE THE RIGHT LENS

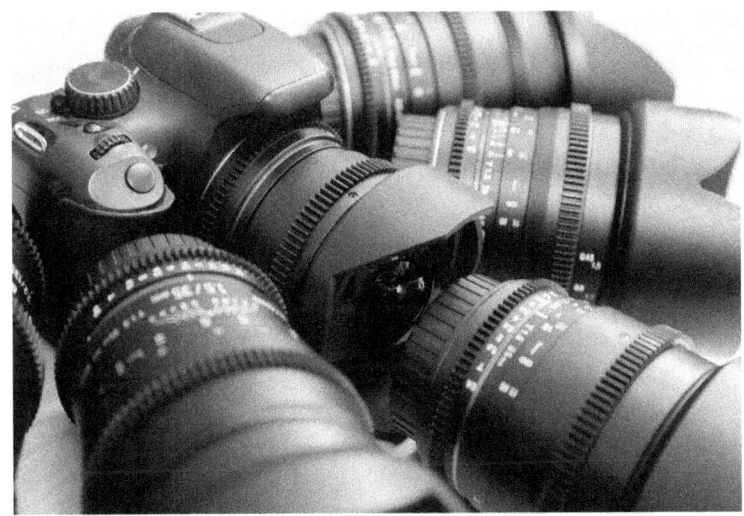

Now that you're a DSLR photographer (or planning to become one), you're suddenly confronted by what seems to be an overwhelming number of lens choices. The process of choosing the right lens, however, is easier than you think – and this section will present some of the basics.

1. Since Canon, Nikon and Sony dominate the DSLR photography market, it's likely your DSLR camera is from one of these manufacturers. Your first smart move, regardless of which manufacturer's DSLR you own, is to use only the lenses made by the same company. All three companies, especially Canon and Nikon, offer

plenty of lenses; many of which you'll never purchase unless you become a very serious amateur or a professional.

2. There are also some photography equipment companies that manufacture just lenses. Many of these can be used on a Canon, Nikon and Sony DSLR camera with a compatible lens mount that connects these lenses to these cameras.

3. Often, the lens choice is very simple for a beginner DSLR photographer, as many of the entry-level DSLRs are offered as a kit that includes, in most cases, an 18–55mm lens.

4. As you may be aware, lenses are designated by their focal length, measured in millimeters. Lenses can either be of a fixed focal length – a 35mm, 50mm, 200mm, 500mm, etc. or a zoom lens that provides a range of focal lengths. In the case of the 18–55mm lens in a DSLR kit, it offers focal lengths from 18mm to 55mm. Other common focal-length ranges on zoom lenses are 24–70mm, 28–135mm, 70–200mm, 70–300mm and 100–400mm.

5. A concept that can be a bit confusing, as a new DSLR photographer, is that you must use a lens that is compatible with the size of the sensor in your camera. For the purposes of this section, DSLR cameras are designated as either full-frame or APS-C. A full-frame DSLR, which professionals typically purchase and use, renders an image the same size as traditional 35mm film, or 24mm x 36mm. APS-C, or Advanced Photo System type-C, were developed to offer hobbyists and amateurs a DSLR camera, but at a substantially lower cost than a full-frame DSLR. An APS-C DSLR renders a smaller image, 24mm x 16mm, than

a full-frame sensor, so an APS-C image is often described as being cropped.

For example, a sample of these Canon DSLR cameras had APS-C sensors:

- EOS Rebel T3
- EOS Rebel T5
- EOS Rebel T3i
- EOS Rebel SL1
- EOS Rebel T5i
- EOS 60D
- EOS 60Da
- EOS 70D
- EOS 7D
- EOS 7D Mark II

While the EOS 6D, EOS 5D Mark IV and EOS-1D X are full-frame cameras.

6. Maybe, the most important point to remember when choosing a lens for your DSLR is that Canon, Nikon and Sony have two sets of lenses: one for full-frame DSLRs and the other for APS-C DSLRs. Both sets will have many lenses of the same focal length. APS-C-compatible lenses are also less expensive than their full-frame counterparts. **You can use a full-frame lens on an APS-C DSLR, but you can't use an APS-C lens on a full-frame DSLR.**

7.	Another tricky concept to understand is what's called the equivalent focal length of an EF-S lens (for an APS-C DSLR). As mentioned above, the APS-C image size is cropped or smaller than the full-frame image, 24mm x 16mm versus 24mm x 36mm. Without explaining all the mathematical computations, an APS-C image has a crop factor of 1.6, based on a comparison of the diagonal measurement of each image size. For example, the Canon **EF-S** 18–200 zoom lens is said to have an equivalent focal length of 29–320mm in the 35mm format. Multiply 18 and 200 by 1.6 and the results are 29 and 320.

In actuality, the focal length doesn't change; and the EF-S 18–200 zoom lens won't bring a subject closer. A better term would be "equivalent field of view" because that does change. Attach a full-frame lens to an APS-C DSLR, a 24mm lens, for example. The resulting image would be cropped, the extreme corners eliminated, because the smaller sensor on the APS-C provides a narrower field of view or image capture.

8.	Since it is very unlikely that you will ever buy a full-frame lens, you'll want to look for these designations in the lens name to know that it is an APS-C lens.

- Canon: EF-S (Full-frame lenses are known as EF)

- Nikon: DX (Full-frame lenses are known as FX)

- Sony: DT (Full-frame lenses have no letter designation)

Using Canon's lens selection as an example, it separates its lenses into 9 categories:

- Ultra-wide Zoom: 10–22mm, for example

- Standard Zoom: 18–55mm, for example

- Telephoto Zoom: 70–300mm, for example

- Wide-Angle (Fixed): 24mm, for example

- Standard and Medium Telephoto (Fixed): 85mm, for example

- Telephoto (Fixed): 300mm, for example

- Super Telephoto (Fixed): 800mm, for example

- Macro: 60mm, for example

- Tilt-Shift: 45mm, for example

Of these lenses most are EF, or full-frame, and the rest are EF-S, or APS-C; and a handful of the EF-S lenses are in the standard zoom category. Canon and the other manufacturers place most of the lower-cost APS-C lenses that beginners or hobbyists would buy in this one category because these lenses will generally cover any kind of photography you will shoot.

You may be asking, "Why would I want to spend the additional money to buy a full-frame lens?" There are three primary reasons: First full-frame lenses are typically "faster," meaning their widest aperture (the smallest f-stop number) is wider than the widest on a similar APS-C lens. For example, the widest aperture on a Canon **EF-S** 55–250mm telephoto zoom lens (for an APS-C DSLR) is f/4.5 while the Canon **EF** 70–200mm telephoto zoom lens (for a full-frame DSLR) has f/2.8 as its widest aperture. As mentioned earlier, professionals need a "faster" lens and can justify spending the money. As a beginner or even an experienced DSLR hobbyist, there is no meaningful reason to pay that much more for a lens with a wider aperture since your photos don't require the same level of quality as a professional's.

The second reason a Canon EF lens costs more is that the quality of construction is better since professionals require a lens that will last longer and be more resilient to the weather and shooting conditions. A third reason is the number, type and configuration of the glass elements inside the lens as well as other features, which will be explained later.

LEARN WHY LENS FILTERS ARE ESSENTIAL TO BETTER PHOTOGRAPHY

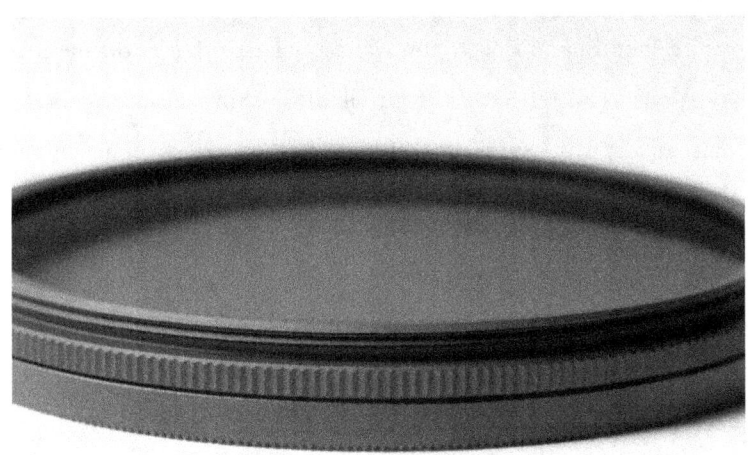

Lens filters are important tools in your arsenal of photography equipment for lens protection, to reduce glare and reflections and to enhance the creativity of your images. Although there are a number of filter types, as a beginner or hobbyist DSLR photographer, you should consider the following 3 as essential.

1. A **UV filter** is an absolute must. In fact, you shouldn't take your camera anywhere or use it under any conditions, indoors or outdoors, without a UV filter on the front of the lens. The greatest benefit of a UV filter is to place an additional layer of protective glass between the bumps, bruises and battering of the outside world and the otherwise exposed front glass element of any lens. Let your fingerprints and any dust, dirt,

moisture or scratches occur on the outside of the UV filter since it can be replaced for next to nothing, compared to a new lens or having the front element replaced. Another pointer: don't be cheap when buying a UV filter; make sure it's from a quality manufacturer and has MRC, or multi-resistant coating.

2.   A **polarizing filter** works the same as a pair of sunglasses, so whenever you're shooting outdoors, you want a polarizing filter on the front of your lens. The reflections from all those shiny surfaces – bodies of water; glass; white surfaces; polished surfaces; reflective metals, such as aluminum, silver, etc. – are controlled as well as glare from the sun or other bright light sources.

A polarizing filter also has creative uses: improving color saturation, which includes the sky, so it isn't a weak, muted space in your photos, and to add contrast. This is the creative element that often distinguishes professional images from amateur photos, so learn how to use a polarizing filter to enhance the contrast. Be conscious of the fact that a polarizing filter reduces the amount of light entering a lens approximately the equivalent of 2 stops, so take that into consideration when calculating your exposure. You might find it helpful to take some test images with a polarizing filter to understand how it affects your photos.

3.   A **neutral density (ND) filter** also causes less light to enter the lens. Whenever you're shooting during the brightest time of the day and you can't choose reasonable exposure values (aperture, shutter speed and ISO), you can use a neutral density filter as an exposure aid. Situations where this is helpful include any motion you want to impart to a photo,

such as a waterfall, or you find it necessary to select large apertures when using a flash, so a scene or subject won't be overexposed.

Neutral density filters are also available in a number of variations. Instead of a single glass element of the same density, the element could have a gradation of density, which is known as a graduated neutral density (GND) filter. A GND filter can either have a distinct line or edge or a soft, or gradual, transition between two gradations of density.

Landscape photographers typically use GND filter when the scene has significant contrast because the sky is normally the brightest portion of the image. The denser or darker part of the filter can be rotated to the top, so less light enters the lens from the sky. The bottom portion is less dense since the foreground is the darker portion of the image. The hard-edge GND is used when the horizon line in a photo is distinct while the soft-edge GND is used when the horizon line is less visible or not an obvious straight line. Both hard-edge and soft-edge GNDs are usually rectangular and must be used with a lens holder.

OTHER LENS FILTER TYPES

- Color filters were popular during the days of film photography to correct colors or they could reduce the effect of one color and allow one or other colors to be emphasized. They don't have much of an application for digital photography because it's easier to create these effects with editing software.

- Close-up filters are used in macrophotography and are often called diopters. A close-up filter is a less expensive method for focusing on and photographing small objects without having to buy expensive macro lenses. Be aware that close-up filters retard image quality, so they don't produce photos as sharp or as clear as a true macro lens.

- You may also find companies that offer star filters that create star-like points from bright light sources or reflections; diffusion filters that are typically used for portrait photography to soften skin tones; and infrared filters that don't allow infrared light into the camera, which results in some interesting effects.

FILTER SHAPES, SIZES AND MOUNTS

It may be obvious by now that most of the filters you're ever apt to use are round and have a screw or thread-type mount to attach to the front of a lens. Plus, round filters come in different sizes to match the size of a lens' front glass element. There are approximately 19 different sizes, but some of these are for specialty lenses, such as a fisheye or a super telephoto.

Landscape photographers, especially when using graduated neutral density filters, prefer square or rectangular filters that are placed in a filter holder, which screws into the same threads a round filter would on the front of a lens. Of course, the shape of a square or rectangular filter conforms to the shape of a photo and in the same proportions.

Some of the well-known and highly respected lens filter manufacturers, include Tiffen, Singh Ray and Hoya, but there are many others. As a beginner or hobbyist, your best value is to acquire a lens filter kit that will include 2 or more of the essential filters you should have. As mentioned above, it's best to buy above-average to top-of-the-line filters.

SHINING SOME LIGHT ON THE SECRET WORLD INSIDE A LENS

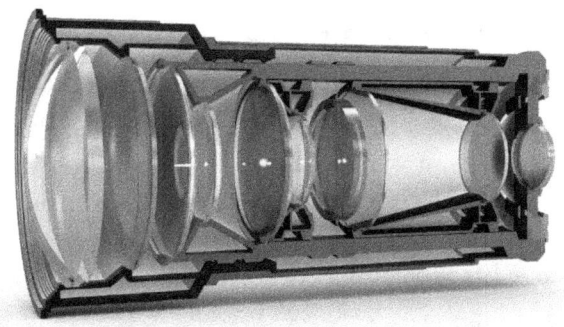

You hold it in your hands and you can look through either end, but what is occurring inside a photo lens when it is in use can seem to be a mysterious secret. Without going too far into the science of optics, it's important that you understand how a lens works because that knowledge can help you to choose the right lens and shoot better photos.

PLENTY OF GLASS

The light rays that enter a lens pass through a number of pieces of glass, or elements, that are of different shapes and sizes. Their primary purpose is to reduce the amount of aberration. Aberration is the degree to which the points of the image transmitted via the light rays do not match when they reach the digital sensor. When the lens elements cause too much aberration then the image will be blurred or the contrast will be weak or colors won't align correctly, which is known as chromatic aberration.

Glass elements in a lens are typically described as being so many elements in so many groups. A separate lens is or two or more elements that are joined considered a group. More elements and more groups are not necessarily better than fewer elements and groups; it depends on the specific lens. The tradeoff is that more elements may result in fewer optical defects, such as aberrations, but more elements also means more glass surfaces through which the light must pass, which create reflections and other problems.

These Canon lenses have various numbers of elements groups:

- Canon EF 28mm f/2.8 – 9 elements in 7 groups

- Canon EF 50mm f/1.2 – 8 elements in 6 groups

- Canon EF 300mm f/2.8 – 15 elements in 11 groups

- Canon EF 24–70mm f/2.8 – 18 elements in 13 groups

Some lenses have what are called aspherical glass elements. This simply means the surface of the element is not spherical; and spherical elements are often the culprits that cause more aberration. Aspherical elements are purposely made with an uneven or complex curved surface, which reduces aberrations and can improve resolution.

SOME IMPRECISION IS NATURAL

Because the light rays are passing through a number of glass elements of various shapes and sizes, it's impossible to transfer the real-life image to the sensor perfectly. Aberration and chromatic aberration are just two of the problems that are evident from the very best lenses.

If you ever notice that the corners of your photos appear darker than the rest of the image, then you are witnessing vignetting. Some vignetting occurs naturally because of the angle of the light rays entering the lens.

Entry-level or lower-priced DSLRs often suffer from this kind of vignetting because the camera software is unable to record as much light in the corners of images. Lenses with a greater number of glass elements can create vignetting because the light must pass through so much glass. This is why professional photographers are willing pay extra for lenses with apertures as wide as f/2.8 or less. The lens is so open at these apertures that more light can reach the corners and there is virtually no discernable vignetting.

DECIPHERING THE NAME OF A CANON AND NIKON LENS

Does your head ache whenever you read the names of lenses? Focal length and f/stop are probably terms you already understand, but the rest of the letters aren't that difficult to understand when you refer to the handy guide below of Canon and Nikon lenses. The other lens manufacturers have similar nomenclature.

CANON

- EF – Electro-Focus. These are Canon's professional-grade lenses and EF indicates they have an electric mount instead of a mechanical mount. The mount is electrical because these lenses have an auto-focus motor in the lens and must be able to communicate with the camera.

- EF-S – Electro-Focus for S-type camera bodies, or those with AFS-C, or cropped, sensors. If you own an entry-level or lower-priced Canon DSLRs, then these are typically the lenses you buy. Remember, an S-type camera body can use EF lenses, although the image will be cropped, but you can't put an EF-S lens on an EF body.

- USM – Ultra-Sonic Motor. This is an acronym for Canon's best auto-focus motor because they are quiet, fast and precise.

- L – This letter signifies a professional-grade EF lens. It's generally understood that L also refers to ultra-low dispersion glass elements, which gives these lenses exceptional optical functionality. L lenses are also identified by their red ring.

- IS – Image Stabilization. This is another built-in system, but this one detects camera shake or other motion, and then adjusts for it. The IS system is particularly helpful when shooting under low light conditions that require slower shutter speeds and handholding your camera, compared to a non-IS lens.

NIKON

- F – F Mount. You won't see the letter F in Nikon lens' names since all Nikon lenses are built with the F-type mount.

- FX and DX – FX signifies a lens specifically for full-frame cameras, but, again, Nikon doesn't actually use FX in any name. DX refers to lenses for cameras with APS-C, or cropped, sensors, similar to Canon's EF-S. Like Canon, an FX lens can be mounted to a DX body, but unlike Canon a DX lens works on an FX body, although the image is limited to the center of the frame as well as fewer pixels are utilized.

- AF-S – Auto-Focus Silent. This is Nikon's equivalent of Canon's USM and is also known as SWM, for Silent Wave Motor, which is the built-in auto-focus motor.

- AF – Auto-Focus. These Nikon lenses also have a built-in auto-focus motor, but it makes a slight noise, compared to AF-S motors. Typically, the AF designation is used on older Nikon lenses.

- D – Distance. Newer Nikon lenses with the Auto-Focus Silent motor have this feature. Take a meter reading with a D lens and it will communicate the focus distance to the camera.

- ED – Extra Low Dispersion. Like Canon's L designation, a lens with an ED element reduces light dispersion. You'll find ED lenses that are for professionals as well as amateurs.

- G – Nikon adds this letter to all of its newest lenses and it simple means it doesn't have a physical aperture ring. It makes these lenses lighter and smaller, but not compatible with older Nikon cameras.

- VR – Vibration Reduction. This is Nikon's image stabilization system and provides the same benefits as Canon IS lenses.

Take the time to understand how the inside of a lens works and Canon, Nikon and the other manufacturers' lens names to make the right choice, the wise choice, of your next and all future lenses.

7 WAYS TO BE MORE CREATIVE
WITH A WIDE-ANGLE LENS

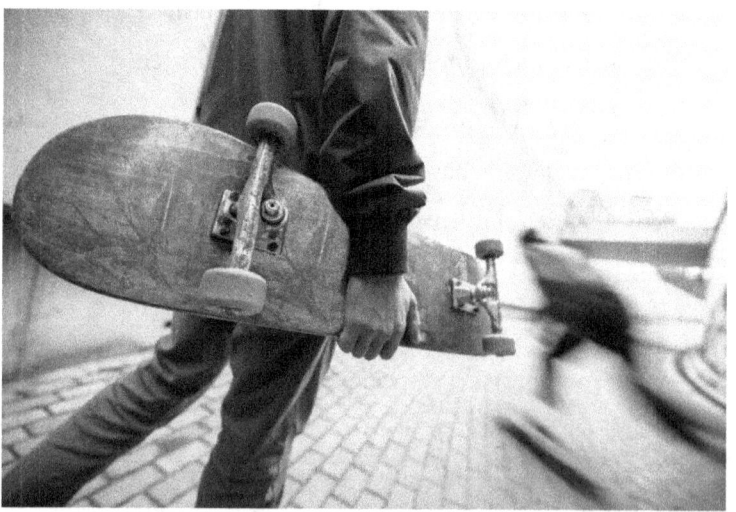

We talked that lenses for your DSLR or mirrorless camera can be categorized in many ways, but there are three types by focal length: wide-angle, normal or telephoto.

- Normal is the equivalent of how your eyes see the world, which is almost a 180-degree field of view, and is considered approximately 50mm. Focal lengths to 85mm also reproduce your vision with just a bit of telephoto starting to occur. Focal lengths from 70 to 85mm focal are considered the prime range for portraits.

- Telephoto, like a telescope, appears to bring distant objects closer, but has a narrower field of view than what you see with your eyes. Technically, any focal length beyond 50mm starts to create the telephoto effect, but in practical terms, lenses with focal lengths of more than 85mm are thought of as telephoto.

- Wide-angle provides a field of view wider than what your eyes would see "normally." Before the wide-angle view is noticeably, you need a 42mm focal length or wider. The wide-angle focal length is further subdivided into ultra-wide-angle, which is approximately 13 to 20mm, and then fisheye, which can be grouped as 8 to 10mm for a circular image and 15 to 16mm to fill the frame with the image.

It's important to remember that the lines between these groups are fuzzy, so there is some overlap. Plus, 2 or all 3 of these focal length categories can be found on zoom lenses, such as 24–70mm or 18–250mm.

All of these focal lengths have creative uses, but the wide-angle lens offers quite a range of creative opportunities because it distorts the "normal" view of your eyes.

1. The Landscape Lens

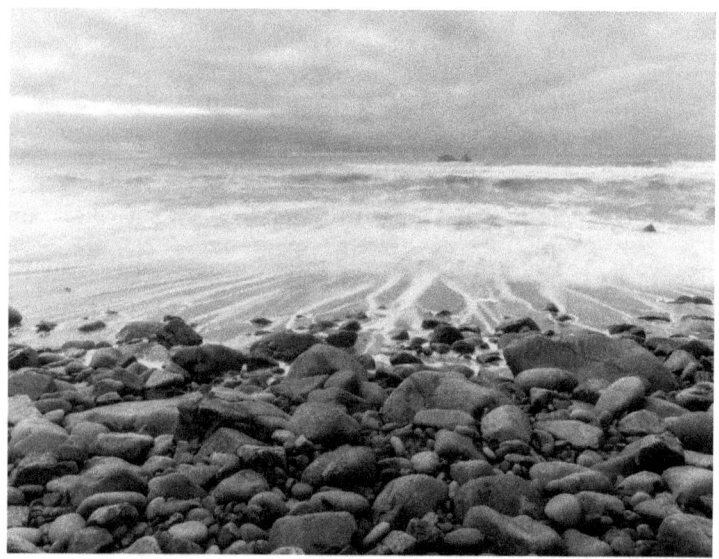

If the 70 to 85mm focal length is perfect for portraits, then wide-angle focal lengths make for the best landscapes. This is a primary distinction between the typical amateur's landscape photo and a professional's. Think of the landscape "snapshots" that you've seen or maybe even shot yourself. Typically, it's a wide view of a lake, the ocean or a mountain range and probably using a normal focal length. All objects in the photo are in the distance – not very creative and, therefore, not very interesting.

With a wide-angle lens, however, it's quite easy to compose interesting, even dramatic and spectacular landscapes. The secret is to find a shooting location with a small object or group of objects of interest in the foreground: wildflowers, an animal skull, a piece of driftwood, a distinctive rock or formation, with that lake, ocean, mountain range, open prairie, desert or stand of trees in the background. Lower your camera position by kneeling or using a tripod, so the foreground object/objects fills the lower portion of the frame. From this lower angle, you can add or eliminate as much of the sky as you want. If the sky has streaks of clouds colored by the sunset, then that is an element you will want in the frame; however, if the sky is just blue, or filled with clouds, then you may want to frame your landscape with little or no sky.

2. Interiors

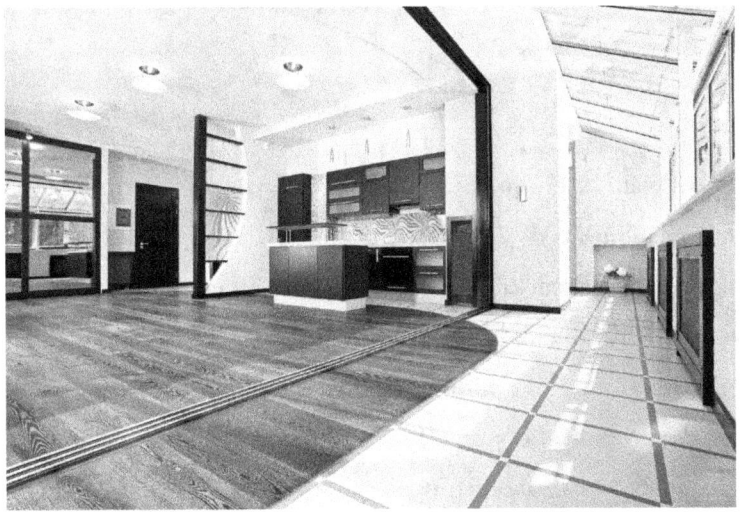

You may have experienced how difficult it is to capture all of a room with a normal focal length, even cramming your body into a corner of the room. A wide-angle lens solves this dilemma, as it is what all professional architectural photographers use to show a majority of an interior space. You'll take much better pictures of Christmas morning at the tree or your child's birthday party with a wide-angle lens or using a wide-angle focal length. Your photos can still highlight a specific person or object in the room, but also show all the activity occurring around the primary subject.

3.   Manipulating the Relationship of 2 Subjects or Objects

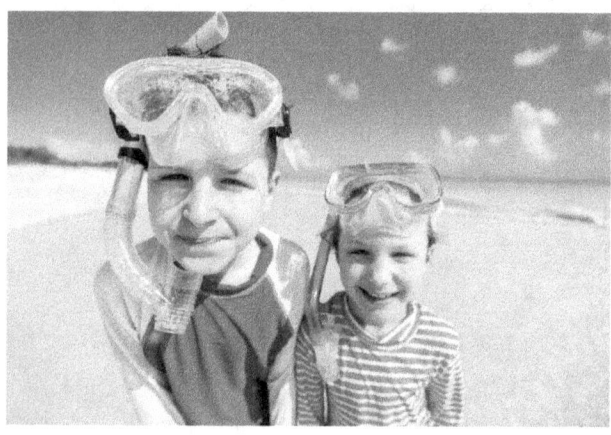

A wide-angle lens or focal length allows you to be creative with the physical relationship of 2 subjects or objects. For example, you want to photograph your small child with a puppy or kitten. With the pet in the foreground and the child behind, you can move to a low position, even laying on the ground, and with a wide-angle lens close to the puppy or kitten make it the prominent object in the frame. Your child fills the background, with an outstretched hand petting the animal.

4.   A Street Tool

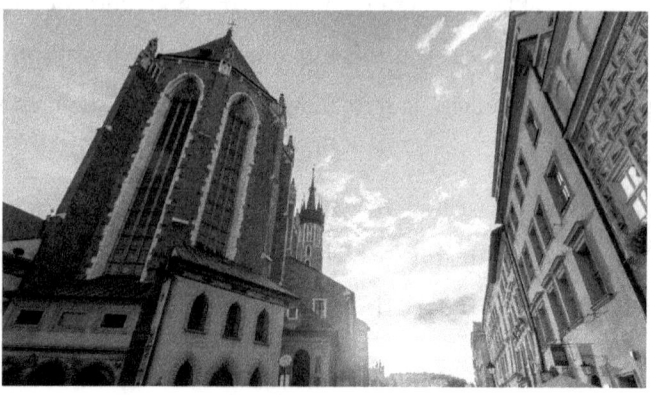

Street photography is another genre where you want to use a wide-angle lens, especially if you plan to shoot from the hip, surreptitiously, as you walk along a street. Many of the people, places and activities you'll find on the street also lend themselves to wide-angle photography. Often, you're working in a confined space, so you need a wide focal length to include everyone in the frame as well as enough of the background to identify the place.

5. A Travel Companion

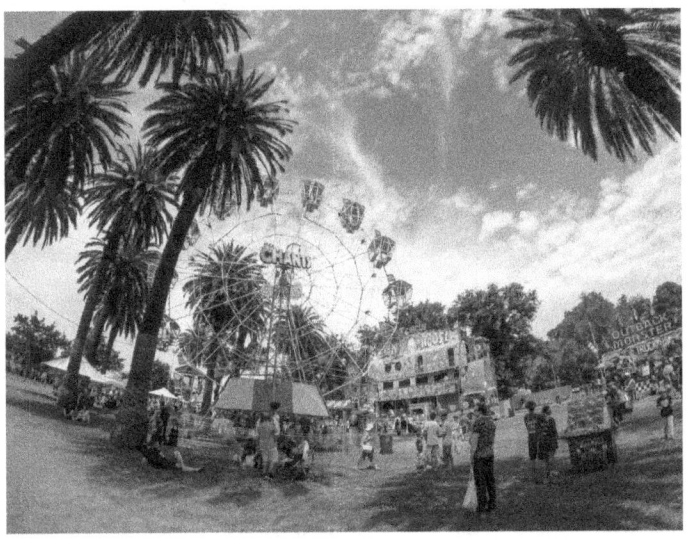

For many of the same reasons as street photography, a wide-angle lens produces better travel images. It allows you to enter a particular activity, such as a street fair or carnival, and be close enough to participants to show their entire costumes, but also part of the carnival environment. Using a wide-angle lens while traveling also forces you to interact with people instead of taking their pictures from a distance with a telephoto lens. After all, this is one of the primary reasons for traveling: meeting new people, experiencing different cultures.

6.   A Different Kind of Portrait

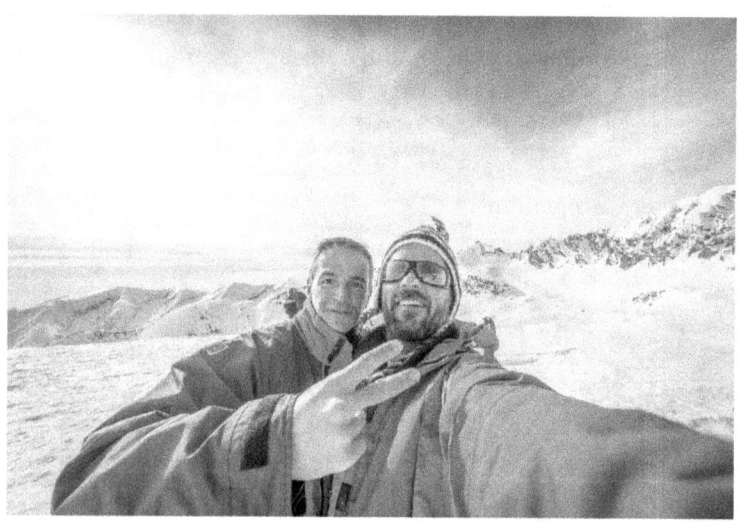

Now, you wouldn't shoot formal portraits or a professional person's headshot for their LinkedIn page with a wide-angle lens. The facial distortions are likely to be unflattering; however, a wide-angle lens is useful when shooting casual portraits and there wouldn't be any group selfies without a wide-angle lens or focal length. Whether you're with your significant other at a picnic for two, playing in the backyard with your kids or at a party or family gathering, use a wide-angle lens to create images with unusual perspectives like the child and puppy/kitty example above. Your significant other is opening the bottle of wine at the picnic. Position the camera very low relative to the bottle of wine, which is in the foreground. The wide-angle view allows you to include his hands working the corkscrew and the concentration on his face above and behind the bottle.

7. Move Closer: The Primary Rule of Wide-Angle Photography

Regardless of what kind of image or subjects and objects you're shooting with a wide-angle focal length, you must move closer to the primary subject or object. Otherwise, it is simply just another object in the frame and relatively the same size as all other subjects and/or objects. In fact, you'll discover that you'll have to force yourself to move as close as you can. The general guideline is to reduce the distance between the primary subject or object and your camera by 50%, and in many cases, you'll want to move even closer.

You're sure to enjoy wide-angle photography and notice improvement in your images and receive more kudos from family and friends. It takes some practice, however, and consciously thinking about your composition before just randomly firing the shutter.

MIRRORLESS CAMERA VS. DSLR

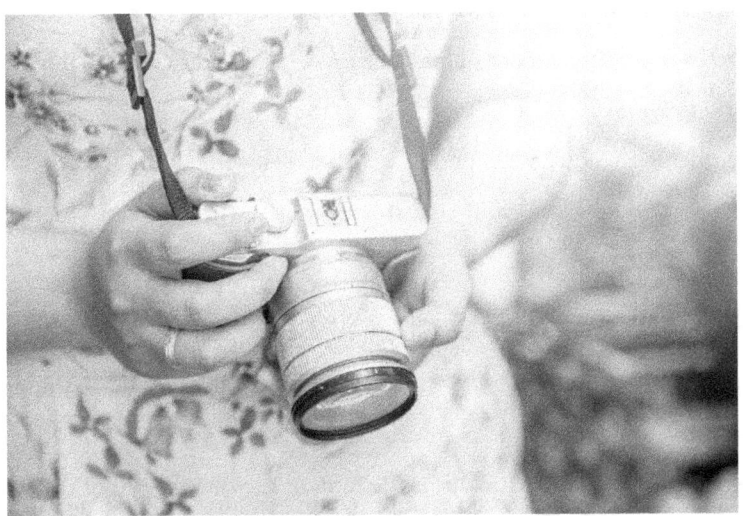

If you're contemplating the purchase of a new camera and advancing beyond your smartphone or a compact camera, then you have two choices to consider: a DSLR (digital single-lens reflex) or a mirrorless interchangeable lens system (MILS). Before explaining the reasons you might want to buy one instead of the other, some background information is required.

As you may know, a DSLR, in its basic form, is the digital version of the classic SLR film camera. Both are so named because there is a mirror just inside the camera body set at an angle, so the light coming through the lens reflects upwards to the pentaprism at the top center of most DSLRs, allowing you to see and compose a photo with your eye to the viewfinder. The mirror will flip to a horizontal position when you press the shutter button, so the light strikes the sensor to record the image.

A mirrorless camera, as the name implies, has no mirror. Instead of the light from the lens reflecting off a mirror, the light rays strike the sensor directly, allowing you to view and compose the image on the LCD screen on the back of the camera. This "live view" is the same as the Live View feature of a DSLR camera. Considering the proliferation of smartphones, you probably already have experience with the viewing system of a mirrorless camera since that is how your smartphone works when in photo mode.

The first mirrorless camera was introduced during March 2004, and not from a major camera manufacturer, but Epson, best known for its printers. Eventually, camera companies started to design and manufacture MILS cameras, with Olympus and Kodak being the first to develop a specific system, called Four Thirds. This is the ratio of the dimensions of the sensor, which had its origination in the ratio of the traditional TV screen. The Micro Four Thirds system is simply a smaller version of a Four Thirds camera.

REASON #1: SIZE AND WEIGHT

One of the goals of the companies that developed MILS cameras was to offer photographers a camera that was smaller and lighter than a DSLR, but allowed for the interchanging of lenses, and could produces images of a similar quality. If you've shopped for a DSLR and felt many of the models seemed heavy, then a MILS camera may be a better alternative for you. Many professional photographers will tell you that they leave their DSLRs at home when traveling for leisure or on vacation with the family and shoot these kinds of images with a smaller, lighter mirrorless camera instead.

REASON #2: SENSOR SIZE

Because there are a number of sensor sizes for mirrorless cameras, let's start with DSLRs as the foundation of understanding the differences. The physical sensor size of a full-frame DSLR, which is considered a professional-grade camera, is 36 x 24mm, the same size as the traditional 35mm film frame. DSLRs for hobbyists and enthusiasts typically have an APS-C sensor that produces a cropped version of the image of a full-frame camera, either a factor of 1.5x or 1.6x. Unfortunately, the major DSLR camera manufacturers couldn't agree on a constant size for an APS-C sensor, so Canon's is 22.2 x 14.8 mm and all others are 23.5 to 23.7 x 15.6mm.

MILS cameras have six different size sensors. The smallest is 6.17 x 4.55mm, also known as 1/2.3-inch, and found in the Pentax Q. The Nikon 1 Series has the 1-inch sensor (12.8 x 9.6mm) while Panasonic and Olympus cameras have the Micro Four Thirds sensor, or 17.3 x 13mm. Some MILS cameras have APC-S-size sensors. The Canon EOS M has the Canon-specific size, 22.2 x 14.8mm. Sony and Fujifilm MILS cameras have the 23.5 x 15.6mm APS-C sensor size. The Leica M MILS camera is equipped with a full-frame sensor.

Ultimately, choosing a camera based on sensor size depends on the quality of images you want to capture. The larger the physical size of the sensor the better quality you can expect. Therefore, if most of your photography will be casual, but you want the option of using different lenses, then you may want to choose a MILS camera with a sensor smaller than the APS-C sizes. If you want photos of greater quality, in terms of contrast, exposure control, color saturation, white balance and other specifications, then choose a MILS model with an APS-C sensor. It will be the equivalent of an entry to mid-level DSLR, but in a lighter and smaller camera body.

REASON #3: LENS SELECTION

No doubt, Sony, Olympus, Panasonic and the other major MILS camera players will increase the number of available lenses as the mirrorless camera continues to grow in popularity. If you need the widest selection of lenses, however, because of the unique kinds of images you shoot, then a DSLR will be a better choice, at least during the near term.

REASON #4: LIVE VIEW QUALITY

As mentioned above, you view and compose a photo with a MILS camera on the rear LCD screen and what you see will typically be a better representation of your final image than Live View on a DSLR because a

MILS camera has an electronic viewfinder. Unlike the viewfinder of a DSLR, the MILS's electronic viewfinder allows you see what your photo will look like with various exposure, white balance and other adjustments.

MIRRORLESS LIMITATIONS

Finally, if you consider buying an MILS camera, then be aware that its battery life is shorter than a DSLR and the auto-focusing system an MILS uses is slower and less accurate than that in a DSLR. This statement may become inaccurate as the MILS technology progresses.

RAW VS. JPEG FORMATS. WHICH ONE IS BETTER?

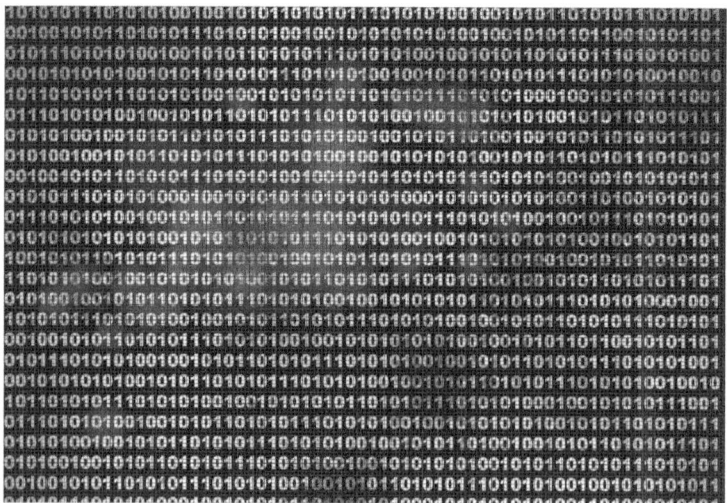

This is a very good question and one that often stumps the new or hobbyist DSLR photographer. Digital photography technology may be a wonderful advancement, but it means you must think about your photos digitally, as that is how your camera's sensor captures them. The pictures you take are not negative or positive film, but a digital file – either RAW or JPEG.

Now, it's not the purpose here to bore you with a highly technical explanation of these file types. If the science interests you, then there are many online sources that will provide a thorough explanation. Basic understanding of RAW and JPEG files is all you actually need as an amateur DSLR photographer.

1. Digital is information

At a basic level, digital is information. A bit is the fundamental unit of information and is expressed as either 0 or 1, while a byte could be considered a "digital word," as it typically consists of any combination of 8 bits. The primary difference between RAW and JPEG is that RAW files include all the digital information of a photo; JPEGs do not.

2. RAW means raw

Your camera captures RAW images in their "rawest" form. The camera doesn't process them in any way, but simple records all of the digital information of a photo. For this reason, a RAW file image viewed on your camera's LCD screen or a computer screen will appear dark, with little or no contrast. It wouldn't be an image you'd want to share with anyone and certainly wouldn't be ready to print, use in a magazine or post on a Website or social media. For RAW files to be useful, they must be processed with photo editing software, such as Photoshop or Lightroom (there are many others, too).

3. When you should shoot RAW files

You can never go wrong always shooting RAW files, because you will have the entire spectrum of digital information about each photo. The only actual downside is RAW files are considerably larger than JPEG files, which means the memory card in your camera won't hold as many RAW files.

Whenever you're shooting in RAW, therefore, you should have extra memory cards with you because you are likely to fill the first one and need an empty one.

- Shoot RAW files when you don't have much control of the photography environment. You may be photographing an event or a street carnival during a vacation where people are moving, the amount of light is constantly changing, the backgrounds are different, etc. Under these conditions, it's difficult to almost impossible to take the time to make sure every image is properly exposed.

- Shoot RAW files when your compositions have High Dynamic range. This simply means that an image includes a wide range of tonal quality from very bright whites (or highlights) to very dark areas (or shadows). Typically, landscapes, nature, architecture, outdoor sports and action will have a High Dynamic range. By shooting in RAW, you're assured of capturing all that digital information, so when you process the image in editing software, you're able to adjust and manipulate the highlights and shadows to create the best-looking photos.

4. JPEG is your friend

Make no mistake – RAW files are the best; however, JPEG files also have their uses, especially as a DSLR beginner or hobbyist. First, JPEG is an acronym for Joint Photographic Experts Group, which is the scientific body that established the technical standard for JPEG. Remember, your camera simply captures a RAW file and doesn't process the image; however, when you are shooting in JPEG your camera actually processes the digital information of the RAW file, and then compresses that information, making a smaller JPEG file.

Your camera uses its exposure and other settings and, during JPEG processing, will adjust the highlights and shadows to render a pleasing contrast across the image as well as reducing any digital noise and actually sharpening the image. Essentially, a JPEG is a finished image in the camera, compared to a RAW file that isn't finished until processed with editing software.

It's important to remember that once a JPEG file is created, the digital information of the RAW file your camera didn't use can't be retrieved; it's lost forever. With this processing and compression, a JPEG file doesn't have the High Dynamic range of a RAW file, which is why most professionals don't shoot in JPEG because they may need that entire High Dynamic range to create the exact image they want during the editing process.

- As a beginner or hobbyist DSLR photographer, you want to shoot most of your photos as JPEGs, since they tend to be casual photos of your family and friends, family events, vacations, etc. Not only don't you need all the digital information of a RAW file as a professional would, but also you're able to show and share your photos immediately; and they will have enough contrast, color saturation and sharpness to be pleasing to the casual observer.

- Another reason to shoot in JPEG is for use on the Web or social media where small files are all you need. The large files created from a RAW image are slow to load and many Websites and social media have limits on the size of file you can post.

- Whenever you're shooting an action sequence, and using burst mode on your camera, you want to shoot in JPEG. In RAW, your camera's buffer would fill quickly and you wouldn't be able to continue shooting in burst mode until the camera had moved the large RAW files from the buffer to the memory card.

- Even memory cards with the most capacity have a limit, so by shooting in JPEG, more photos can be stored on a card. Under most shooting conditions this is not a problem until you find yourself somewhere in the backcountry shooting landscapes or nature from dawn to dusk or on an all-day vacation excursion. You inserted a small memory card in your camera before your left on your photography adventure and forgot to bring extras, or the extra cards in your pocket also have small capacities.

Once you include post-production with editing software as part of your photography skills, you may want to shoot some RAW images to learn how to use the software and create highly dynamic finished photos.

MEMORY CARDS FOR YOUR DSLR

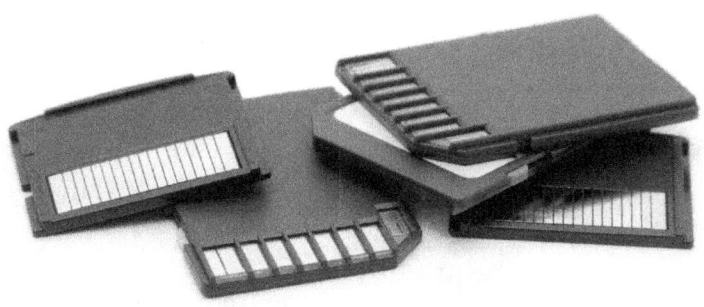

For all its technological prowess, your DSLR camera (and most of them) doesn't have the capability to store the images you shoot. That's the job of the memory card (or cards) you insert in the slot (or slots) on the outside of your camera. Refer to your camera's manual to learn where the slot is located and what kind of card the manufacturer recommends. Even with this information, understanding and selecting the right memory card can easily be confusing and overwhelming – so let's fix that here.

The first point to understand is that both the cheapest and most expensive card records the same image quality of your photos. The problem with a cheap card is that it typically records slower and isn't as dependable as higher-priced cards.

What you need to know next is the 2 primary descriptions of a memory card: format and speed.

1. Format

It's likely your camera manual will recommend one of two types of memory cards: SD, or Secure Digital, or CF, or Compact Flash. Within each type, there are a number of varieties.

- The SD Standard card will store as much as 2GB.

- The SDHC (High Capacity) will store 2GB to 32GB.

- The SDXC (Xtra Capacity) will stores 32BG to 2TB.

The CompactFlash format is now more than 20 years old; and, although many cameras were able to use them, today they are typically only used on professional-level DSLRs and professional HD video cameras. These cards are available in storage capacities from 2GB to 128GB.

There are also a number of other formats you might see while shopping for and buying a memory card. The Memory Stick was originally a Sony variation on memory cards and many Sony digital cameras use the Memory Stick Duo; however, most of them will also accept SD cards. UHS-I standard SDHC cards are a relatively new product from SanDisk, one of the major memory card manufacturers. The purpose of this new card was to provide professional photographers and videographers with a card that had a write speed as fast as 45 MB/sec or faster. The CFast 2.0 standard advances the capabilities of the common CompactFlash format to even faster read and write speeds of as much as 450 MB/sec and 350 MB/sec, respectively.

2. Speed

The second major characteristic of memory cards is the speed at which data is written to the card as well as how fast the data can be read. The industry uses a common classification system of 2, 4, 6 or 10. These numbers are expressed as X MB/sec, or the capability to write a set amount of data, measured in megapixels, per second. Memory cards are also assigned a maximum write speed, such as 30 MB/sec. The importance of the read speed is how long you must wait for all the images (and their data) to be transferred to another device, most commonly a computer. How the card connects to a computer and the speed of the hard drive or SSD storage will also affect the read speed.

HOW TO CHOOSE THE RIGHT CARD FOR YOUR CAMERA

Choosing the right memory card has very much to do with what level of photographer you are and what you shoot. If you're new to DSLR photography and/or a part-time hobbyist, then an SD or SDHC card of 16GB to 32GB is probably all you need. Of course, it depends on what the manufacturer of your camera recommends and the file type, compression and resolution of the images you are shooting.

Before purchasing a card, it's best to visit the Website of a few of the well-known manufacturers, where you'll find tables with the number of images the various card types can typically hold. If most of your photos are casual images of family members, friends and social activities, then you may not need a card with much more than 2 MB/sec or 4 MB/sec write speed.

At the enthusiast, amateur or even semi-professional level, you definitely need an SDHC or SDXC card; but, again, it depends on your camera and what subject matter you are shooting. If you spend a considerable amount of time selecting a good landscape location and setting up a tripod, etc., then you probably won't be taking as many images as a wedding photographer or a photojournalist. These photographers not only need a high-capacity card, but also one that writes quickly, especially if they are using the continuous shooting mode.

Full-time professionals also need the best cards in terms of data capacity and write speed for many of the same reasons above, but primarily because most, if not all, of their images will be in the RAW file format, which results in a high volume of data capture. The cards with the highest capacity and fastest write speeds are also an absolute necessity for serious videographers, especially professionals, as they are shooting multiple takes of the same scene and/or enough video to create a 5-, 10-, 20-minute or longer final presentations. Some professionals will advise that you use a number of smaller cards instead of one with a very large capacity, so all your images are not vulnerable to card failure (although this rarely happens) or having that single card become damaged by accident or being immersed in water.

Although there are many well-respected memory card manufacturers, many amateurs and professionals use Kingston, Lexar, Transcend and SanDisk cards.

INTRODUCTION TO FLASH PHOTOGRAPHY

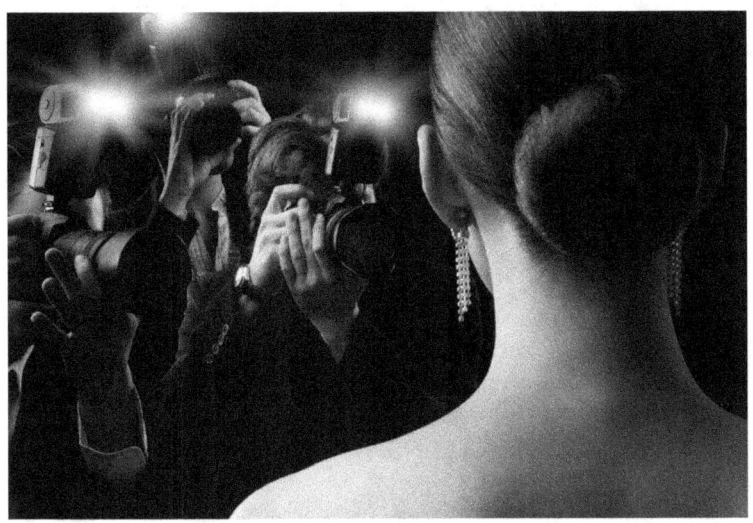

Before you "graduated" to a DSLR camera, you probably didn't pay much attention to the flash on your smartphone or compact camera. It worked automatically much like the camera, so you didn't need to know much about flash photography and how it worked. Now, you've entered a whole new world and, although your DSLR can operate automatically, you're learning that much of the creativity, excitement and passion of DSLR photography occurs when you take control of the camera. The same goes for a flash unit.

Although sunlight provides plenty of light for most photography, there are numerous situations, indoors and outdoors, when you require artificial light, in the form of a flash, to illuminate a scene or subject adequately and expose it properly. There is so much more DSLR photography to experience and images to create once you understand and are able to take control of flash photography.

Many DSLRs come with a built-in flash unit that is often located at the top middle of the camera, which pops from a compartment, and then retracts into the compartment when not needed. The pop-up flash is a convenient feature when shooting casual photos of family members and friends and for family events and vacations, but they have limited power and, therefore, limit the kinds of pictures you can light with it. As you desire to spread your wings as a DSLR photographer, you'll want to consider a separate flash unit eventually, so you can do more with your camera and push the creative envelope.

THE 3 BASIC SPECIFICATIONS OF A FLASH

- **Sync speed** – Most DSLRs have a sync speed of $1/250^{th}$ of a second, although some can be different, so be sure you know the sync speed of your camera. Sync speed is a rather simple concept: it is the shutter speed you must use to be sure the light from the flash is synchronized with the opening of the shutter. If you select a shutter speed that is not the sync speed, you're likely to have a photo that is half black. This is because the shutter curtains are still moving when the light from the flash enters the camera, so you've taken a picture of the curtain.

- **Guide number** – While sync speed relates to shutter speed, the guide number relates to what aperture, or f/stop, you must select for your lens, so enough light will illuminate a subject at a given distance. For example, the guide number for the built-in flash on the Canon EOS 60D is 43 feet at ISO 100. If you selected an aperture of f/4, then the subject would have to be approximately 10 to 11 feet from the flash to be illuminated correctly. The guide number is divided by the f/stop, or 43 divided by 4 is 10.75 feet. If you know the distance to your subject,

7 feet for example, you can divide the guide number by the distance to calculate the correct aperture. 43 divided by 7 is approximately 6, so you'd select an aperture of f/5.6.

The guide number on a separate flash unit can be much larger. For example, the Canon Speedlite 430EX II has a guide number of 141 feet at ISO 100. At an aperture of f/4, your subject could be at a distance of 35 feet and would be correctly illuminated. If he or she were only 7 feet distance, then your aperture would be f/22. Although the built-in flash on a DSLR is convenient, you can see by these examples that a separate flash unit has much more power, illuminating subjects at a much greater distance.

Obviously, if you don't make the guide number calculation, then the wrong aperture wouldn't allow enough light to enter the camera, creating an underexposed image; and conversely, if the aperture is too wide, then too much light will reflect from the subject into the camera, causing an overexposed photo.

Another point to remember is that the guide number is at ISO 100. If you increase the ISO number, then the guide number increases too. Using the guide number of 43 feet above, the guide number would increase to 60.2 feet (or a factor of 1.4) at ISO 200 and 86 feet (or a factor of 2) at ISO 400.

- **Flash Metering Modes** – Your DSLR uses one of three flash metering modes, which reads the light of the flash to determine the correct duration of light to expose the scene or subject correctly.

TTL, or Through-the-Lens, is the mode that measures the light of the flash as it travels through the lens and strikes a separate flash sensor in the camera. It reads the exposure and shortens or lengthens the duration of the flash, so the right amount of light creates a correct exposure.

A-TTL, or Advanced Through-the-Lens, works essentially the same as TTL, except an extremely fast pre-flash of light is fired that is often infrared and thus invisible. It determines the correct f/stop, which the camera selects prior to the full flash of light. The duration of the flash matches how much light is required according to the pre-determined f/stop setting.

E-TTL, or Evaluative-Through-the Lens, is Canon's name for its flash metering system (Nikon calls its I-TTL, or Intelligent-Through-the Lens). It uses a pre-flash of light, as with A-TTL, to determine the correct f/stop; however, instead of a separate flash sensor reading the light to control the duration of the flash of light, the camera's main sensor (that typically reads the ambient, or natural light, when not using a flash) also monitors the light of the flash.

YOUR MOST IMPORTANT COMPOSITIONAL TOOL: THE RULE OF THIRDS

Much of what makes a photograph more compositionally pleasing and creative is based on principles that painters and illustrators learned centuries ago. One of these is the Rule of Thirds.

The concept is not difficult to understand. When you look through the viewfinder, think of a grid of two parallel vertical and horizontal lines superimposed on your image, exactly like a Tic-Tac-Toe layout. Many DSLRs come with this feature that you can select in the camera menu. Those master painters and illustrators of long ago discovered – and science has subsequently confirmed – that the points where the lines intersect and the individual lines are where the human eye is naturally attracted. Moving you or your camera, so the subject or object, or its dominant feature, is positioned at these points or along these lines typically results in a much more interesting and creative image.

1. Portrait Perfect

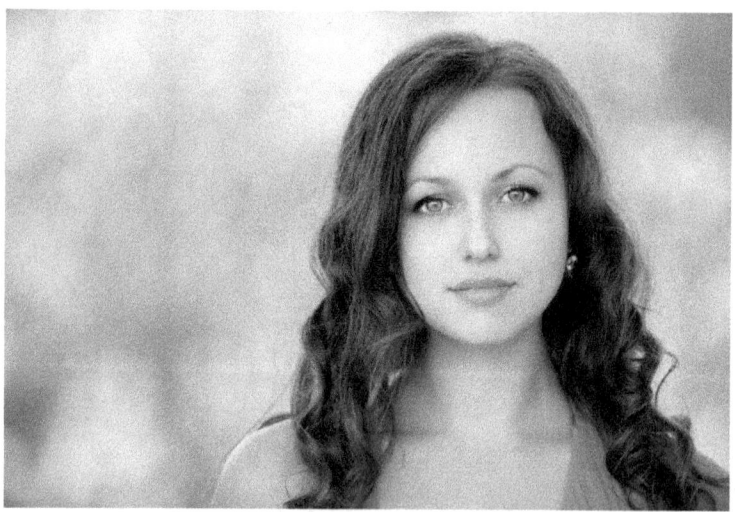

Although it may seem logical to position a person, either his or her body or face, in the center of the frame, you'll quickly discover that placing them along either the right or left vertical line in the grid will improve the look of the photo significantly. The "empty" right or left two-thirds allows more of the background to be seen, even if quite defocused and indistinguishable. You can use this technique to create a balance with another object. For example, you're photographing a person at the seashore. You could position him or her along the right vertical grid line and a lighthouse in the background, slightly defocused, along the left grid line. You're on vacation and plan to photograph your travel companion with an interesting road sign. Instead of placing him or her in front of the sign in the center of the frame, position him or her to the right or left with the sign in the opposite third. You could also shoot this photo from a low angle with the person's face prominent in the lower left or right third with part of the sign behind and above your subject in the other third.

2.   The Eyes Have It

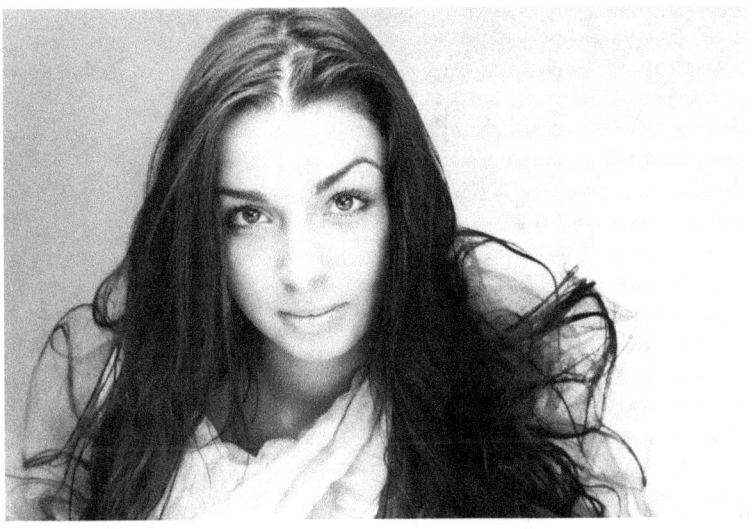

Another common mistake of novice photographers is not only to position a subject in the center of the frame, but also his or her eyes on the horizontal line that cuts the image in half. Your subject will be more pleased about his or her portrait if the eyes are aligned with the top horizontal line of the grid, remembering also to place his or her head to the right or left. You can also experiment with photographing a person with his or her eyes aligned with the bottom horizontal line. Only the top half of the subject's head will be in the shot, but since the eyes are the most important facial features, just seeing them can result in a very interesting photo. You can also ask your subject to try different facial expressions – a happy face, a sad face, a scowl, etc. – that will only be communicated through the eyes and the lines on the forehead.

When the subject's eyes are aligned with either horizontal line, he or she doesn't necessarily have to be looking at the camera. Ask the person to look toward the opposite side of the frame, as if looking off camera. This will imply something of interest outside the frame that will leave viewers guessing as to what it is. In the example above, with the subject's eyes aligned along the bottom horizontal line, you can ask him or her to look up, so the eyes are staring into the space above his or her head.

3.   Dynamic Diagonals

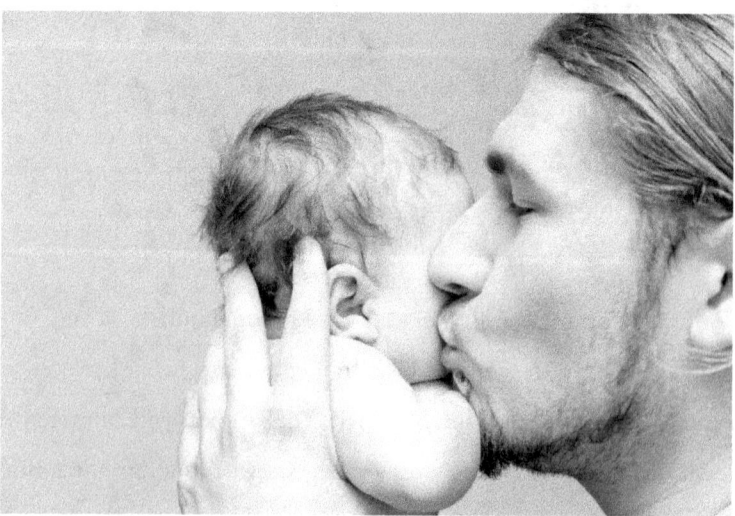

The Rule of Thirds also allows you to introduce a secondary object into the frame; and positioning it at the opposite and upper or lower-line intersections creates a natural diagonal element to the photo. For example, a woman is positioned in the right third of the frame, turned almost 90 degrees to the camera. In the lower left of the frame, she is holding a rose and is looking down at it. Or, a father is positioned similarly and he holds his newborn child in his hands to the lower right or left. This diagonal concept also applies to photos of inanimate objects. Instead of positioning a pot of flowers in the garden in the center of the frame, move it to the right or left, with the blooms to the top. Place a hand trowel, a pair of soiled garden gloves or a similar gardening implement or accessory in the lower right or left and slightly in front of the flowerpot.

4. No Half Horizon

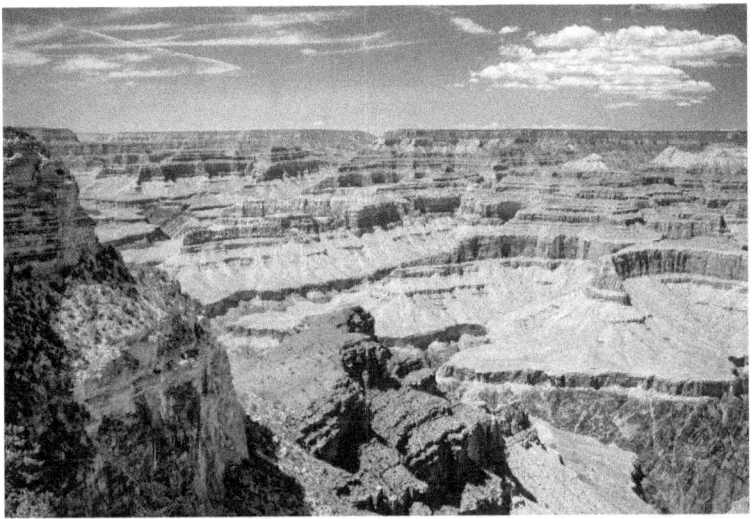

The Rule of Thirds also applies to the horizon line in a landscape, seascape, cityscape or other wide view images that show the natural horizon line. A sure sign that an inexperienced photographer shot a picture is with the horizon line centered across the photo. Your pictures will be much better if you move the camera or you, so the horizon is aligned with the top or bottom horizontal line in the Rule of Thirds grid. By eliminating most of the sky, you're able to introduce more elements into the bottom third of the frame. Think of photographing the Grand Canyon or any scene from a height. You want most of the frame to be the Canyon, not the sky. Conversely, if you want to emphasize interesting cloud formations above the sea or a city, then you'd want the natural horizon to align with the lower horizontal line of the grid.

5. Learn to Lead

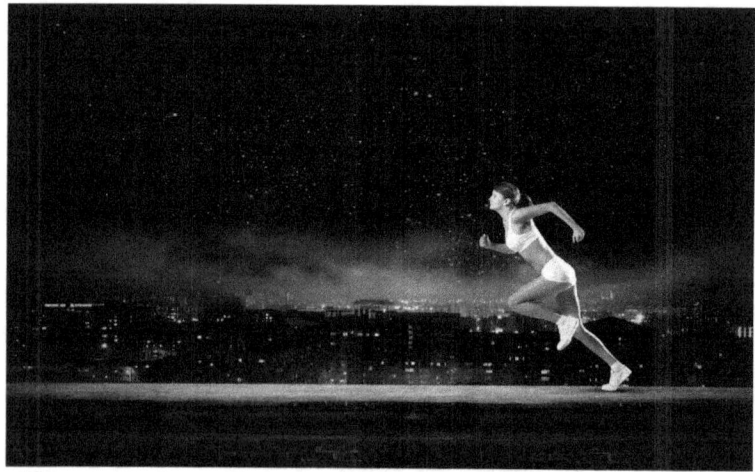

When photographing any object or subject in motion across the image – a sprinter, a racehorse, a racecar, a bird, etc. – position it in the side of the frame from the direction from which it is coming. By leaving the other two-thirds of the frame empty, you are giving the object or subject room to run into the frame. It's often called leading the subject. This helps to communicate the idea of motion to the viewer's eye better than the object or subject in the middle of the frame.

6. The Old Cliché Applies

You know, the one that states, "all rules are meant to be broken." There will be specific kinds of composition when you want to break the Rule of Thirds, typically when centering the object or subject helps to emphasis the story it is telling. For example, you want to capture your entire family seated at a long table at Thanksgiving, with the table piled with food and everyone's face in anticipation of the feast. By standing on a chair or ladder and shooting with a wide-angle lens, the best composition would place the food-laden table at the center of the frame, with your family members seated to each side.

You'll find it helpful to plan one or more practice photo shoots where you photograph objects or subjects according to the Rule of Thirds, without much concern for the rest of the image. You'll become more conscious of the Rule of Thirds and think about it as you compose every future photograph.

BASIC SHAPES ARE THE BUILDING BLOCKS OF YOUR PHOTOS

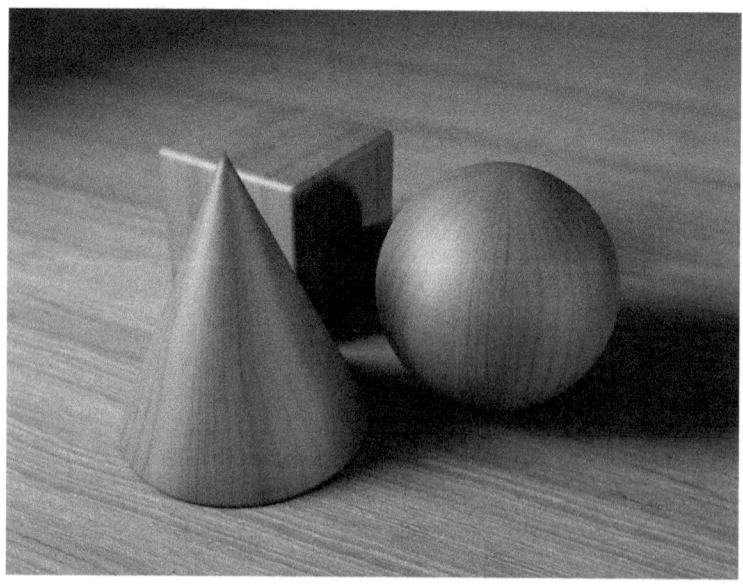

It's often the case with new photographers and even DSLR hobbyists and enthusiasts with some experience to concern themselves first with the identification or definition of the objects they see through the viewfinder when composing a photo. Their mind-speak says, "I am photographing a building, a person, a face, a variety of melons in the market," etc. You must certainly recognize what you are shooting, but you should start the process of composing a photo by first identifying the basic shapes that you see.

A skyscraper is not a building, but a long rectangle; the human body is also a rectangle, but it can be posed to appear triangular; the human face is an oval; melons are round, but in three dimensions they can be elliptical or spherical. The two primary purposes for looking for basic shapes are first to compose an image with shapes that complement or contrast with each other; and secondly, to help you simplify your compositions. This is often a major dividing line between amateur and professional images: the amateur typically includes too many objects in a composition while the professional strives to reduce them to a minimum, thus emphasizing those few to a maximum.

At an even more subtle level, the professional is also looking at the shape of the open space between objects, whether they are in close proximity or at a great distance from each other. Photographing a city skyline, for example, will include many long vertical rectangles – skyscrapers – and the space between them will also appear to be long vertical rectangles. You might create a more interesting photo if you find a position and angle that allows the open space to appear as a square of sky or background between two skyscrapers.

Another example is composing a cityscape image with a single, modern skyscraper in the middle background and the rounded arch of an entryway or memorial in a park in the foreground or just the top of the dome of a classically designed building, such as a capitol building, museum, university library, etc. A similar contrast is a photograph on a beach, with the roundness of a beach ball or the sweeping arc or diagonal of a driftwood branch in the foreground and the narrow rectangle of a lighthouse in the distance.

The Rule of Thirds is also often important to recognizing the shape of the open space between basic shapes. The Rule states that the best place in the frame for the primary object or subject is either aligned with the two vertical and horizontal lines that divide the frame into a tic-tac-toe board or where those lines cross. In a landscape photo, you may photograph a cliff face at right angles, so the face aligns with the vertical Rule-of-Thirds line in the left third of the image. The space to the right of the rectangular shape of that part of the cliff seen in the frame may be an open square of sky with just the top half of the circular setting sun in the distance and its low light reflected off the cliff face. The basic square shape to the right of the cliff could also be a river that appears as a straight line, but diagonal from the lower left to the upper right, dividing the square into two right triangles.

A primary compositional technique of landscape photography is to position your camera low with a wide-angle lens and with a smaller object or collection of objects in the foreground in contrast with a broad lake stretching to the horizon or a grand wall of snow-capped mountains in the background. Recognizing basic shapes, and then positioning your camera, correctly, can help you compose complementary or contrasting landscape images. The rounded shape of delicate wildflowers in the foreground contrasts with a stand of dark green pine trees in the background, with each tree perfectly straight and vertical.

The wide-angle lens you typically use for many types of landscape images will cause naturally straight lines to curve because of optical distortion. These curved lines suggest arcs or create a curved edge to otherwise straight-sided objects. The viewer will find these curved lines more pleasing and will subconsciously lead his or her eye into the heart of your image.

A few examples of diagonal lines have already been mentioned above, but look for diagonal lines that become the sides of triangular shapes. From a high angle, a road enters the frame from the lower right and a train track from the lower left. They intersect in the top third of the frame (following the Rule of Thirds) and create a triangle, with its broad base across the bottom of the image, causing the eye to move towards the top of the triangle. There are also triangular shapes to the right and left and above where the road and tracks cross.

Lines that intersect at right angles will create square spaces. The horizontal branch of a tree and the vertical shape of a tree behind it can result in a square space where a primary object or subject is framed for emphasis. Naturally occurring square objects will be more difficult to find, but there are many human-made square patterns, in the tiles of an interior space or the layout of a public park or backyard garden. During your travels, look for old or interesting homes with series of square windows or an outdoor café with square tables, photographed from above with only one person sitting at one table.

An aid to helping you recognize shapes first as you compose photos is to print a series of your photos or purchase the print version of a few photography magazines. Use different color markers to outline the basic shapes you find in the photos, and then study their complementary and contrasting nature. You can even take these into the field to make the basic shapes in the scenes you photograph become clear and distinct and to use them to compose better images.

8 WORST MISTAKES BEGINNER DSLR PHOTOGRAPHERS MAKE

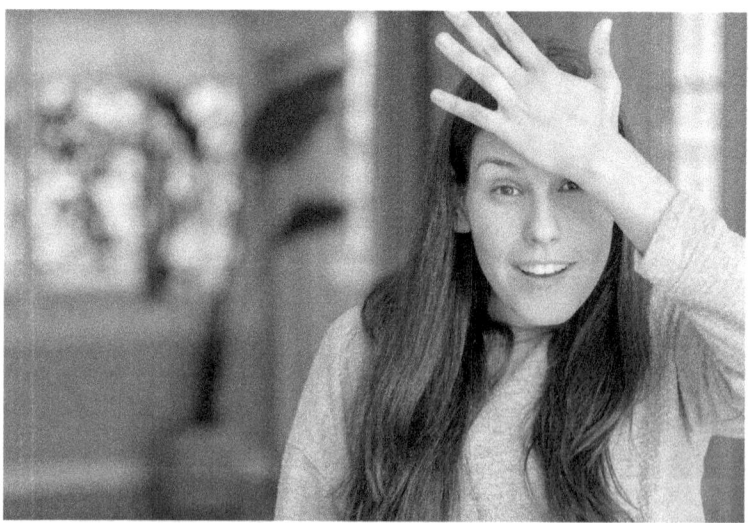

You may have discovered by now that DSLR photography is not meant to be easy. You must be willing to study and practice various concepts and techniques and spend time learning your camera's controls, so you can take better pictures and also maximize the return on your investment in a DSLR camera.

No doubt, you've stumbled and made mistakes as you advance into the world of DSLR photography; and that's OK because making mistakes is often the best way to learn. This section highlights a number of the most-common mistakes of DSLR beginners; some of which you may have already made while others are just waiting to jump up and bite you. Read through them carefully and start to apply them to your shooting sessions and you're almost sure to see better results.

1. Standing too far from the primary subject – You've seen (and are no doubt guilty) of photos with the subject – family members and friends – so far from the camera that it is difficult to identify him or her. Often, these are vacation shots in which the photographer wants to include some notable attraction or architecture, so people viewing the photos will know where it was shot. You'll greatly improve your photos, however, if you move closer to your subject; in fact, your plan should be to shoot essentially the same image at various distances from the subject.

2. Shooting all photos from a standing position – This is a companion mistake to #1 above. You can move closer to your subject in those common vacation shots, and then crotch down to shoot from a lower angle to include enough of a Disneyland attraction or the Eiffel Tower in the background to identify the location. You don't want to be shooting from a low angle at your subject's feet, as the steep angle will result in a strange photo, but a few feet to the front or to either side.

3. Photographing people with a light source behind them – Another "classic" vacation photo mistake is placing the subject between your camera and the primary light source, usually the sun. When your camera's light meter reads the light reflected from the front of the subject, usually in a deep shadow, the bright sky or background would

be extremely overexposed. Conversely, if the camera reads the bright light source, it will be correctly exposed, but your subject will be an indistinguishable dark blob. To correct this mistake, first notice the direction of the light source, and then position your subject and camera, so the light strikes the front of the subject at a slight angle. Now the light reflected from the subject and the background will be of a similar exposure.

4. Keeping the camera steady – Although relatively small and light, considering all their capabilities, DSLR cameras are still larger and heavier than that camera phone or compact camera you've been using. Your pictures can become blurry and less than sharp if you don't hold your DSLR correctly. Unlike a compact camera, you shouldn't hold a DSLR with a hand at each end of the camera. Instead, grip the right end of the camera with the fingers of the right hand and the index finger positioned to depress the shutter release button. The fingers of the left hand are on the lens, holding it and controlling zoom and/or manual focus.

Since you may often be shooting in auto mode, you may not notice when the camera adjusts the shutter to a slow speed. You should be conscious, however, of the shutter speed because once it reaches 1/60 or 1/30 of a second, you will need additional camera support, especially as a DSLR beginner. Find a vertical surface, a wall or a doorframe, and brace your body against it to help steady your camera. At 1/30 of a second, you will probably want to use a tripod, again because of your inexperience.

5. Failing to pay attention to lines – Every photo you take has some lines within it: the edge of objects, buildings, roadways, etc. You want to be sure that all lines appear parallel in the frame; otherwise your photos will look strange. Before you take any picture, look for the lines, and then move you and your camera and/or your subject (if possible), so the lines look natural.

6. Causing the red-eye effect – This beginner's mistake is also probably familiar to you. A picture is taken using a flash and for some reason the subject or subject's eyes appear with a red glow. Typically, the photographer is standing directly in front of the subject, so the flash enters the light in a relatively straight line and strikes the back of the eye, and then is reflected back to the camera also in a straight line – and you have the red-eye effect. The solution is relatively simple: Ask your subject not to look directly into the camera, but at a slight angle, over your shoulder, for example. If you are using a separate flash unit, then you can hold it at a higher angle off the camera, so the light enters your subject's eyes at an angle.

7. Avoiding the "magic hours" – Don't be surprised if you read about "magic hours" more than once in the book. If you watch TV shows and movies carefully, you'll discover that most of the time exteriors are shot during early morning or late afternoon. There is enough light, but it is muted, subdued, because the sun is low in the sky. During these times of the day, you can capture more dramatic photos and unique compositions that are impossible during midday. This mistake is one of the biggest differences between amateurs and professionals.

8.   Forgetting to carry extra batteries and memory cards – If you haven't discovered it yet, then you will soon: DSLR photography is an adventure of discovery. It's easy for the one hour you planned to shoot to become two, three or more hours because you've found so many interesting scenes and subjects to shoot. Suddenly, in the middle of your euphoria, your batteries become weak and/or your memory card is filled to capacity – and you forgot to bring extras with you! Make it a rule: always bring extra batteries and memory cards with you; they can easily be carried in your pocket.

6 IDEAS TO ADVANCE FROM A BEGINNER
TO AN INTERMEDIATE PHOTOGRAPHER

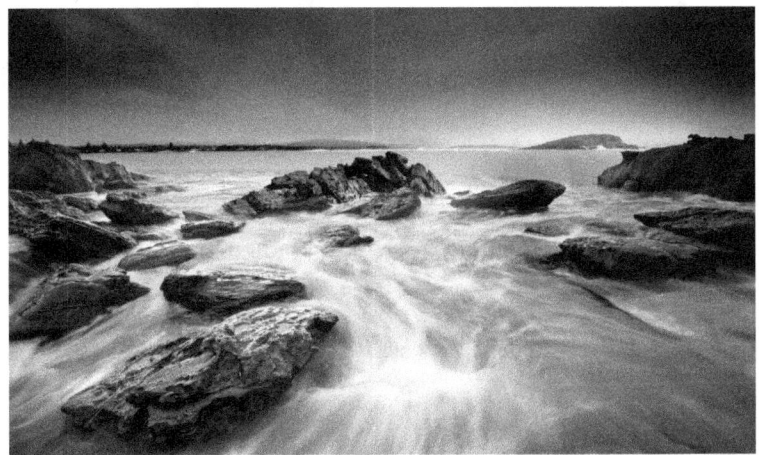

Many people, even those who buy a DSLR or mirrorless camera, are happy to be a casual or hobbyist photographer, shooting mostly pictures of their family, friends and family events and travel. If that is your choice, then make sure you have plenty of fun taking such photos and sharing them on social media.

Maybe, when you decided to spend some significant money for a camera, lens and other gear, your intentions were to be at least semi-serious about photography. Or, maybe once you first had that new camera in your hands, you realized it was a powerful creative tool and you were suddenly inspired to see how much more you could do with it than just casual images.

However, you arrived at the conclusion that you wanted to advance beyond a beginner photographer, there are a number of ways to achieve this goal and some of those ideas are presented here.

1.   Education and a Helping Hand

Being a student of photography is the #1 method to becoming a better photographer. Fortunately, for you, the photography community offers an amazing array of books, videos, seminars and workshops – and many are free or very affordable.

You'll make it much easier to choose the best books, videos, seminars and workshops, if you first join your local photography club. Many clubs have a regular seminar schedule conducted by either local pros or visiting photographers. Experienced and accomplished photographers are very generous with their time and knowledge for beginners who want to become intermediates. Your local photography club may have a mentoring program or can help you find a local photographer that is eager to guide you.

Another kind of education that will be very helpful is to attend summer adult art classes. Because photography is an extension of fine-arts drawing and painting, these classes will teach you about the basics of perspective, composition and color as well as a better understanding of the shapes of the human body that will improve your portrait photos.

As a complement to art classes, check throughout the year for fine arts and photography exhibits at local galleries and museums. You'll find many of the best examples of the techniques you'll learn in an art class and find it easier to apply those techniques to your photography.

2. Become an Everyday Shooter

There's an old adage in the writing community, "the writer writes," which means you can't call yourself a writer unless you are writing almost all the time. The same applies to photography, "the photographer photographs," so your camera should travel with you virtually everywhere you go. The better photos you want to capture are in the everyday world and you can't shoot them if your camera is at home.

It's not always easy with your busy schedule to find some shooting time every day, but if it's only for a half-hour, even 15 minutes, it's another step forward. For example, dusk into twilight is one of the magic hours of the day when the low light is especially conducive to more creative images. If you just concentrated on spending that brief time to learn how to use the magic hour light, then you would take a big step forward.

3. Let Landscapes Inspire You

You'll find a number of tips and tricks for landscape photography and you should read them; however, there are a few other ideas and concepts to understand to take your landscape images to the next level. Maybe, the most important of which is that you must be prepared to do some traveling and hiking into the backcountry to find the best landscape subject matter. Shooting from the side of the road or the convenient viewing site in the park where all the tourists are standing shoulder to shoulder with their cameras is for beginners. Load your backpack, pull on the hiking boots and take a trek to where the tourists never go.

Cameras, lens, etc. are only the tools; you are the creative master, but there is some additional gear that will help you create better landscape images. A fast, wide-angle lens; a tripod and remote shutter release or trigger; and a filter kit that includes a UV, polarizing and neutral density filters are good starters. In terms of camera use, learn the hyperfocal focusing technique and shoot only RAW files, so your camera captures all the data for each image.

4. Tell a Story with your Travel Photography

Let the hobbyists and tourists take the snapshots, simply recording what they see. Your goal is to tell a story with your travel photos; and you'll start to be a more accomplished photographer when you first take the time to study the scene or area where you plan to shoot. If it's a busy city street or a bustling marketplace, then stroll a few hundred yards in both directions to observe the people, the activities that are occurring, the direction of the light, interesting backgrounds, etc. Then, you're ready to shoot and reveal the true essence of a place, its people and their culture.

5. Sports Shots Success

It's likely you bought a DSLR or mirrorless camera to shoot photos and videos of your kids' sports competition, which is still an excellent opportunity to apply advance techniques to move beyond a beginner. After all, you won't be receiving a call from *Sports Illustrated* or ESPN anytime soon, but that doesn't mean photos of your daughter's soccer match can't emulate some of the same qualities of pro sports images.

To take total control of sports photography and show you are working hard to advance your skills, learn how to select exposure and focus manually.

Yes, often, the auto-exposure and auto-focus functions of your camera will do a good job, but there are many moments in a sporting event that requires manual shooting skills to capture the best images.

6. Master Editing Software

A major sign you are moving beyond a beginner photographer is learning how to use editing software, whether its Photoshop, Lightroom or any of the other excellent products available. Like traditional film photography, very few photos are totally created and finalized in the camera. Film photographers need a darkroom to add the final creative touches and editing software serves the same purpose for digital photographers. For example, the best landscape images are often created as much in post-production as during the shoot, which is the reason you should always shoot RAW files.

BE A STORYTELLER, AND NOT
JUST A PICTURE TAKER

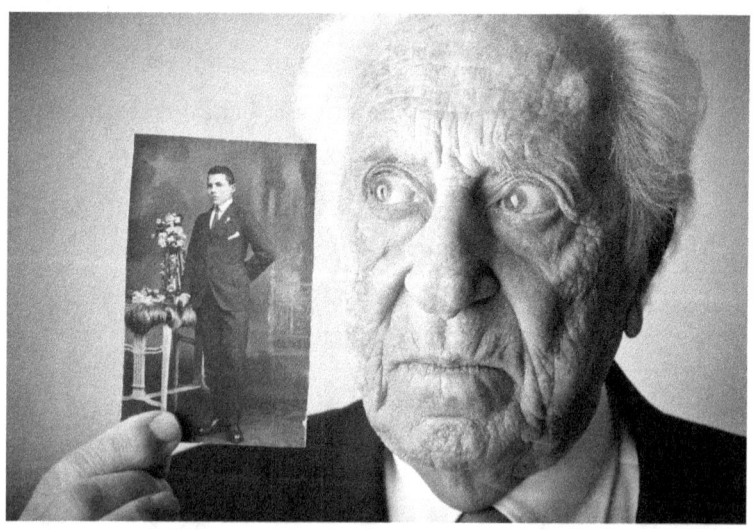

When do you know that you are becoming a better DSLR photographer?

Is it having thousands of dollars of equipment filling a camera bag? Not unless you know how to use all that equipment and are realizing the value of having spent all that money.

Is it using all your free time to explore the world and take many pictures? It's possible, if a succession of photos during a period of time shows improvement.

Whenever people in your life tell you that your photos are interesting, even outstanding? It could be, especially if those comments are coming from accomplished, even professional, photographers, and not just your mother (with all due respect to your mother).

Maybe, a better sign that you're advancing your photography skills is when you can tell stories with a single photo or a small group of related images. When others recognize the story in your photographs and connect with your images through any or all of the 5 basic storytelling elements – Mood, Emotion, Narrative, Idea and Message – you've definitely taken a large step forward. Understanding these 5 elements, looking for them in the scenes and subjects you photograph and then capturing them in a compelling and creative manner will mark you as a photographic storyteller.

1. Mood

Mood is often the rapport between the subject and the environment in which you are photographing he, she or it. The subject doesn't necessarily have to be human or animate. Even the way you photograph an inanimate subject could reveal its relationship with the background, the foreground, other objects, etc. The challenge is to show the subject and whatever else is in the frame as parts of a greater whole, a synergy; or they are dependent on each other.

2. Emotion

Emotion is a human characteristic, and we're discovering that other species of animals can express and feel sympathy and/or empathy for another's emotional state. Although you can stage an emotional facial expression or body posture, capturing a spontaneous or unexpected emotion, much as a photojournalist does, is another sign your skills are improving. Other elements in a composition can cause your subject to respond emotionally: to the unknown, to something new, to a natural environment, etc.

3. Narration

This is a particularly challenging storytelling element for photographers to convey because still photos have no narration, either with graphics or an audio soundtrack, such as a movie or TV show. Narration is not necessarily words either. A woman in a loose gown is standing or walking under a tree during a strong wind. The implied movement of the limbs and the flow of her gown and hair in the direction of the wind could cause viewers of your photo to "hear" the sound of the wind in their mind.

Narration in a still photo can also be communicated if the subject is reacting to an object in the frame or one outside the frame. A child is holding a balloon, but all you show in the photo is the string from her hand, but cropped by the edge of the frame. As she looks up, viewers' eyes are drawn upward too and her stare and the string tell the story of a little girl and her balloon. An even more compelling story would be the little girl having just released her end of the string, positioned just above her fingers. She is also looking up, but with an emotion of anguish on her face. Now, the silent narration communicates the little girl's loss of her balloon and how she feels about it.

4. Idea

Although some authors are able to write the first sentence of a novel and allow the story to develop from those few words, most writers have a story in mind, even loosely, before writing the first word. If you expect your photos to tell a story, then you too must have an idea in mind for your photo and the story it will tell. It's not just the story elements that must be part of your plan, but also how you will photograph it. See the vision, the composition, in your mind, and then think about the place you must shoot it as well as what equipment will be necessary, the lighting, the exposure, etc.

5. Message

The message element of your photo story is often an underlying truth or universal human belief. While the narration may reveal what is occurring either within or outside the frame of the photo, the message could be revealing why it is happening and what it means, not only to the subject in the photo, but also to anyone viewing it. Your idea for your storytelling photo and the elements you use and how you arrange them often determine the message. For an even greater challenge, try to compose an image with a message that isn't easily discernable or is open to interpretation. Now, you've given the viewer some control of his or her interaction with your photo story. It may communicate different messages to different people or they may have to view your photo on multiple occasions for the message finally to penetrate their minds or understand the personal message that only means something to the individual.

With these 5 storytelling elements in mind, you are then ready to put them into practice. Set yourself the goal of planning 5 separate photo sessions where you try to shoot images that use just one of these elements. Study and compare your images to understand how you were able to reveal these elements photographically. Then, go one step farther and start to apply multiple storytelling elements to a single composition. With this approach, you'll slowly, but steadily, become a photographer that can tell interesting and compelling stories and signal the advancement of your skills to a new level.

PROFESSIONAL TIPS AND TRICKS FOR VARIOUS TYPES OF PHOTOGRAPHY

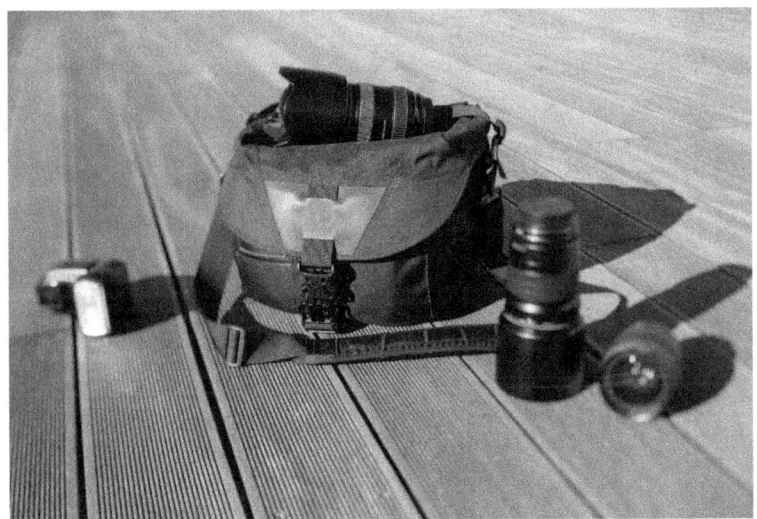

This section of the book is concerned with the aspects of photography other than the technical stuff and practical stuff. In this section we will delve into the meat of the vocation or avocation depending on your use of your skills.

Here we will go over almost everything else that you didn't learn in the last section. Think of the following chapters as a review of camera settings and adjustments but with the inclusion of the elements of photography.

Look around you, and in doing so notice that your senses are perceiving everything there is to know about the world. Now it is time to capture as much of that as you can. Your subject matter is able to be recorded with a camera according to physical attributes such as size, shape and color, but not directly in regards to touch, taste, sound and smell. These are things about subjects that cannot exactly captured, or so you might think. Here you will learn techniques that can be used with a camera to convey feelings, emotions, texture, function, and yes, even smell and sound.

Subject matter is very important, as it contains many properties which we will learn to exploit and capture visually with pictures. Doing so takes knowledge of the subject. What is the subject? Is it animal or plant, inanimate, or animate?

Perhaps it as a combination of subjects, or elements of a single photo. You will learn techniques involved in different types of photography ranging from sports to macro photography of tiny subjects like insects or the details of a flower. Animals often require long-distance photography, perhaps using telephoto lenses, depending upon the size of the animal. Scenics, landscapes, seascapes or architecture, such as buildings, churches, landscaped properties, trains, cars and street scenes all require techniques which may be unique, or at least require different lenses. These techniques are taught here, as are the skills involved.

In this section you will learn how to select the proper lens for the subject, how to modify the lighting, either natural or artificial, to set the mood you desire, or to capture the feelings you want your photo to convey.

How do you successfully photograph snow scenes and what are the required settings to render the snow white and not grey as often results when using automatic exposure. Learn why natural lighting is so important for seascapes, why cloudy days are sometimes better for photography than sunny days. You will learn how to use proper DOF, or depth of field, to achieve focus either near, for closeups, far, for scenics, or in between. Become a moon and star photographer, using exposures measured in seconds or minutes. Learn to understand people photography at parties, weddings, concerts and more. How do portraits portray the mood and feelings of the subject.

Learn tricks to take waterfall photos that instill a feeling of calm and peace, or the tenseness associated with falling and rushing. Taking pictures of rain drops in a puddle and how you can create an image that almost conveys sound. Photographing food in ways that suggests sizzles, popping, and brings the smells to mind. Experiment with capturing contrast with seasonal photography, emphasizing change, like from winter to spring, or photographing old buildings, showing decay. It's all here, in this most informative section. Let's get going!

PORTRAIT PHOTOGRAPHY: 6 TIPS TO SHOOT BETTER PORTRAIT PHOTOS

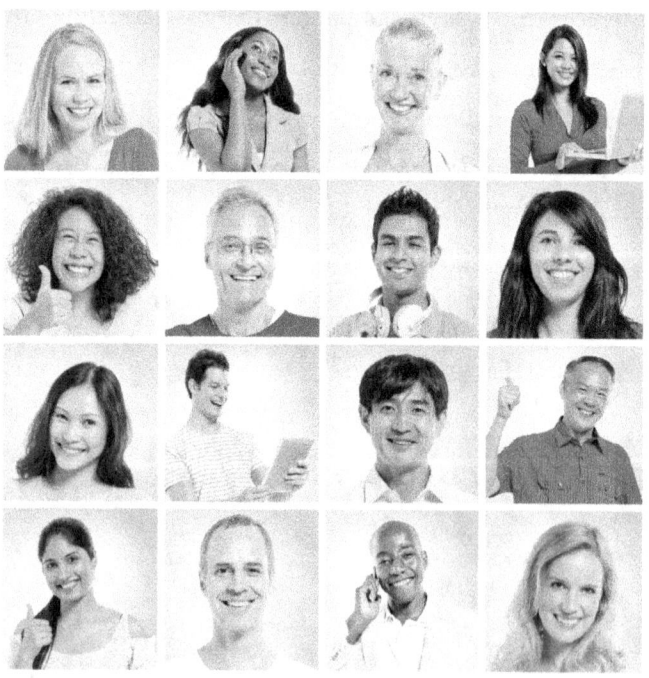

When you decided to buy a DSLR camera, you probably wanted its expanded capabilities to photograph many different kinds of subject matter – with a possible emphasis on one or more types: portraits, landscapes, pets, travel, close-ups, architecture, street life, events, etc. Of all these, however, you will certainly be taking plenty of pictures of family members and friends, and maybe even strangers when traveling or shooting on the streets or at events. Portraits, therefore, is the first subject matter to learn how to shoot better, and what you learn will help you with other kinds of photographic subjects.

1. The right lens.

Although there is not one focal length that is "perfect" for shooting portraits, in most cases, you want a lens with a focal length that is slightly telephoto. On a DSLR camera, a 50mm lens is considered "normal," or reproduces much the same field of view as your eye. Any focal length smaller than 50mm is considered a wide-angle lens and any focal length longer than 50mm is called a telephoto lens. Professional portrait photographers would likely choose a lens of 85mm, 105mm, 135mm or even 200mm.

A wide-angle lens creates distortions, which can be fun if your goal is an unusual portrait. A 50mm lens will also cause distortions, such as enlarging the nose, if you stand close to your subject; however, a 50mm lens might be the right choice if you are shooting a full-length portrait from a distance of 6 feet or more. A lens that is just a bit telephoto, however, slightly compresses the image, so those distortions don't appear. With an 85mm or 105mm lens, you can stand farther from your subject, turn the camera to a vertical orientation and fill the frame with their face or a neck-up composition. A single focal-length lens can be expensive, so a more economical choice would be a telephoto zoom lens of 28–135mm or 70–200mm.

2. Choose a portrait location.

Since it is likely your first portraits with your DSLR camera will be informal and not in a studio setting with multiple lights, you'll want to choose a pleasing location. The location you choose is dependent on the light source. We will later explain the use of flash photography, so for our purposes here, available, or ambient, light will illuminate your first portraits. If you want to shoot indoors, then your best choice is to position your subject at a slight angle looking through a large window that allows plenty of light to strike his or her face. Never shoot a portrait with the person standing directly in front of the window, which creates a silhouette effect.

When shooting portraits outdoors, don't place the person in direct sunlight or when the sun is the highest in the sky, as that will tend to create dark shadows, especially in his or her eye sockets. Schedule your portrait for either early or late during the day when the sun is low, or place your subject in a shaded location, under a tree or an umbrella on the beach.

3. Posing your subject.

Often, what makes a portrait photographer a professional is that he or she knows how to pose a subject, so he or she looks his or her best. As a first-time portrait photographer, however, keep it simple, and shoot from a position that is at a small angle to your subject. Photographing parallel to his or her face can, again, cause distortions and he or she won't be pleased with the results. It's likely the person knows his or her best side or you can make that determination and that is the side you want closer to the camera. It's also a good idea to have the subject lean forward a bit with the back straight.

Your subject could be standing or sitting in a chair or on the ground. Regardless of his or her body position, make sure you are shooting at eye level. You may have to lower yourself to one knee or even sit on the ground with them. Obtuse angles above or below your subject can also create distortions or unpleasing photos.

4. Check for arm and leg angles.

A common mistake of beginner portrait photographers is forgetting to check the subject's arm and leg angles if you are shooting a wider view and will show all or part of the arms and legs. Make sure the angle is less than 90 degrees. If the portrait won't include all of the subject's arms and/or legs, then crop the appendages between the joints. When you crop the arms or legs at the joint, it creates an amputated look.

5. Focus on the eyes.

Another common error of first-time portraits is failing to focus on the eyes – and the eye closest to the camera. Don't hesitate to spend some extra time to be absolutely sure you have the correct focus point.

6. Be conscious of the depth of field.

In most portraits, you want the background not to be in focus, which helps to give your photo more three-dimensionality and projects the person from the frame. As explained in the depth-of-field (DOF) section, aperture is typically the primary factor that determines depth of field; however, your distance from the subject will also affect DOF, which is especially important in portrait photography. The DOF will be shallower when you stand closer to your subject. You must choose a distance in combination with the aperture or f-stop. Choose too wide an aperture (smaller f-stop number) and stand close to your subject and his or her eyes may be in focus, but not the tip of the nose. Choose a small aperture and stand farther from your subject and too much of the background and/or foreground may be in focus. It's likely an f-stop in the middle of the aperture range (f/5.6 to f/11) will be best, but you may need to experiment a bit to pick the right aperture and distance from your subject.

For your first few portrait photography sessions, you may want to ask a friend or family member to serve as a "test" subject. Take a series of photos with different poses at different distances from your subject and at different apertures, and then compare the results. When you determine the best combination of distance and aperture, you can then take the actual portrait photo that your subject will want to use on social media, for example, and share with his or her family and friends.

PORTRAIT PHOTOGRAPHY: POSING TIPS FOR MALE AND FEMALE PORTRAIT PHOTOGRAPHY

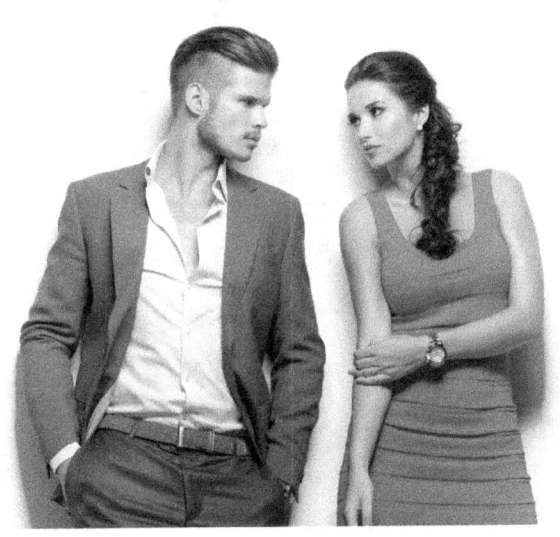

Although you may have no aspiration to become a professional portrait or fashion photographer, you can present your family members and friends with better, more pleasing, portraits of themselves when you apply any of the following posing techniques. Some of these tips apply both to women and men, but there are some differences.

POSING THE FEMALE BODY

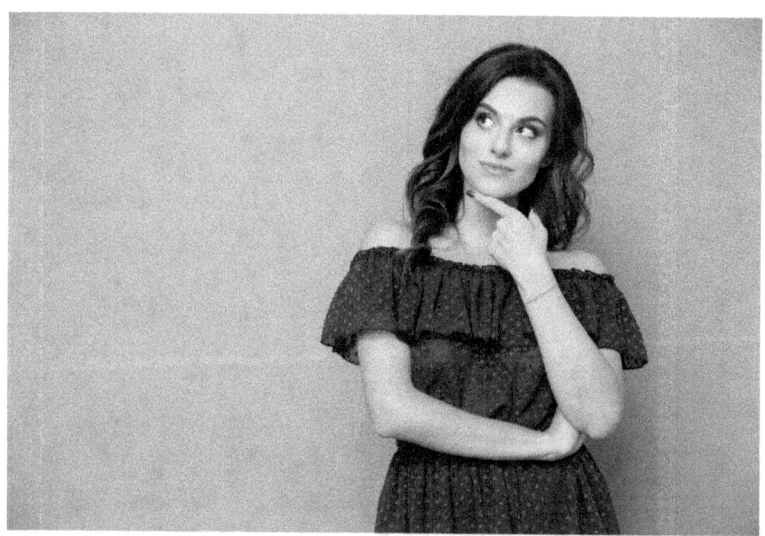

1. The 1-2-3 posing technique

Start the posing process of a woman by arranging her body in a pyramidal shape, or the 1-2-3 pose. Never pose a woman's body parallel to the camera, as this will overemphasize the shoulders; instead her body should be turned 45 degrees to the camera and primary light source. Don't have her turn at a greater angle or her nose will protrude beyond the rear cheek line of her face. This will cause the nose to look larger. Have her turn her head back, so it is approximately 20 degrees beyond the position of the camera. Her arms are positioned on either side of her body to create the sides of the pyramid. You know she is posed correctly when you notice the primary light source falling across her body and illuminating the face attractively.

2. Make the face the dominant skin area.

Your subject may have pleasing upper arms, but for a better portrait, you don't want those large areas of skin competing with the face. Everyone's attention should be on her face when viewing the image.

3. Forward from the vertical

A portrait subject should appear to be projected towards the camera. With her back straight, position your subject with a slight forward lean and thrust of her chin. Place your camera at a bit of a higher angle to minimize the fullness of the chin or a double chin.

4. Favor the high shoulder.

For the best portraits of women, it is preferable that the head is tilted toward the high shoulder.

5. Use the model's pose.

By posing the woman like a model, her body will assume an "S" curve, which complements the female form. First, ask her to shift her weight to her back foot and point the front foot towards the camera. Then, she should bend one knee toward the other leg.

6. Don't show parts of the body no one wants to see.

To minimize the view of the lower abdomen in a full-length portrait, instruct the subject to raise the leg closest to the camera just a bit. When you are shooting a seated portrait of a woman, make sure the legs are next to each other. Look for exposed armpits, and then hide them with a different arm position or camera angle.

7. Posing the arms.

Whenever the arms (or legs) are bent, they should appear to be less than a 90-degree angle, which creates a balance with the other parts of her body. Whether composing in the camera or editing in post-production, arms and legs should always be cropped between the joints. When the edge of the frame crosses the elbow or knee, it creates the amputation look.

8. Posing the hands.

Hands can be very expressive in a female portrait, so start by posing them separated. Then, make sure the hand closest to the camera isn't too close. If the subject has her hands above her waist, then her fingers should be pointed downwards, below her waist pointed upwards. You always want a side view of the hands, since the backs present too much skin area.

9. Posing plus-size women.

A fundamental portrait photography technique is the use of a slight telephoto focal length to avoid unpleasing distortions of the nose and chin. This is an absolute must when photographing plus-size women since the compression of the telephoto focal length will understate her size and shape. Shooting from a low angle is particularly unflattering to larger women.

Finally, do your best to pose and photograph a plus-size woman as you would any other woman. Use your creativity to capture attractive full-length portraits, reassuring her that you'll make her look her best.

POSING THE MALE BODY

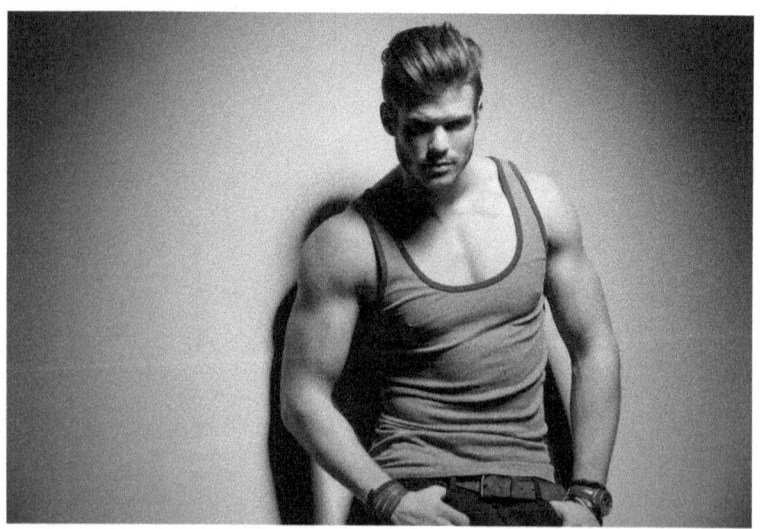

1.   Show the man.

While women want to present their femininity, men want to emphasize their masculinity, athleticism or profession. When younger men are photographed, they can wear tighter clothing or even be shirtless. Business/professional men will likely be dressed in a suit or apparel that identifies their profession. The primary body pose for men is their torso parallel to the camera, revealing their broad shoulders and chest, back straight, thighs half open and their weight on both legs or more of it on either leg.

2.   The lower shoulder is the men's shoulder.

While women look better with the head tilted towards the higher shoulder, for men, it is the lower shoulder, and with the chin slightly lowered.

3.   Positioning a man's arms and hands

There are many acceptable and attractive poses of a man's arms and hands. These include relaxed fists; thumbs in his front pockets; fingers flat in the back pockets and the thumbs outside the pockets; and across the upper chest. Nothing ruins a male portrait more than the arms and hands dangling on either side of the body or the hands covering the crotch area.

4.   A well-fitted suit

For men who wish to wear a suit, it shouldn't be an old or being worn for the first time. Ask him to choose a suit he has worn a few times, which has allowed it to assumed the shape of his body.

THE MOST-IMPORTANT POSING TECHNIQUE

The eyes are central.

Ultimately, almost every portrait photo is about the eyes. They are the best way to express the personality and emotion of the subject. Instruct a female subject to change her vision angle, so there is white visible on both sides of her pupils and a bit more on one side than the other. Never allow the eye farthest from the camera to be half-covered. A man's eyes should be looking in the same direction as the nose.

PORTRAIT PHOTOGRAPHY: HOW TO REVEAL A SUBJECT'S PERSONALITY IN A LIFESTYLE PORTRAIT

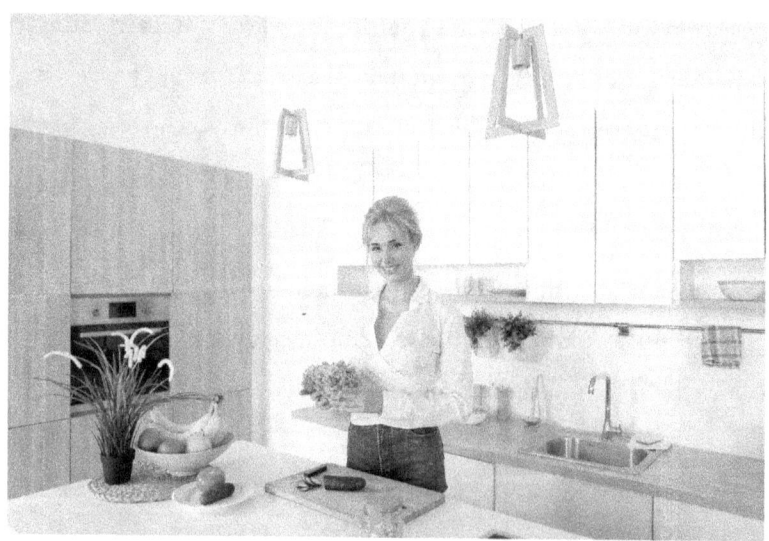

When you think about photographing a person's portrait, two choices are more likely to come to mind: a casual picture that you might take at the spur of the moment, such as during a vacation or family gathering, or a more-planned photo that has many of the similarities of professional portrait work. There is a third choice, however, that may result in more interesting pictures and subjects more pleased with the results. Lifestyle portraits, if planned and photographed correctly, will reveal more of the personality of the subject, not just an image of his or her physical features, but also who he or she is, his or her passions, profession, occupation, work, hobbies and interests.

Many people are shy or uncomfortable with a professional photographer shooting a formal portrait in a studio. The environment is unfamiliar, the lights are hot and it typically takes more time than the subject expected. Some people think formal portraits are stiff looking, reduce them to an object and force them to dress formally when they almost never do.

Think of how much more interesting a lifestyle portrait of your aunt, for example, in her crafts-and-hobby room would be and how she would be more comfortable and relaxed because it's a place she enjoys being. Her smile and her posture would be more natural. Your son may enjoy skateboarding and the joy and elation he experiences when sticking a good trick or landing says much more about him than those typical school portraits.

In addition, when you plan a lifestyle portrait session with a family member or a friend, you have the opportunity to be closer and to understand what they enjoy most in life; and he or she will also come to understand why you are so passionate about photography.

The best lifestyle portraits are not usually spontaneous or candid, although they can happen. Carefully planning a lifestyle portrait session is more likely to result in great photos and it's an excellent opportunity for you to learn how to organize a shoot like a professional. Follow these tips and you may be receiving requests from people in your life for lifestyle portraits.

1.   Know your subject

You may think you know your aunt, your son, friends, co-workers and other people in your life that could be excellent subjects for a lifestyle portrait, but you must know them even better to capture their true personality and passions. So, the first step in planning a lifestyle portrait shoot is to spend some time with the subject, especially during the activities, hobbies, etc. that help to define who he or she is. You may also want to talk to the people closest to him or her to see your subject through their eyes. They are very likely to share information or insights about your subject that he or she hasn't shared with you, or personality traits of which your subject is unaware. All these details and perspectives will help you start to organize your thoughts about the kind of lifestyle portraits that are possible and the best locations. Another benefit of spending time with your subject is that he or she will become more comfortable with the idea of being photographed and his or her confidence that you will create pleasing photos.

Although you may want your first few lifestyle portraits to be of family members and friends to make it easier, consider asking strangers to be subjects too, especially if they have unusual hobbies or occupations that will both challenge your skills and allow you to capture some unique images.

2. Location scouting

A major part of your planning is the location for the lifestyle portrait. If your subject's passion is woodworking, gardening, scrapbooking or other hobbies, then the location is rather obvious. Spend some of your time with your subject in the place where he or she enjoys these hobbies or activities. You want to pay careful attention to the lighting, the best positions and angles for your camera, the look of the background, etc. You may even want to bring your camera and ask your subject to stand in certain places, hold certain tools or whatever he or she creates to help you determine camera positions and angles, without actually taking any pictures.

Lifestyle portraits of other people may be more appropriate where they work. This may be more difficult, as their employer wouldn't want their work and the workplace disrupted, but you might be able to schedule your lifestyle portrait session during off-hours. Your subject may work construction, drive a truck, be a doctor or nurse, operate heavy machinery in a factory, etc. Again, you may have to seek permission to photograph them during the workday.

3.   Portrait setup

Although you've talked with your subject and scouted the best location for the lifestyle portrait, you may need some time to re-arrange the setting. You don't want your uncle's woodworking shop to look too pristine and clean, but also you don't want it to look too cluttered; so you may have to eliminate or add props or other elements to your photos.

You also want to strike the right balance with the apparel your subject is wearing, and how clean it is. If your subject is a painter, then his or her well-used smock covered in paint dabs and some paint on his or her fingers or even face is a much truer representation of his or her lifestyle than totally clean clothing.

Although you may have determined good positions and angles for your camera, and maybe on a tripod, try some unusual angles too. Stand opposite your uncle planning a piece of wood in a vise and capture the wood chips popping in the air in front of his face. If you're photographing your skateboarding son at a skateboard park, lie in the bottom of the run and photograph him jumping over your position.

Lifestyle portraits can be fun for you and your subject and force you to stretch your creativity. Who knows; you might discover that you do such a great job photographing people in lifestyle settings that someone may be willing to pay you for similar pictures.

LANDSCAPE PHOTOGRAPHY: CAPTURE PROFESSIONALLY-LOOKING LANDSCAPE PHOTOS

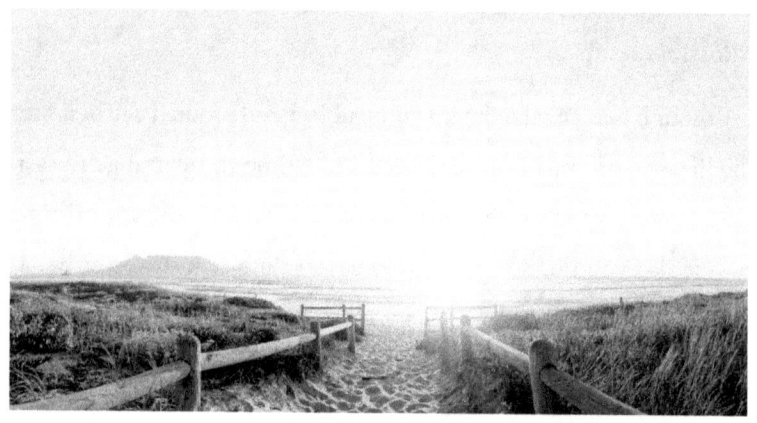

Landscape photography is certainly one of the major reasons people buy a digital camera. It's a great outdoor activity and a primary subject matter during vacations and travel. If you've been bitten by the landscape photography bug, then the ideas here should help you bring home some above-average images similar to professional's.

Landscape photography is a very broad topic, as it can include the world's most spectacular mountains, serene seashores, mysterious jungles, dense forests and endless deserts and require many days to hike to these locations. You can also find and photograph interesting landscapes within your neighborhood, the local city park or a nearby state park without a long trek into the wilderness. In fact, it's probably better to start with local landscapes first to learn the basics. Plus, it's a great opportunity to develop your photographer's eye to notice a good view to photograph even in the most common and familiar locations.

WHAT MAKES A GOOD LANDSCAPE TO PHOTOGRAPH

There are no hard-and-fast rules about a good landscape for your camera; often, it has more to do with the lens you are using, the light conditions and the composition of the image. In many cases, you'll want to use a wide-angle lens for landscapes simply so you have a wider view of a scene, but it also allows you to compose one of the better types of landscape images.

You've probably seen thousands of amateur landscape photos shot on vacation of a mountain range, lake, etc.; and likely many of them are yours. The problem with these images is that the subject of interest is at a long distance. A better technique is to compose a landscape of contrasts. The mountain, lake or ocean in the background is fine, but the secret is to find a small object of interest in the foreground to include in your landscape that complements and contrasts with the background. Position you and your camera so there is an interesting piece of driftwood in the foreground for the seashore landscape or a small group of colorful wildflowers on the near shore of the lake that extends into the background.

You'll need a wide-angle lens to include both the foreground subject and background in the photo; and you'll want to position yourself low to the ground, so the foreground subject is prominent. Plus, it's best if it is to the right or left in the frame and not directly in the middle. Don't be surprised if you must walk through an area for a considerable amount of time to find this juxtaposition of foreground and background subjects of interest. A variation of this theme is to compose a landscape from a high place, such as a ridge or cliff looking across a prairie or desert, for example. In this case, you may not need a foreground subject because the angle of your camera can eliminate most of the sky and fill the viewfinder with the expansive landscape spread before you.

The third element to take into account when choosing a landscape view is the light. Shooting during the brightest part of the day, when the sky is high in the sky, can make the landscape look flat, since the light reflects from all the various surfaces evenly. It's often better to shoot during the early morning or late afternoon, or what motion picture directors call the "magic hours". Not only can the sky be more dramatic with how the rising or setting sun affects the sky and clouds, but also your scene is more likely to have contrasting brightly lit and dark shadowed areas. The colors of rocks, vegetation and water will often be more or less saturated, also creating contrasts in your landscape image.

Additional Equipment that Will Enhance Your Landscape Photos

Yes, you can shoot very good landscapes with just your camera, but you should seriously consider adding a tripod to your photo gear. With a tripod, you're able to shoot more photos at slower shutter speeds, especially during those early and late periods of the day, which provides you with more exposure control and choices that lead to more interesting landscape images. You'll also want a shutter release cable or wireless shutter control, so you don't have to touch the camera to snap the shutter. Doing so at slow shutter speeds will likely blur your images.

Filters can also greatly improve the quality and dramatic effect of your landscape photos. You definitely want a polarizing filter on the front of your lens, which can give the sky more contrast and make colors look more intense and saturated. We already explained the use of lens filters in the book, but there are many other types of filters that should also be part of your gear if you expect to be a serious landscape photographer.

Study and Learn

Whether you're attracted to landscape photography or any of the other types of photography, you'll progress faster if you study the images of the world's best landscape photographers and attend one or more seminars. Spend some time on the Internet to discover who are the best, and then visit their Websites to view their portfolios. There is likely to be more than one source of landscape photography seminars in your community that are not formal photography classes, although some colleges also offer amateur classes that are not part of a curriculum. Again, you can do an Internet search or check with your local photography club, which either offers seminars or can recommend the right one for you.

Landscape photography is fun, adventurous and can attract plenty of attention from your family and friends when you put into practice the tips in this book. As you improve, you can make prints to decorate your home or office, and give them gifts.

LANDSCAPE PHOTOGRAPHY: PANORAMA TIPS FOR CREATING SPECTACULAR LANDSCAPES

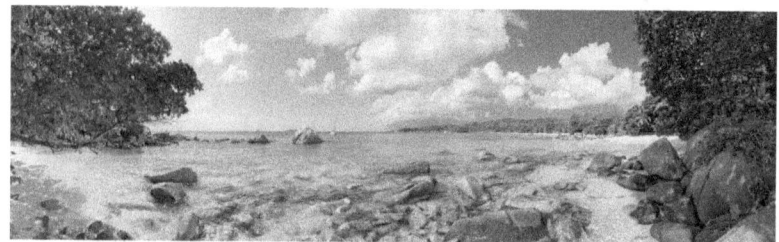

Digital photography technology has made creating panoramic landscapes much easier than the days of film photography, when specialized and very expensive cameras were required and photographers spent hours in the darkroom.

In simplest terms, a panorama image consists of two or more photos that are stitched together in editing software to create a much wider view of a scene than a wide-angle lens could capture. Although panoramic techniques are primarily used in landscape and nature photography, they could also help you create a grand wide image of a family gathering, a party or a wedding; a sporting event; or an action adventure. Panoramas don't necessarily have to be horizontal; separate images of a waterfalls or a cliff face can be stitched together vertically.

1. Seeing beyond your eyes' field of view.

One of the reasons panoramic photos are so interesting and spectacular is that they show much more than what we can see with the natural field of view of our eyes. This is a challenge for the photographer, however, as you must be able to view a scene, often turning your head and/or body right and left to discover the panoramic vision that requires multiple photos. Panoramic images have a much different aspect ratio than the typical 3:2 or 4:3 of a single photo, so the finished image is often very long and narrow (or tall and narrow).

You might find an open landscape, such as a desert or a plain that will be enhanced by including a single tree, distant butte or other isolated feature in the right or left third of the frame. Showing a much wider view of the stark landscape and the single object may have much more impact that simply framing the object and what landscape is seen in a single image.

2. Equipment Requirements

- **Tripod**: A tripod is absolutely essential because each of the separate photos must be shot level and overlap as precisely as possible in the camera. Choose a tripod with a built-in level or acquire a small level you can attach or place on the tripod.

- **Ballhead**: The tripod must be outfitted with a ballhead, which makes it much easier to ensure the preciseness of the image overlap and smoothly and accurately pan the camera to the exact position for the next image. Although a ballhead is very helpful, it requires that you level the tripod clamp and legs. Leveling the tripod legs makes the ballhead-panning base also level for each successive photo, and then leveling the tripod clamp will keep the camera parallel to the panning base of the tripod.

- **L-Plate:** You may also want to use what is called an L-plate, attaching it directly to your camera instead of the ballhead. The reason is that you can move the camera in either horizontal or vertical orientation without having to recompose the image. With an L-plate, the camera only moves and not the entire ballhead/camera configuration.

Some of the well-known manufacturers of ball heads and L-plates are also most of the top tripod manufacturers, including Manfrotto, Vanguard, Sirui and Really Right Stuff. Remember, if you're not ready to invest in a ballhead, then they can be rented for a weekend or a vacation at a reasonable rate.

- **Lens:** Although a wide-angle lens is often used for landscape photography, it will actually cause problems in panorama photography. Because of the distortion that is evident in the corners of wide-angle images, it will be necessary to crop the corners. If you haven't overlapped the images enough, then the results may be images that don't stitch together precisely. For panoramas, it's better to use a telephoto focal length that eliminates any distortions.

- **Filters:** Of course, you want an UV filter on your lens for its protective qualities, but a polarizing filter can be problematic. Yes, it can create a more dramatic sky, but it can also cause the color of the sky to be slightly different in each image. If a polarizer enhances the image, then it can be used and any uneven sky color corrected with editing software. An ND, or neutral density filter, will help your panoramas just as it would for any single landscape photo; however, graduated neutral density filters are tricky. Like a polarizer, if they add value to your images, then give ND filters a try, but typically you might find it better and easier to apply the ND-filter effect during post-production.

3. Shoot in Manual Modes

Just as you must keep the view of the multiple images level, the exposure and focus of each photo that will be stitched together to create the panorama must also be consistent and precise. To maintain total control, therefore, you want to determine exposure values and focus manually. The aperture is the most important exposure value, and it should be f/8 or narrower, so there is plenty of depth of field. This will typically result in the need for slower shutter speeds, so a remote wireless shutter trigger should be added to your equipment package.

4. Image Overlapping

At a minimum, overlap the multiple images at least 25 percent and as much as 50 percent, so you have plenty of excess with which to work in post-production. You'll also find it useful to select a fixed object in each photo to help you align the images and choose the stitching line.

5. On the Computer

With your multiple images shot and loaded into editing software, you're ready to stitch them together. The photo-merge feature in Photoshop will do this automatically, but you're likely to create a better final image with layer masking.

Give yourself plenty of space at one side of each opened photo, and then begin adding each image right to left or left to right as different layers and overlapped. Once the initial panorama has been assembled, zoom to 100% to help you align them precisely. You'll find that using the horizon line is easiest and most accurate.

Apply a layer mask to the photo that is the top layer and then eliminate the overlap to reveal the next layered image. Continue this process for all the images and you should have a precisely assembled panorama. Make sure to inspect it carefully for any distortions or other flaws before flattening the layers. It can be saved as a TIFF file and then image editing can commence to finalize the panorama photo.

LANDSCAPE PHOTOGRAPHY: CAPTURING THE SPIRIT OF THE SEASHORE IN PICTURES

Humans' compulsion to go to the sea is literally in our DNA. As a fetus, we live in a saltwater environment, the amniotic fluid. Whether to sail the waters, swim in the surf or to relax on the beach, people are attracted by the overwhelming spirit of the sea—the place where life began and emerged to occupy the land. It is, therefore, a special subject matter for all photographers and rife with both spectacular and subtle imagery. It is where light, water and air mix magically for some of your most creative photos.

Clearly, the seashore is a vacation destination and, by all means, you should photograph your visits and fun there with family and friends; however, here we reveal how to photograph the seashore as the primary subject matter of your photos, and not as a backdrop to a vacation.

It All Begins with Light

Ask any veteran fisherman or sailor about the light and the sea and he or she are sure to tell you that regardless of how often they've sailed its waters, the light expresses itself in unique and endless varieties. The winter light is different from the summer light; the morning light is different than the evening light. For the photographer, this creates a journey of discovery: to choose various days and times of day to visit the seashore and photograph the environment in the special light of the moment.

As with most of the best landscape photos, including those of the seashore, the diffused light of sunrise and sunset, and even twilight, after the sun has disappeared, are more likely to make your photos magical. During those first moments of morning sunlight, thinly veiled mist and heavy fog often accent the seashore. Put yourself in the midst of the mist or a fog and capture ghostly silhouettes of lighthouses, traditional fishermen putting to sea or a distant passing ship. Position yourself at a great height and photograph the thick fog enveloping the seashore as the brilliant sunrise illuminates the top of the fog.

It's only natural to photograph the sun as it rises or sets at the horizon line of the sea, but don't overlook photographing the seashore when the sun rises or sets in the opposite direction. An entirely different kind of lighting effect occurs. Find a point of land that allows you to put the sea behind you, but a seashore or harbor in front of you, with the sun rising or setting in the distance.

Composing Seashore Images

The seashore is a landscape, often called a seascape, so the most fundamental landscape compositional technique applies to your photos there: Frame your seascape with an object in the immediate foreground to give your photo scale and shoot from a low angle with a bit of a wide-angle focal length. The enormous expanse of sky, water and sand can confuse the mind because there is no recognizable object to provide perspective. Common objects are driftwood, small rocks and tall sea towers of rock thrusting from the sand, a dune with sparse vegetation, a shell and even a crab that holds its position, seemingly posing for your photograph.

Position yourself so a progression of rocks, driftwood or old pilings that disappear into the sea are diagonal elements in the frame from the bottom right corner across the right third of the image, leading the viewer's eye to the horizon line and the grand vista of the sea and sky. It's important to be aware of the horizon line in all your seashore photos. Remember the Rule of Thirds and place the horizon line so it aligns with either of the two horizontal lines that separate your photo into thirds. A low-angle composition will include more sky while a camera position at the top of a cliff overlooking the beach will reduce the sky and, at a certain angle, eliminate it completely, so your photo is entirely the seashore and the first few hundred feet of sea.

Just as the light at the seashore can be significantly different during certain days and times, and during the various seasons, the tidal activity of the sea changes from low to high tide everyday. Consider photographing a seascape from the exact same position and angle during low and high tides. The compositional elements are likely to be quite different although the view is eerily the same. In addition, don't limit yourself to photographing the seashore from just the beach or land. Consider walking a few feet into the sea to shoot back toward the shore and/or from a low angle. Make sure your camera is properly protected by renting an underwater housing that will allow to be even more creative in the shallows of the sea around rocks, coral, etc.

Exposure Control

The low light of sunrise and sunset will typically require a slow shutter speed since you want a wide aperture setting for maximum depth of field and a normal ISO setting to eliminate any digital noise. You'll need a tripod and remote shutter release trigger for any shutter speeds slower than 1/30 of a second. Although you can easily shoot a series of photos at different shutter speeds (bracketing) to make sure you capture the one with the best balanced exposure, you may find a separate light meter helpful, as the bright light of the sun and the darkness of the sky may confuse the meter in your camera.

Varying shutter speeds allow you to photograph the subtlety of the waves. You may be shooting on a low beach where the waves gently roll across the sand with only a few inches of height or you may choose a rocky coast where the sea dashes against the rocks, creating spectacularly soaring waves and spray. Faster shutter speeds will freeze the water while slower speeds – a half-second to a few seconds – will cause the waves and water to blur, giving it a mystical quality.

Bring Your Filter Kit

Of course, whenever you're shooting outdoors, you want an UV filter on the front of the lens, primarily as protection. A polarizing filter will help to emphasize clouds. It's a graduated neutral density (GND) and a neutral density (ND) filter that will give you even more control of the light and create dramatic effects. A GND filter balances the light of bright sky and darker foreground, and is particularly useful during sunrise and sunset. Use the ND filter when shooting at a slow shutter speed, so enough light enters the camera and you can keep the best aperture and ISO settings. A ND filter will also help you when you want to capture the motion of the waves.

PET PHOTOGRAPHY

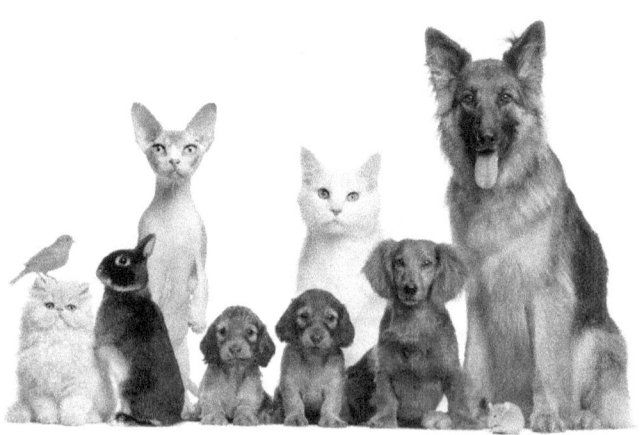

According to one of the American Pet Product Association's National Pet Owners Surveys, 68 percent of US households own a pet, or 82.5 million households. The survey also estimates there are 95.6 cats and 83.3 million dogs that are pets in these households, plus millions of birds, horses, freshwater and saltwater fish, reptiles and small animals.

As they have for thousands of years, pets are integral members of human households and today many are considered equal members of the family. If you're a pet owner, then it's not surprising that you would want to photograph it (or them) often with your DSLR camera. Even if you're not a pet owner, it's likely family members or friends who are may ask you to photograph theirs once they see you with your DSLR.

Pets are excellent photographic subjects. Not just because you can capture their personalities, but also because photographing them is a great learning experience, challenging your current photography skills and providing numerous opportunities to improve what you already know and to learn new skills.

If you want to take the best possible pictures of your pet(s), then the first step is to forget your camera and spend some quality time simply observing your pet; even take some notes that will prove to be helpful when you do begin to photograph it. Because we consider them members of the family, we are concentrated on enjoying their company and not actually studying what they do and how they react to a broad range of situations. The better you understand your pet, the better photos you are likely to take; and you can start by observing its resting and active periods of the day.

- Where is your pet's favorite place to rest? For your dog, is it the doggie bed, a sunny warm spot on the floor or a favorite chair? Does your cat like to stretch across a windowsill, on top of a bookshelf or your bed? Once you determine the place or places, note the time of day and how long it remains there as well as the lighting and the background.

  These are likely to be the best moments to plan a "formal" portrait of your pet. You know they won't move much and they will be in a comfortable position.

- Virtually all pets have active periods. Dogs like to sniff and dig in the backyard, accompany you on a walk or run or play with other dogs at the local dog park. Even if your cat only lives indoors, there will be times during the day when it scampers through the house, explores its environment, plays with toys and is willing to interact with you. These may be some of the best times to photograph your pet because it is focused on whatever activity has attracted its attention, acting spontaneous and more likely to be oblivious to you and your camera.

PET PHOTOGRAPHY TIPS

Quite likely, the most important skill you need to photograph your pet has nothing to do with photography; it is patience. Although they are not human, pets are individuals, with their own personality, energy level and favorite activities. Regardless of how well you've trained your dog, your bird or other pet, it still has a mind of its own – and cats, of course, are almost totally independently minded.

Don't expect your pet, therefore, to cooperate with your efforts to photograph it. You may start a photography session, thinking you know this is your pet's rest period and it will remain in its current position for an appropriate amount of time and, suddenly, it decides differently. Your pet photography session may end before it even started; but you can't be frustrated. If you're lucky, then maybe your pet has just decided to rest in another place today, but you may also discover that today is not the day to photograph your pet and you must simply put your camera back in the bag and try again tomorrow.

When it comes to the right lens to photograph your pet, you may want to use a wide-angle lens or wide-angle focal length on a zoom lens to make it easier to keep your pet in the frame. You may also want to use a telephoto focal length, from 85mm to 200mm. Just as when you are shooting human

おをを

portraits, you need a bit of telephoto focal length, so there are no facial or body distortion. You may also need the longer focal lengths, so you can photograph farther from your pet, either because of its position or because it is uncomfortable with the camera and lens close to its face.

When your pet does cooperate, you and your camera's positions are critical to the quality of the images you take. To photograph pets successfully, you must be willing to shoot at their level. This may require shooting from your knees, laying on the floor or the backyard or using a ladder to bring your camera to the eye level of your cat perched on top of the bookshelf. This is a great general photography lesson because as you progress, you'll come to learn that many of the best photographs can't be captured standing with the camera to your eye. Most of them are found at a high or low angle. This is one of the most common errors of amateurs.

If you want to position your pet in a specific place in a specific pose, then you might find the task much easier if you entice it with a bit of food or add its favorite toy to the shot. Not only will the food or toy take its attention from you, but also allow it to relax and possible provide some cute or interesting interactive photos. Including a family member in the picture can also help to relax your pet and the person can control it.

Finally, be careful about using a flash or bright photography lights to photograph your pet. The flash may surprise it and make it more difficult to photograph it today or during the future, as it may associate your camera with an unpleasant experience and become uncooperative whenever you want to photograph it again. If you plan to use a flash, then you might want to fire it a few times in different directions, to see how your pet reacts. Once your pet becomes familiar with the light, it is more likely to allow you to flash it directly at its face.

Taking pictures of your pet is an excellent learning experience and, of course, captures memories just as important as any in your family.

TRAVEL PHOTOGRAPHY: TIPS FOR BRINGING HOME BETTER TRAVEL PHOTOS

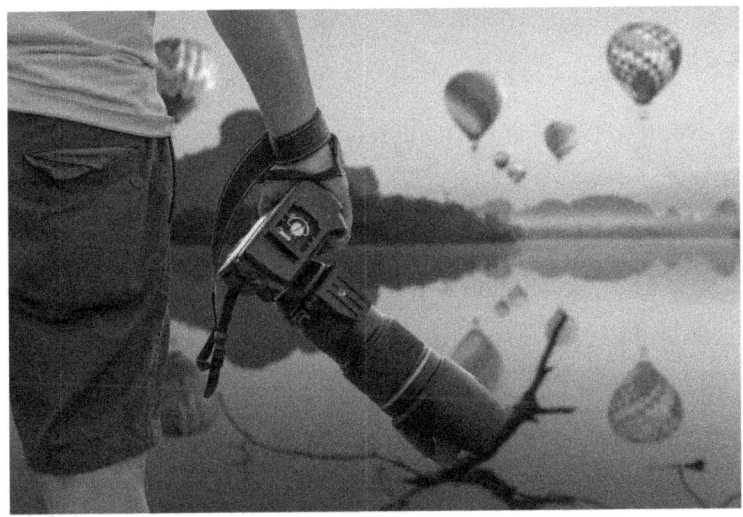

What better reason to own and learn how to use a digital camera then to take great pictures during vacations and travel! Photography and travel have been synonymous almost as soon as cameras were small enough to move from one place to another. It would also seem insane not to take a camera with you when traveling; and even in the era of the smartphone, the best and most interesting pictures are only possible with a DSLR.

1. Plan your travel photography just like you plan your trip.

Before you head to a familiar destination or someplace you've never been, you'd be smart to plan and prepare your photography. Not only is it practical, but also a great learning experience because it's exactly what professionals do whenever they receive a new assignment.

- No doubt, you chose your destination because there are sites you want to see and activities you want to experience. As part of your travel planning, make conscious notes of what you want to photograph, the best times of the day and best angles to photograph them, so you'll bring home images that are much more than what the millions of tourists have shot.

- Spend some time online viewing professionals' photos of these same places, activities and events to learn how you can make your photos special. You don't want to copy the pros, but to use your limited time wisely, so you're in the best place at the best time. Social media, photography forums and travel Websites are other excellent sources of information and insights from photographers and people who have been where you are planning to travel.

- You also want to understand the local weather patterns where you're traveling. If it rains every afternoon in a tropical locale, then you won't want to plan a photo trip during that part of the day, OR there may be interesting photos to capture during the rain that the tourists avoid by staying indoors.

- Learn about the local culture and any special events occurring during your visit. Make sure you understand local customs about photographing people on the street or entering and photographing at museums, art galleries and religious sites.

2. Think like Goldilocks when deciding what equipment to pack.

Luggage and weight are always a consideration when traveling and now you are adding your DSLR camera and accompanying equipment to your baggage, which is why you want to take "just enough, but not too much," as Goldilocks might advise.

- Start by reducing your lens selection to a minimum. Zoom lenses are preferable to fixed focal lengths. Depending on your photography plans, a small zoom, such as 18–55mm, may be just right for most of your photos. You may also want to consider a larger telephoto, 55–250mm. The best guideline is to pack no more than two lenses.

- If you're planning to photograph landscapes or nature images during your travels, then a tripod is probably a must; but be absolutely sure you will use it.

- You'll also want to pack extra memory cards, batteries and possibly a filter kit. A protective rain cover made specifically for cameras and photography will take little room and add almost no weight, but could prove to be very valuable. A separate flash unit is probably unnecessary unless you are planning to shoot where a flash will be required.

- It's best to use a camera bag and not pack your camera and other equipment with your personal items. Choose a bag with enough room, but not too large, and be aware of safety and security issues.

- An alternative is to rent some of the equipment either at your destination or from a photography rental company in the United States, which will ship the equipment to your hotel, so it's waiting for you. It's more affordable than you might think.

3. Enjoy the travel photography experience.

- Try to be more like a traveler than a tourist. As a traveler, you will immerse yourself in the local culture instead of being a part of the pack of tourists who only visit the standard attractions. Now, you may also want to photograph some of these attractions, but try not to follow the crowd. Purposely walk in a different direction than the tourists to find more interesting and unique angles and views. Another option is to visit the most-popular sites during the times of the day when the tourists aren't present.

- Dress so you can more easily blend with the local people; wear subdued colors and the garments and styles they are wearing, if possible. It is the everyday life of the locals and the activities on the streets that truly represent a place, not the tourist attractions.

- You might also find it very helpful to engage a guide and/or translator. He or she is more likely to know the true nature of the city or country and where you will capture excellent photos of the people and the culture. A guide will also make it easier for you to approach locals and ask them to pose for a picture.

- You may find it advantageous to take your camera and just start walking with no itinerary or specific destination in mind. Often, the best travel photos are spontaneous and unexpected, but you must be willing to become part of the local activities to discover what is most interesting and unique about a place and its people.

- If you've brought your laptop or have access to a computer and an Internet connection at your hotel, then reserve some time at the end of every day to download the photos from your camera. Consider emailing your photos to yourself, so you have backups that are not with you.

SAN FRANCISCO PHOTOGRAPHY: ICONIC, ECLECTIC, DYNAMIC AND SOMETIMES ECCENTRIC

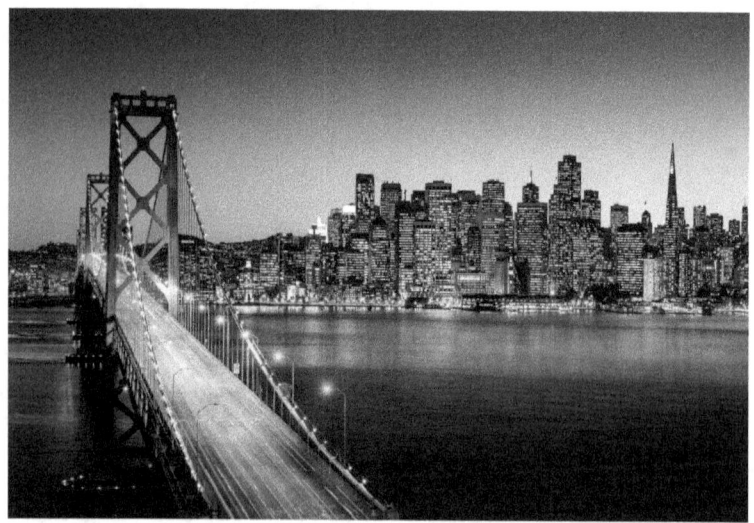

B ehind the sophistication and cool, San Francisco, "the city by the bay," is at its roots a Wild-West-kind of town. It's the place where the adventurous, westward moving people of the late 19th century – entrepreneurs, both legitimate and otherwise, and characters and eccentrics of all sorts – had to stop because they couldn't go any farther west. This colorful history has made San Francisco quite distinctive from Los Angeles and almost any other American city.

When photographing San Francisco, you can assume one of two mindsets or, if you have the time, a combination of both. If you've never visited San Francisco, then you're sure to be attracted to the city's iconic places, which is also where the greatest concentration of tourists can be found. If Fisherman's Wharf, Pier 39 and Ghirardelli Square; Chinatown; Alcatraz Island; Lombard Street; a cable car ride; and other famous attractions are the only blimps on your radar, then, by all means, enjoy and photograph them liberally to remind you of your visit.

The second mindset is to avoid most of the tourist hot spots (because many of them require quite a bit of time with the large crowds) and concentrate on the places with fewer tourists, but just as interesting, and maybe more so. The bigger challenge of photographing any city like San Francisco is to capture the life of the city and not necessarily just its places and attractions.

WEATHER WATCH

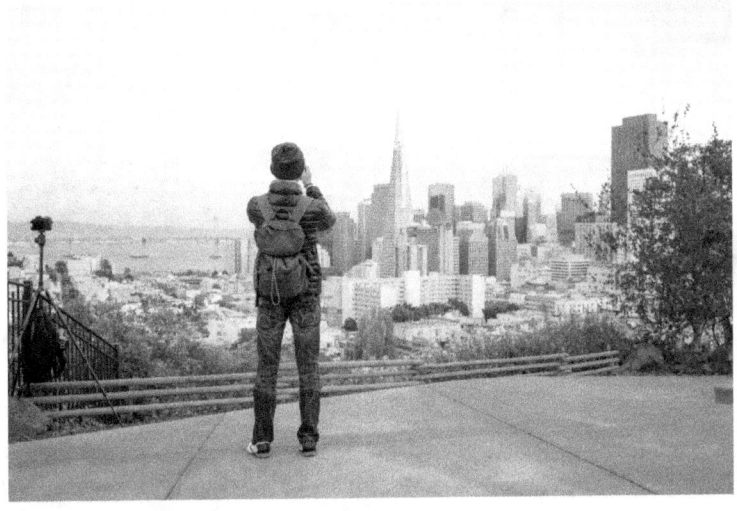

187

Regardless of which way you plan to approach San Francisco photography, you must understand the weather, both to pick the right time of the year and to bring the right clothes, especially if you plan to be shooting from many exterior locations. The warmest, sunniest time of the year is not the summer months, but September and October. November through March is the rainiest period. Even during the summer, you best have a jacket, and not a thin one, as daytime temperatures average in the mid-60s, but it can feel much cooler with brisk sea winds and chilly, damp fog.

Naturally, there are much fewer tourists during winter and early spring and, therefore, lower hotel rates. Not only will you save money during these periods, but they're better for photos with fog and mist.

WALK THE BRIDGE

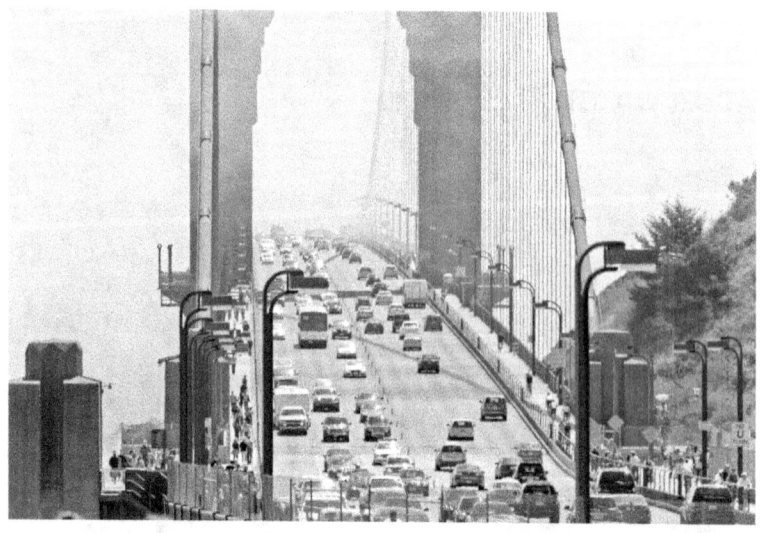

San Francisco's most iconic symbol is the Golden Gate Bridge. No doubt, it will be a star attraction in many of your images, but you'll gain a much greater appreciation of this engineering marvel and find opportunities for incredible close-ups of the structure and photographs of the surrounding panorama when you walk the bridge. It's an intrepid adventure, so you need a good pair of shoes and the time. The upside is that you won't find many tourists on the walkway.

VICTORIAN NEIGHBORHOODS

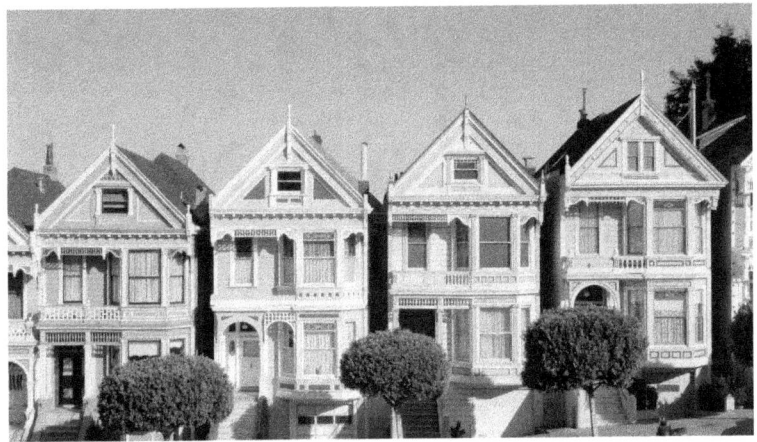

The Transamerica Pyramid may dominate the San Francisco skyline, but of equal architectural interest are the colorfully painted and "gingerbreaded" 19th-century Victorian homes. Alamo Square is likely the most famous of these neighborhoods primarily because of the Painted Ladies, or Six Sisters. As an added bonus, Alamo Square just happens to be situated to afford incredible views of much of the city and the bay. Here is where you want to be during the magic hours of sunrise and sunset when the tourists are still in bed or at dinner.

THE 49-MILE DRIVE

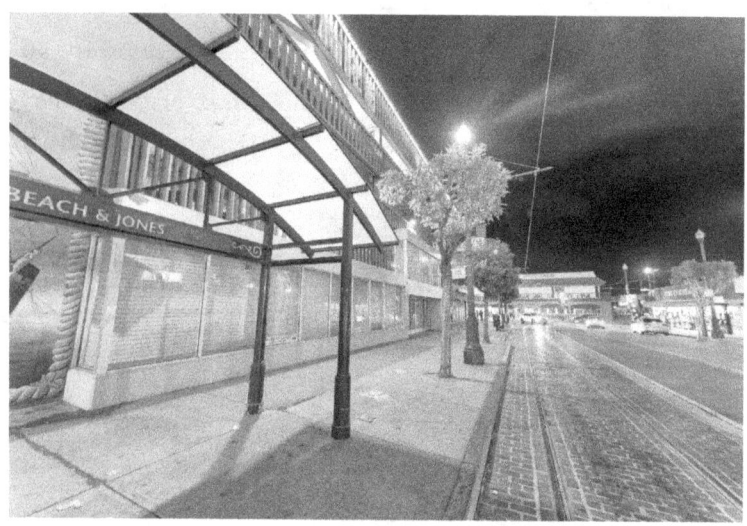

The 49-Mile Drive winds its way through and around San Francisco, and will provide you with both excellent shooting locations of the city as well as allowing you to be closer to the real city. Reportedly, parts of the Drive will take you to rather common neighborhoods, but this is where you may find special street images of life and people. Its recommended that you walk the Chinatown-Union Square-North Beach-waterfront portion, as the one-way streets and congestion will require you to pay too much attention to your driving.

FOOD, GLORIOUS FOOD

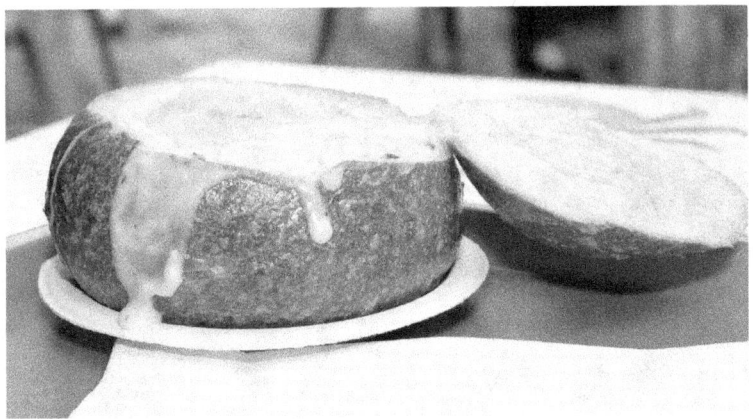

San Francisco is equally known for its eclectic mix of restaurants, cuisines, local ingredients and the wines of the nearby Sonoma Valley. If you're a foodie and/or foodie photographer, then your entire visit could focus solely on stuffing your face and your camera's memory cards with image of restaurant décor and close-ups of whatever you order.

Again, there's no reason to avoid the tourist eateries, although some are better than others; but you are apt to discover and photograph some rare treats and places where only the locals eat with a bit of prior research and a good gastronomic plan.

GOLDEN GATE PARK

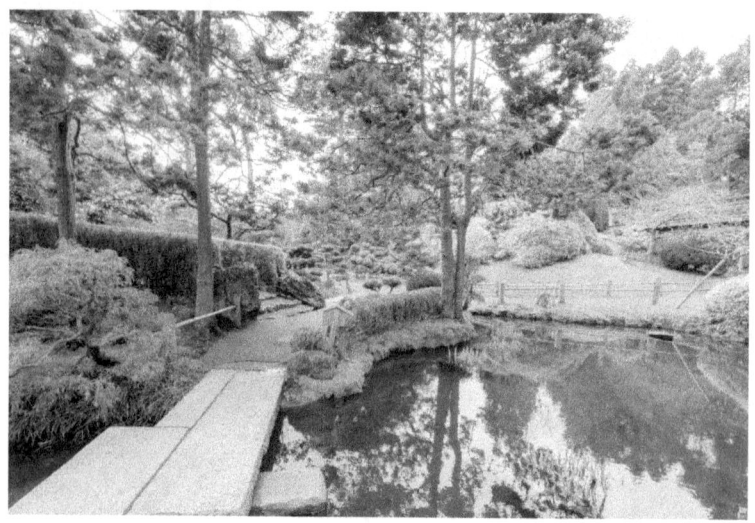

If your San Francisco visit is a family affair, then a good respite from the packed tourist attractions is Golden Gate Park. Take a break from your hectic schedule for a casual family picnic and the opportunity to photograph your kids' enjoyment and play in this beautifully, natural environment. Many people find the Japanese Tea Garden the primary attraction, but you may find more photographic subjects if you include the San Francisco Botanical Garden, California Academy of Science and Conservatory of Flowers.

SAVOR SAUSALITO

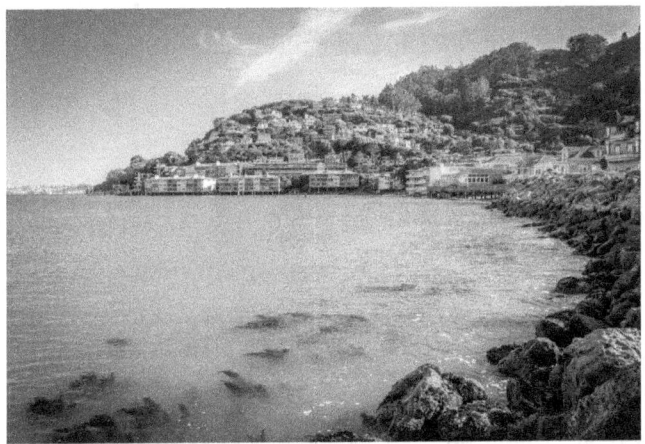

Another great diversion from San Francisco proper is to drive across the Golden Gate Bridge or take a ferry to Sausalito. It's laidback vibe of small shops and waterside restaurants present different kinds of scenes and subjects for your camera. Plus, it's an ideal location for photographing the city and at an angle you wouldn't otherwise have.

NIGHTTIME IS THE RIGHT TIME

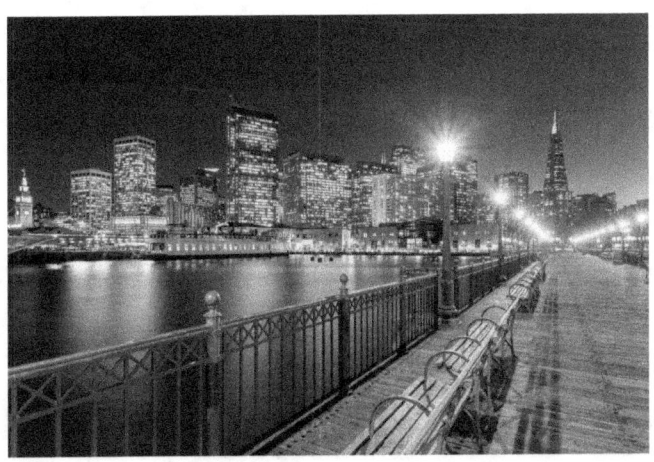

San Francisco sparkles and shines at night, especially when you have a front row seat for your camera of the Bay Lights on the Bay Bridge. Fortunately, the city decided to make this light show a permanent fixture, but, unfortunately, it will be dark from March 2015 to February 2016 to make this possible.

Of course, you can wander the streets to find the nightlife and highly photogenic street activities, but you might find Vantigo's City Lights Tour a better option. Just you and 5 others occupy a restored Volkswagen van and spend 2 hours touring the city – and with adult beverages and snacks.

As with any of the world's great cities, San Francisco offers much more than you can see, experience and photograph during a single visit. Whether yours is a full-blown tourist trip or a serious photography adventure, plan carefully, dress appropriately and bring homes some of your best photos ever.

BABY PHOTOGRAPHY: CREATE LASTING MEMORIES WITH THESE BABY PHOTOGRAPHY TIPS

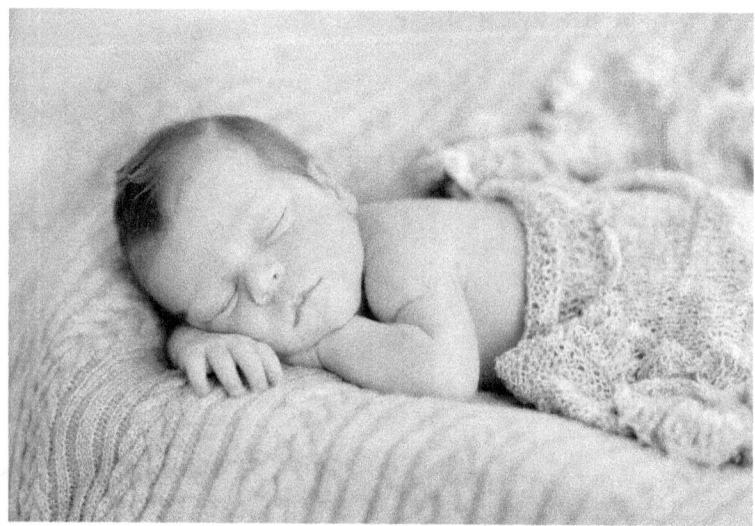

An important lesson for every parent is that children grow quickly. Today, they are infants; in a blink of an eye, they're toddlers; and turn away for an instant and they're romping, running and playing 3-year-olds. Capturing these early years is an excellent reason for buying a DSLR camera and using it to capture these moments before they disappear. Whether you're a new parent, grandparent, aunt or uncle, the following tips will help you take better-than-average pictures of infants.

1. Patience is key.

Much like photographing pets, taking pictures of infants requires infinite patience. Obviously, they won't understand or respond to any kind of directions on your part; so you may have a vision of how you want to photograph them, but don't be surprised if your vision goes "poof". As with pets, your baby may decide just as you're ready to start shooting his or her pictures that today is not the day for photography.

2. Plan, plan and plan some more.

Because you must anticipate very little time to capture the images you'd like to have, you need to plan thoroughly for your infant's photo sessions. You may discover a few spontaneous moments during the average day when you can snap a cute picture or two, but if your goal is more "formal" portraits of your child, then planning is required.

- Timing is paramount since most babies live rather strict regimens, with designated sleep and nap times and feedings. Avoid scheduling a photo session just before a sleep or nap period, as that is when an infant is likely to be tired, look sleepy and be uncooperative.

- Think about the long term too. You may want to schedule photo sessions with your baby every 30 or 60 days, so you have a series of images to show how he or she has grown. Once he or she is a year old, then the sessions could be every 90 days or twice a year.

- Look for locations where the child is already comfortable: a bed, the floor of a room or even outside on a blanket in the shade of a tree. You can even place the child in these settings and simply observe him or her and check your watch to determine how much time they are willing to be there without wanting to be held.

- As mentioned in the section about pet photography, check the natural light and the background of the shooting locations to be sure they will contribute to good compositions.

- You may even want to shoot some practice shots in these locations with a similar-sized object to represent your baby to check the lighting and background and determine the proper exposure.

- It's also a good idea to place the infant in the places you would like to photograph him or her in advance of the actual photo session day and time. This allows you to try different outfits and to determine which toys are more likely to keep him or her occupied and smiling and happy during the shoot. You may also want to place your camera in front of and next to the child for a few minutes and snap the shutter a few times, so they are familiar with what is otherwise a strange object to him or her.

- Just as with pets, if you plan to use any artificial lights, especially a flash unit, you'll want to fire it a few times in various directions and at the baby, again, so he or she becomes familiar with it and isn't suddenly surprised during the actual shoot.

- Plan some sessions for photographs with the infant and parents, other siblings, grandparents, aunts, uncles, etc. Don't expect to take all these photographs during one "super" session, however, as your baby is unlikely to have the energy and could be stressed from all the people, shuffling them in and out of the photos, etc.

3. Manage the photo session like a pro.

You may have no aspirations for becoming a professional photographer, but you can still practice some of the same session management strategies that a pro would use to maximize the results.

- Remember, you're photographing an infant; accidents can happen. Make sure there are towels, diapers and other baby supplies at hand. Select in advance more than one blanket or other spread on which you plan to photograph the baby in case the first must be replaced.

- Your lens options are essentially the same as photographing pets, and for the same reasons. Shooting with a slight telephoto focal length means you don't have to place the lens and camera immediately in front of the infant's face. You can also try some images with a wide-angle focal length to see how the baby responds and to capture some unusual angles and views.

- As with pets, you must also be prepared to bring the camera to the eye level of your infant, so you will probably have to lie on the floor. Consider renting a mini-tripod, which allows you to place the camera just a few inches from the floor.

- You should already be aware that your infant's attention span is short as well as his or her energy level and willingness to be cute. This is why it is critical to plan well in advance, so you can capture the images you want during short, 5-minute-or-less sessions. Then, allow the child to rest for 5 minutes.

- As mentioned above, provide the child with the toys he or she likes the most; but also consider photographs with a puppy, kitten or baby chick. Again, you would want to introduce these to your child prior to the shoot, so you know they won't scare him or her and you can observe how he or she interacts with the baby animals.

- You may also want to consider acquiring some of the photographic aids that are made specifically to help hold infant's attention, such as Shutter Buddies.

Photographing your infant is an excellent opportunity to hone your skills and learn how to work with people (babies in this case), so you can preserve the best memories of your child's early years.

TIPS FOR PHOTOGRAPHING
LIFE ON THE STREETS

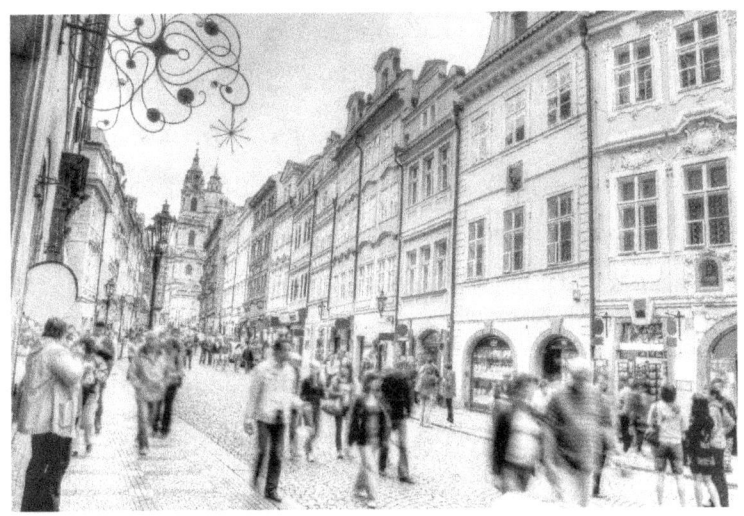

The myriad of activities, spontaneous human emotions and interactions and unique environments of the street are often the best representations of the true life of your city or the cities where you travel. Photographing street life is also an excellent laboratory to practice your skills because everything is unpredictable; you have virtually no control as you would when shooting portraits, landscapes and many other types of pictures. You do have control of you and your camera, however, and these tips will help you use that control to capture exciting, dramatic and even gritty images of what's happening on the streets today.

1. Preparing for the unknown.

Assuming you're a beginner photographer and have no experience wandering the streets of a city taking pictures of the people and places there, there are some preparatory steps you should take.

- You might find it very helpful to visit some of the streets of your city first without your camera. You may be or think you are familiar with these streets, but it's likely you've driven or walked them many times without consciously observing what is occurring. Take a walk on one or more streets you think may have interesting subjects and objects and pause occasionally just to watch, and even take notes (but don't be arrested for loitering). If there is a sidewalk café, then sit for a while to observe. To be thoroughly prepared, visit these streets during different times of the day to notice the amount of foot and vehicular traffic, the lighting, etc.

- Don't just look for the wide views of street activity; notice also small objects, such as signs, architectural elements, etc. that define the street or the neighborhood.

- It's also a good idea to visit the streets you think are best for your photo session, with your camera; but, again, not to take pictures, but simply to test angles and points-of-view and to determine in advance the correct exposures for the different lighting conditions.

■ Obviously, you want to be careful about which streets and during what times you shoot pictures, but neither can you be afraid to immerse yourself in the street life to capture the best images. An excellent strategy is to invite a friend to accompany you. First, he or she can pay attention to the people near you when you have the camera at your eye. Second, you can use him or her as a decoy. Make it look as if you are photographing him or her, but then, with a slight movement of your body and camera, you can take a picture of another person or an interaction or activity without being noticed.

2. **Less equipment, better photos.**

■ In most cases, leave your camera bag at home because life on the streets occurs too quickly to be fumbling with lenses, etc. As a beginner, your best lens choice is a zoom lens and with enough telephoto focal length, so you can shoot from a distance, such as 70–200mm. Don't forget to attach a polarizing filter. As you acquire more street photography experience, you can start to use a zoom lens with a shorter focal length, such as 24–105mm, or even wide-angle, fixed focal-length lenses.

3. **People are the prize.**

No doubt, your observations and notes will show that the people on the street are the most interesting subjects to photograph; however, there are guidelines, protocols, to taking their pictures.

■ Respect for people's privacy is of the utmost importance, especially when traveling to international locations where there might be specific cultural "rules" about photographing people. In many places, it is often considered bad form to offer payment to convince someone to allow you to take his or her picture. You'll also earn more respect when you treat your subject as a human. If he or she has given you permission for a photograph, then show them the image(s) on your camera's LCD screen. Even consider exchanging email addresses, so you can send him or her copies.

- The best strategy is always to ask permission before taking anyone's picture. Now, this is not always possible on a crowded street and when you are shooting from a distance with a telephoto lens. You can also gesture to the person and show him or her your camera, which is a message that crosses language barriers. Once he or she acknowledges your presence and gives some sign of agreement, then you can take his or her picture.

- You are more likely to win people's trust and gain their permission to photograph them if you dress less like a tourist and more like the locals. In addition, people will respond more positively to your request if you are alone instead of part of a tourist group.

- If you find interesting storefronts or even interiors, then make sure to ask permission of the owners or managers first, and then offer to provide them with copies they could use for their advertising and/or social media.

- If a police officer or security guard stops you, then calmly explain you're an amateur photographer learning how to shoot life on the street for private purposes and present a valid ID.

4. **Don't be confined by the rules.**

    ▪ Again, because the street life occurs so quickly, you don't have time to think about and follow all the "rules" of photography. Having determined the right exposure in advance for the place and time you're shooting, just start shooting and occasionally check the results through the playback mode.

    ▪ As you gain experience, you can start to shoot images with the camera at your hip or above your head, as you walk and stop to release the shutter. Low angles are also excellent perspectives for street photography. Be careful with this one, but crouch between parked cars and frame the parallel space on the sidewalk and snap pictures as people walk into the frame.

    ▪ Street photography is such a great learning experience because it requires you to be more open-minded and just as spontaneous as what is occurring around you. You may discover many of your images are blurred, have high contrast, without adequate light and not "perfectly" framed. Just go with the flow and you may take home some images that will wow everyone.

CAPTURING ARCHITECTURE AND FUNCTION OF BUILDINGS AND STRUCTURES

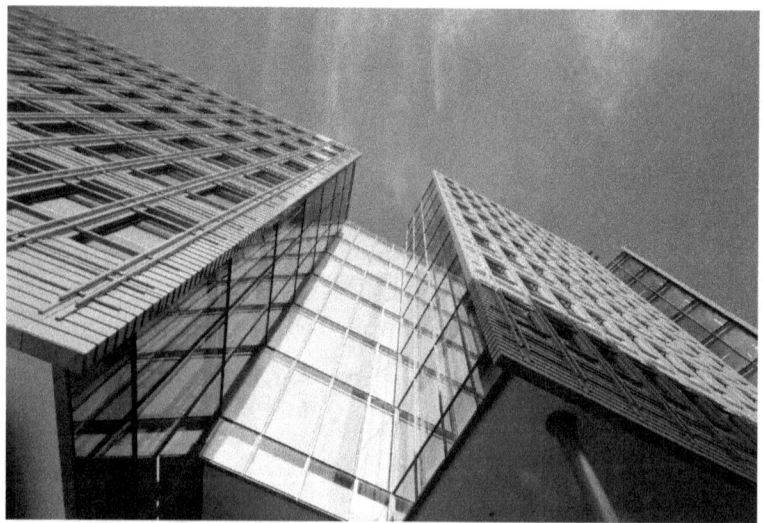

Studying and recording the details of one art form – architecture – with another – photography – can teach you much about form and function and how best to capture them with lighting and composition. Follow these tips to learn how to photograph not just buildings and structures, but the essential elements of their architecture.

1. **Architecture is everywhere you look.**

Humans are often described as makers, creators and builders and the structures we design and create reveal much about our nature and our needs. Whether the architecture is familiar and somewhat standardized like the homes on a street; the glass-enclosed edifices of skyscrapers; government and university buildings that reflect architectural styles of the past; or the unusual, unique and extremely modern-looking structures for museums, art galleries, stadiums and other public or private uses, they can be interesting and enjoyable subjects to photograph. Plus, they never move or blink and complain about how much time you spend photographing them, but they can surprise you when shot from various angles and under different lighting conditions.

2. **Raise your architectural acumen.**

To photograph architecture successfully doesn't require that you spend hours learning about different styles or the most-honored structures in the world, but some research will prepare you to take more than the typical photos of buildings.

- You can start with some online research that makes it easy to understand the basics, and then it's a good idea to explore your neighborhood and your city to discover these basic elements in their structures.

- Form and function are the terms most-often associated with architecture and are rather simple to understand. You may have also heard it said that "form follows function," meaning the functional use of a building dictates its design, shape, size, etc.

Office buildings must use space efficiently to accommodate the most people at work. A museum or art gallery not only requires large and tall rooms for the paintings and sculptures displayed there, but also designed to allow a maximum number of people to move through the rooms easily and be able to see the exhibits.

- The other fundamental elements to notice in architecture are lines, shapes and textures. A building can be viewed and photographed as geometry, placing the camera in positions that emphasize the lines of the structure and how the various shapes that contribute to the overall design complement or contrast each other. Architectural surfaces present various textures that are best photographed very close; so close that no one would know it's a building unless you told them. Plus, the textures of wood, metal and stone can look entirely different as the light angle or camera angle changes.

3. With the camera in your hands.

- This section is not meant to be an overview of the theory and concepts of architecture, so before you become totally bored, it's time to take the theory and concepts into the field and learn how to use them with your camera to bring home outstanding images.

  - ➢ Architectural photography has much in common with landscape photography. For images of an entire structure, you typically want to shoot with a wide-angle lens, or focal length, and at a low angle. Plus, you can compose your architectural images with a smaller object in the foreground to complement the grand view of the building in the background.

> ➢ The building's sign is an obvious example, but it could also be a street cart or food truck that contrasts the small business of the cart or truck with the big business in the skyscraper behind it.

> ➢ A single person sitting in the foreground maybe eating lunch or reading a newspaper creates a feeling of the human being overwhelmed by a massive structure.

> ➢ A foreground grouping of the small products manufactured in the immense factory in the background.

> ➢ A single chicken filling most of the image with a view of hundreds of chickens in the background scampering through the doors of a large chicken-breeding facility.

- You can also photograph architecture with a slightly telephoto focal length, as you would a portrait, to avoid disturbing distortions. This is why it is so important to recognize and understand the lines of a building because you want them to appear parallel in your photos. Non-parallel lines in any photo (unless that is your intention) look strange. By choosing a more distant camera position, you're more likely to record the building's line as parallel.

- What may look like a monotonous, monolithic structure in the light of day can be something amazing when photographed at night with the lights of the city. When you shoot these kinds of images, you'll want to use a tripod, so you can shoot with a slow shutter speed, which allows you to use a smaller aperture, such as f/8, to maximize the depth of field. It will also be unnecessary to increase the ISO setting, so your images are sharp and smooth without any digital noise. You'll also need a shutter release cable or wireless, remote shutter release device.

- Architecture is often rendered better with black-and-white photography because the contrast between light and dark areas are typically more pronounced than in color and it gives a building or structure a dramatic look. Lines, shapes and textures are also more likely to be emphasized in black and white.

- Although architecture can be interesting, even dramatic, during the brightest times of the day, you'll definitely want to schedule some time to photograph buildings and structures during the "magic hours" of sunrise and sunset, too. Don't think it needs to be a sunny day either; an overcast or rainy or snowy day adds weather elements that can also result in more interesting photos.

- Finally, don't limit your architectural photography to city buildings. There are many historical and interesting structures in small towns and industrial areas as well as rural locations: barns, silos, country estates, etc. Make sure you check on any rules or prohibitions about photography any building and ask permission of the owner.

WINTER PHOTOGRAPHY: HOW TO CAPTURE WINTER WONDERLAND PHOTOS

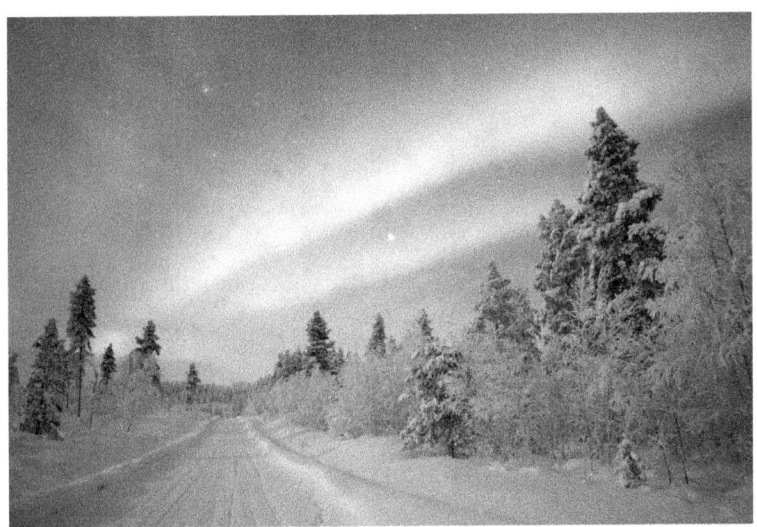

An important truism of photography that you must learn from the beginning is that the subjects and scenes (especially the most interesting) won't come to you, you must be willing to go to them – and even during the cold, ice and snow of winter. Weather can never be a deterrent to a photographer who wants to advance his or her skills and capture the images that can't be taken during any other time of the year.

While most everyone is hiding indoors, you're fortunate to have a reason to be outdoors to enjoy your hobby and some exercise instead of just shoveling snow and scraping the windshield of your car. No doubt, it's a challenge to shoot in the cold, especially when it isn't one of those bright, clear, blue-sky days of winter, but once you take the plunge you'll realize it was worth it and you'll want to go again.

WINTER PHOTOGRAPHY BEGINS WITH PROTECTING YOUR CAMERA

1. Your camera and batteries must be as warm as possible, so keep them in a black, weatherproof camera bag until you're ready to shoot. The black outer surface of the bag will absorb and retain heat.

2. You don't want to expose your camera to the cold temperatures, immediately. Just as the lenses of a pair of room-temperature eyeglasses will fog as soon as they come in contact with the cold air, moisture will cover the outside of your camera and possibly penetrate the interior. You must slowly introduce it to the cold by leaving the camera in the bag and in your unheated garage for approximately a half hour, and then in your car for another 30 minutes.

3. Just because its winter and the light is weaker than during summer doesn't mean you can leave the UV filter at home. Keep it on the front of your lens because during those crisp, sunny winter days, there is more reflective light that could damage the lens.

4. The humidity level, and the resulting moisture, can change quickly during the winter, so don't place your camera bag directly on a patch of snow or ice. The cold will start to penetrate the bag and freeze the

moisture and that could result in a damaged lens, sensor and/or batteries.

5. Take two pairs of gloves with you. One pair you can allow to become wet, but keep the other pair dry and only handle your camera with the dry pair. Just as with #4 above, your camera could easily absorb the snow or frozen moisture on your gloves and that could be a disaster.

6. Pack a dry cloth and keep it dry, and then use it to wipe snow, ice or moisture from your second pair of gloves or the outside of the camera. Never open your camera body outdoors to attempt to dry the inside.

WHERE TO FIND THE MOST-INTERESTING WINTER PHOTOS

1. You can approach winter photography two ways. First, you can just dress warm and head outdoors and be surprised by what you find; or second, check the weather for today and during the next week to determine which days may be best, based on the potential for frost, snowfall, freezing rain and warmer weather that will partially melt ice and snow. The challenge of shooting outdoors may be exciting and inspiring, but with a plan, you'll be able to maximize the limited amount of time you'll want to be in the winter weather.

2. If the forecast calls for frosty conditions, then you'll find some interesting designs on the surfaces of common natural and manmade objects. Look closely and you're apt to see more frost accumulate on edges or any pronounced lines. Frost is also a natural phenomenon that often occurs during early morning, so planning your wintertime shoot during sunrise allows you to capture frost pictures as well as interesting scenes illuminated by the early, low light. If the frosty conditions persist

into the middle of the day, then the slight warmth of the sun may cause some melting; and the same objects and surfaces you photographed during the early morning may present you with a new set of images to capture midday.

3.   Ice is a natural element that will provide you with an incredible number of photographic opportunities. Wait for freezing rain to stop, and you'll discover a coating of ice on most everything outdoors. The end of twigs can become bejeweled and surfaces will shine with reflective light. Once it begins to melt, everything will be dripping. Look for icicles during a warming trend after a heavy snowfall; some will be short, others long and even some doubles and triples.

     Consider visiting the nearby park that has a lake. Not only will the frozen water's surface provide a myriad of interesting patterns and textures, but also look along the edges of the water and how the ice interacts with vegetation, rocks and wood. It will be worth the effort to find a flowing stream that is partially covered by ice. The cold water gives the surfaces of bare rocks a different kind of reflective sheen and there may be small icicles where the water falls over debris.

4.   Snow, of course, is the other major winter weather event; and it will provide you with a huge number of pictures to take. If the snow is heavy, then you'll have many choices of natural landscapes to photograph. It's also fun to photograph people drudging through the snow, an impassable side street where all the parked cars are covered in the snow and children building snowmen and throwing snowballs.

5.   You may want to review the Histogram section. If you're shooting in an outdoors environment where all the surfaces are white, your

camera's light meter may incorrectly read all that reflective light and cause your images to be underexposed.

6. You may also want to consider bringing a tripod with you, so you can shoot at slower shutter speeds since many winter days are very gray with low-light conditions.

Ultimately, the advantage of having a DSLR camera is that it allows you to shoot in any weather condition and in any environment and you're doing yourself a disservice if you only use it when the weather is nice.

WINTER PHOTOGRAPHY: 7 EASY STEPS TO BETTER SKIING PHOTOS DURING YOUR WINTER VACATION

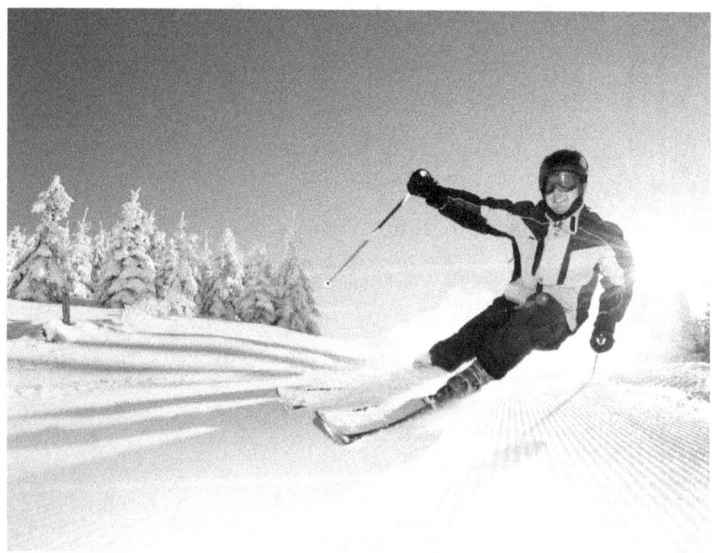

If you're heading to your favorite winter fun spot during the first part of the year, then you have a great opportunity to capture some excellent photos of skiers in action on the slopes. Follow these 7 steps and you and your photos will be the center of attention at the ski lodge.

1. Keep the Gear Simple

For the best skiing photos, you'll likely to be on skis too and far up the slopes, so you don't want be carrying a big, heavy camera bag. You may want to consider acquiring a camera cover to keep the internal mechanism of the camera and lens warm, especially during the coldest days. Plus, buy yourself a pair of thinner gloves that expose your fingertips. It's nigh impossible to handle a DSLR camera with bulky skiing gloves. You'll need a lens with a telephoto focal length because you must shoot from the side of a run, in most cases. Then again, you don't want a large, bulky lens either. Choose a lens of at least 135mm; 200mm would be even better, but it will weigh more.

2. The Action Camera Option

You may also want to consider renting a GoPro or similar action camera for a week or weekend, so you can attach it to your head, your chest, a wrist or even the front of a ski for some amazing action shots. These cameras are much smaller, lighter and also record video and are perfect for selfies and closer photos of your family and friends on the slopes.

3. Safety First

Be careful about stopping in the middle of a ski run to capture photos of skiers passing you, especially if you're on a run for experienced skiers or one with plenty of curves or corners. Such a position should allow you to take some very interesting pictures, but they're not worth injury to you or a skier. The same applies to moguls or ski jumps. You may be able to catch a skier as he or she soars above you lying on your back or crouched low; but don't do this randomly. Plan the shot with your subject, so he or she knows you will be below him or her. Accidents and injuries could occur if skiers aren't aware you are below the mogul or jump.

4.   Be Positioned for Action

Your best position for action shots is to the side of a run, so you can frame skiers as they move past you, either perpendicular or at a slight angle in front of their position. Your goal is to place them in the center of the frame and freeze the action. You may find this quite difficult to accomplish, however, first, if you don't have much experience photographing moving subjects and, second, because skiers are moving so fast relative to your position, you don't have much time to pick one coming down the slope and snapping the shutter at the right moment. You may want to try this random-shooting style because it's good practice and you may be surprised at what you capture.

A better strategy is to coordinate your photo with a skier, so he or she knows where you will be and you know he or she is on the way, so your camera is ready and you're positioned correctly. Friends and family members will be excited to participate since they certainly want great ski photos of themselves to share with everyone.

You and your subject may want to ski the run to decide on the best camera location, such as at a curve. Pick the point on the run where you plan to take the picture and pre-frame and pre-focus your camera for that distance. You won't have time to be fiddling with focus when the skier comes into view. Neither can you rely on your camera's auto-focus system to be able to focus accurately on your subject as he or she flashes past. You'll achieve better results with manual focus. Then, both of you return to the top of the run, with your subject waiting until you're in position. You can stay in contact over your phones or walkie-talkies, with your subject calling you just as he or she is starting the run.

5.   Go Low and Wide for the Spray

Another great ski action composition is to shoot from a low position with a wide-angle lens as a skier approaches your position, and then stops quickly and sharply on the ski edges to create a spray of snow. You'll want to use a wide-angle lens, so the spray fills the foreground and you can tightly frame the entire person with his or her face visible. Again, plan this photo with safety in mind; the person doesn't have to be moving at top speed to create the spray. It's likely the spray of snow will hit you, so as soon as you depress the shutter either turn or curl your body forward to protect your camera from being drenched in wet snow.

6.   Use the Panning Technique

Once you're comfortable with photographing skiers from the side of a run and have some great shots, you may want to try the panning technique, which will impart the illusion of motion.

- Set your shutter speed low; 1/30th of a second is good.
- Instead of waiting for the skier to enter your viewfinder at the pre-determined spot for a photo, follow the skier as soon as you see he or she, panning with him or her as he or she moves past your spot and down the slope.
- During your panning motion, release the shutter when the skier is parallel to you.

- In the resulting shot, the skier should appear mostly in focus, with a bit of blur around the edges of the body, but the background will be much more blurred.

7.   Check Exposure and White Balance

You may not be able to use the auto-exposure mode on your camera since all the white snow, and the reflections if it is sunny, clear and sharp, could fool auto-exposure. Shoot some test images first in lighting conditions that are similar to your skier photos. When planning your shots with your subject skier, take a meter reading of his or her face or your skin and use that exposure for your photos. Determine during your test photos if your camera's auto white balance mode is working correctly too.

You can learn so much when photographing skiers and the fast action of their movements, so be sure to pack your camera when you're hitting the slopes this and every winter.

TAKING PHOTOS AT THE ZOO

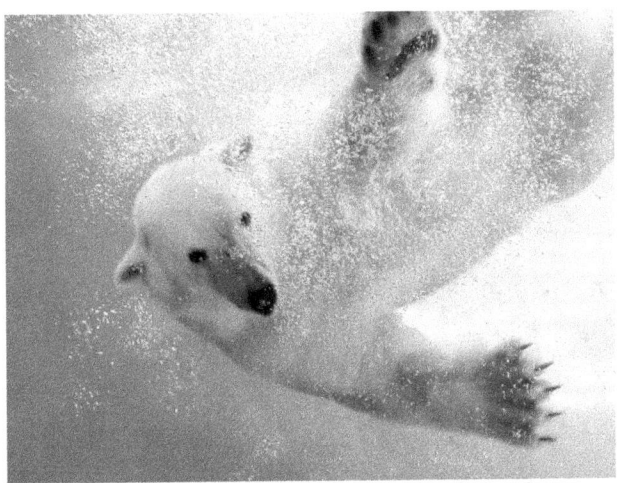

Y ou never know where your photography may take you. Someday, you may find yourself on an African safari in the Masai Mara, photographing the millions of wildebeest, zebras and antelopes on their endless migration, or the Pantanal, the world's largest freshwater wetland, in South America, where the elusive jaguar could appear in front of your camera. To enjoy these photographic adventures and bring home incredible images, you'd want to make sure your skills are well developed, but you'd also want to understand the behavior of wild animals and how best to photograph them.

Before you pack your bags, make your local zoo your first stop. As zoos create more natural habitats for their animals and eliminate the cages, they become excellent learning laboratories for wildlife photography. It's likely you've taken the family to the zoo and snapped pictures of their fun and interaction with animals; and you should continue to do so with your DSLR camera. You'll also find it beneficial, however, to visit the zoo alone, so you can concentrate on just photographing the animals. When you "capture" great photos, your children would love a number of enlargements for their bedroom walls, or to share at school. Follow these tips and you're sure to bring home some winners.

1. Safety First

Obviously, the most important job of the zoo management is to keep the animals and human visitors safe; and this should be your uppermost thought in mind when photographing zoo animals. Make sure you know the rules (you should be able to find them listed on the zoo's Website) about photography. For example, many zoos don't allow the use of a flash. Plus, in your zeal and enthusiasm to take a great shot, DON'T EVER compromise your safety or hold your camera inside a cage or extend the lens through bars or a fence.

2. Do Your Homework

Visit your local zoo's Website to determine which of its animals are housed in natural habitats, as these will probably provide you with unobstructed views and better pictures. Also, take notice of any special exhibits or specific animals for which the zoo is known. A bit more research may reveal smaller zoos in the area that specialize in birds, reptiles or insects.

Since zoos house many more animals than you could shoot during a single visit, you'll want to develop a tentative shot list, based on your research. Then, when you know which animals you plan to photograph, do some additional online research to learn about their behaviors, striking colors and features that could make excellent photos and their interactions as a group.

3. Equip Yourself

Although a wide-angle zoom lens, such as an 18–55mm may prove to be useful when you're allowed close to animals, you'll likely need a telephoto zoom since many of your photos will have to be taken from a distance. A 70–200mm, or even 70–300mm, is a good choice. Remember, you can always rent a lens for a weekend at a very affordable fee; and online rental companies will ship it directly to you.

You'll also want a polarizing filter on the front of every lens to reduce the glare of a bright sun and any reflection off the surface of a big cat's shiny coat or the bright, colorful wing of a bird. A polarizing filter will also help you control reflections if you must shoot through glass or into a water-filled tank to photograph aquatic animals.

4. Watch the Weather and Pick Your Time

Beginner photographers often make the mistake thinking that direct sunlight and the brightest time of the day are best for their pictures. In most cases, both assumptions are wrong. As part of your zoo photo safari planning, make sure you check the weather. A colder, rainy day will probably force most animals indoors, but many may enjoy being outdoors on a warm day with drizzles. A cloudy or partially cloudy day may be your best shooting condition, as the light will be more even and diffuse, so there won't be any harsh shadows.

As has been and will often be mentioned in this book, the best times of the day for most photography is early morning or late afternoon when the sun is less direct. Again, the light is softer, more diffuse. Being one of the first visitors at the zoo in the morning will also allow you to avoid the crowds during the middle of the day. You may also want to bring your tripod on cloudy days or early mornings, so you can shoot at slower shutter speeds and keep the ISO at its normal setting.

5.   Overcoming Shooting Challenges

Zoos do what they can to make the photographing of the animals as easy as possible, but typically you find that you must shoot through a fence (rails or wire mesh) and glass. In addition, many of the natural enclosures place the animals below the level of the walkways and viewing positions for humans.

Fences – The trick with fences is to place the end of the lens as close to the rails or wire mesh as possible, and so you are looking through an opening. Position yourself, so whatever animal you are photographing appears in that opening. You then want your aperture setting to be at its widest, which will narrow the depth of field and likely defocus the rail or wire so much as to be invisible. If part of the fencing does appear in an image, it can always be removed with photo editing software, so don't necessarily discard an excellent composition of an animal just because some of the fence can be seen.

Glass – Reflections aren't the only problem with glass. It's likely to be smeared with fingerprints, so include a cloth among your gear, so you can wipe the glass surface where you want shoot. Attach the lens hood to the lens and gently place it against the surface of the glass. This will help reduce glare. You may want to shoot a test photo or two because your camera's auto focus system may be confused. You might have to shoot with manual focus.

Low habitats – When animal habitats are below your viewing level, then don't shoot from a standing position, but move yourself and your camera as low as possible to reduce the angle.

6. Capture Animals at Their Best

Generally, it's best to frame your images tightly on a single animal or the interesting interaction of two or more animals. This is why a telephoto zoom lens is a necessity. You also want to shoot at wide apertures, so the fencing or other enclosure structure behind the animal becomes blurred. During your research, check on feeding times, since that is when animals tend to be more active.

Even if you never journey to the Masai Mara or the Pantanal, you can create an excellent portfolio of wild animals at your zoo.

HOW TO TAKE PERFECT PHOTOS
OF THE WILDLIFE

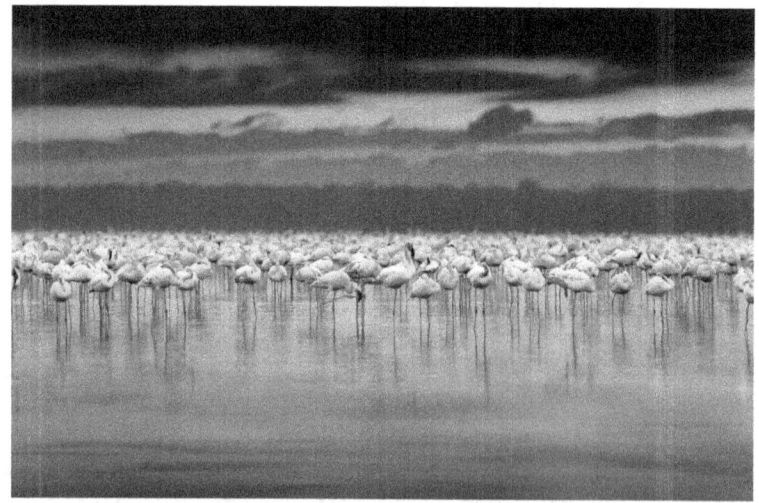

One of the primary reasons you may have bought a digital camera is that it allows you to photograph virtually every kind of scene and subject, and essentially everywhere. Initially, most of your images may be casual shots of family members and friends; but, eventually, you'll start to develop an interest in specific kinds of photography: portraits, landscapes, architecture, pets, travel, etc. Wildlife photography is a category that often excites and fires the imagination of many beginner photographers because it is adventurous and takes you to wild places to photograph animals that you may have only seen in books or at the zoo.

Good for you! Of course, there is a practical, down-to-earth part to wildlife photography that you must understand before running into the woods with your camera. This section will help you approach wildlife photography step-by-step.

1. The wildlife learning curve

You'll spend many wasted hours in the state park or wilderness area, come home with no wildlife photos and be frustrated with your effort unless you spend some quality time learning about the animals that are available to photograph within a reasonable distance of your home. The Internet is your schoolroom, but you can also check with local or national wildlife organizations and/or clubs. State governments and the US government have Websites for their various parks and designated forests and wildlife areas and they usually list and/or explain all the birds, reptiles and mammals you're apt to see in those locations.

2. Practice with a captive audience

Your first wildlife photography challenge shouldn't be grizzly bears in the mountains of Montana or bald eagles nesting along an Alaskan river. Start with photographing animals at your local zoo or a children's petting zoo or a butterfly house. You must first familiarize yourself with animal behavior in general and cut your wildlife photographic teeth on animals in a controlled environment.

3. Start with the small and easy-to-photograph

Again, you can only become frustrated if your first wildlife photography adventure is animals you can only photograph at a great distance and/or run or fly quickly. Develop your skills by shooting snails, frogs and other small creatures that don't move much or certainly fast. Practice skills, such as proper exposure, sharp focusing, depth of field and composition, with these animals, and then try your hand at squirrels, chipmunks and local bird species. You may be itching to photograph the big "glory" animals, such as bears, raptors, buffalo and cats, but developing your skills with smaller species will improve your chances of bringing home the big prizes.

4. The skill of patience

Maybe, the most important skill you can learn by photographing small, slow wildlife first is patience. When shooting wildlife, you essentially have no control of the environment or the animals' behavior. You need a combination of the right equipment, the right location and the right knowledge about the animals you want to photograph to have any opportunity to capture exciting images. Even the best and most honored wildlife photographers will tell you that despite all their experience, they can spend hours, even days, tracking their animal quarry and take no worthwhile photos for publication. As an amateur, you can be assured that this will happen to you – and often.

5. Planning for the weather and your comfort

The pros will also tell you that wildlife photography can be a miserable experience, sitting for hours in foul weather and in uncomfortable positions just waiting for the right shot. Start to develop the habit of checking the weather reports even for your first simple wildlife shoot of small, slow animals and be sure you are dressed for the weather, including a rain suit, a hat, the right footwear, sunblock, a ground cover for sitting, a folding stool, hand warmers; whatever the conditions require. Plus, bring a rain cover for your camera.

6. Specialized equipment

Although you may be able to capture interesting and well-composed images of snails and frogs with a lens of a short focal length, most wildlife photography requires much longer focal lengths, with 300mm often the minimum. Most of the pros are shooting with 500mm, 600mm, 800mm and even the extra-super focal length of 1200mm. Of course, these lenses are very expensive, so renting lenses of these focal lengths will be your only option. You shouldn't even invest in a 300mm telephoto lens until you've discovered a true passion for wildlife photography and you have some shoots under your belt.

Often, a tripod is also an essential piece of equipment, especially with these very long lenses. In addition, animals may not give you the time to bring the camera to your eye and focus before they've moved; so having your camera mounted to a tripod and set for the height of your eye is important.

7. The conditions dictate exposure

The auto-exposure function of your DSLR will be useful shooting wildlife, but be prepared to go fully manual, as weather can change quickly, affecting the light level. Within seconds an animal can move from a brightly lit position to deep shadows or vice versa. These rapid changes can fool auto-exposure, so be careful about relying on it entirely. Lenses with long and very long focal lengths don't have the wide apertures of small lenses, so this will also have an effect of what exposure combinations you can use.

Another tip from the wildlife photography pros is that you can use higher ISO settings, such as 800 or more, to give you more exposure latitude. New DSLRs, even entry-level models, have such an enormous ISO sensitivity range, that ISO 800 on today's camera is the equivalent of ISO 200 on older models. The pros are always willing to have photos with a bit of grain if it means taking the photos they envisioned and those their editors expect them to submit.

8.   Take advantage of every learning opportunity

To succeed at wildlife photography, you must continue to educate yourself: Attend seminars, join your local photography club and accompany an accomplished wildlife photographer as an assistant during his or her shoots and save your money and allocate some vacation time to join a wildlife photography workshop. You'll spend a week with a few other photographers, guided by a professional who knows what to shoot, where to shoot and how to shoot.

MACRO PHOTOGRAPHY TIPS

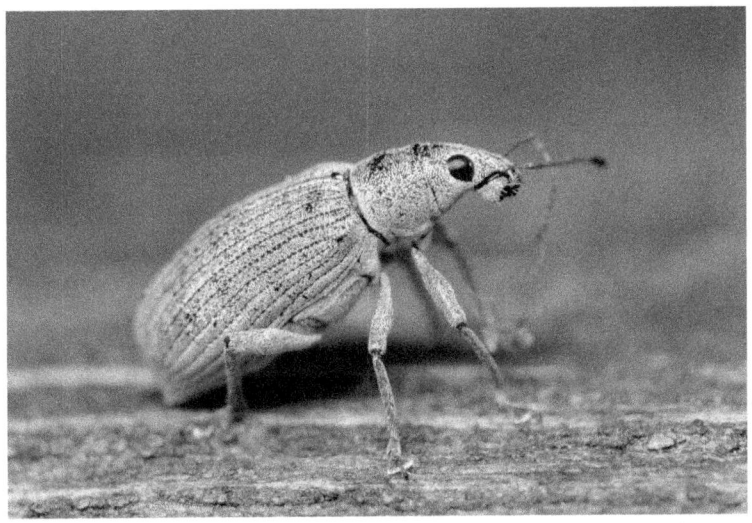

The number of scenes and subjects to photograph with your DSLR camera are truly infinite, but one category that beginners and hobbyists often overlook is the tiny, almost invisible, world of insects, the inside of flowers, the surface details of everyday objects, textures and patterns, etc. You can enter this world and discover many wonders you have never seen or knew existed with the help of macro photography.

1. Magnification and Macro Photography

Macro photography is defined as the capability to photograph an object at a 1:1 magnification ratio. This simply means that an insect, for example, which is one inch in length, will be projected onto your camera's sensor as also one inch in size. If the sensor can only project the insect's image as small as two inches, then the magnification ratio is 1:2.

2. The Lens Difference

Therefore, for true macro photography, you need to use a macro lens because only it provides 1:1 or better magnification. You must be careful, however, because lens manufacturer will use the term "macro" as part of a lens' name to boost the marketing of the product. Typically, these "false" macro lenses have only a 1:3 or 1:4 magnification ratio. They will allow you to capture nice close-up images, but they are not true macro lenses.

Many standard lenses have rather close focusing distances.

- The 18–55mm Canon zoom lens that comes with any of the EOS Rebel DSLR cameras can still achieve focus at 9.8", but it won't be a 1:1 magnification ratio.

- The Canon 24–70mm f/2.8 has a closest focus distance of 1.25 feet.

- The Canon 70–200mm f/4 focuses only as close as 3.9 feet.

- The Canon 60mm f/2.8 macro lens focuses as close as 7.8" and creates a 1:1 magnification ratio.

3. Inexpensive Options

Although macro photography can be an exciting pursuit, you won't actually be sure if it is one of your favorites until you've tried it, and probably more than once. Macro photography can be expensive but you can enter this microscopic world for much less cost with these options.

- Renting a true macro lens for a weekend is very affordable, and will provide you with enough time and opportunities to decide if purchasing a lens is a wise, long-term investment.

- The least-costly option is a reversing ring. It allows you to attach two standard lenses together front-to-front. The end of the lens attached to the camera is the standard mounting end, but the opening at the other end of this two-lens combination is the smaller, or mounting end, of the front lens. This creates a light-gathering device similar to a true macro lens. You can either use a 50mm and a zoom lens or a 50mm and telephoto lens with a fixed focal length of 200mm or more.

- An extension tube is attached to the camera body and then the lens. It is a hollow tube like a lens, but it has no glass elements. By increasing the distance from the camera to the lens with an extension tube, you are able to focus closer on a tiny object; the longer the tube, the closer you can focus. The longest extension tube can cost hundreds of dollars, so, again, this may be an item you'd want to rent.

- A close-up lens is a narrow piece of glass mounted in a ring and looks much like a lens filter. It is attached to the front of a lens and the shape of the glass will give your standard lens more magnification. As a first-time macro PHOTOGRAPHER, YOU CAN PURCHASE A CLOSE-UP LENS FOR LESS THAN $100.

4.   Lighting Your Macro Subject

In a natural setting, there may be enough light to photograph an insect or the interior of a flower, but you may also find yourself in a dark, shadowed area to reach a prize subject. Most standard flash units will produce too much light at such short distances. A better lighting solution is called a ring flash, which attaches to the lens, surrounding it. The entire surface of the ring produces a soft light that evenly illuminates the subject.

You may also be able to use a small piece of aluminum foil or white card stock and place or attached it to a nearby branch to reflect more sunlight into the tight location where you find your subject.

5.   Pay Attention to Depth of Field

Depth of field is a major element of macro photography. Because the distance between the camera and the subject is one of the three factors that determines depth of field and your camera will be very close to your subject, the depth of field will be very shallow, sometimes less than an inch. You may have seen a photo of an insect shot down its body. The head is in focus, but the remainder of the body is not in focus. In this case, the depth of field was so shallow that it was impossible to include the entire insect in the focused depth. You'll want to use the smallest aperture possible (f/11, f/16 or f/22) to create the most depth, but this will require a slow shutter speed. That's why a tripod and a cable shutter release or a wireless remote release (the best) are essential pieces of macro photography equipment.

Achieving precise, sharp focus with such a narrow depth of field can be tricky. Your camera's auto-focus system is essentially of no use, so you must focus manually.

6. Look for Macro Subjects Everywhere

Insects, the inside of flowers and close-ups of other plants are the obvious subject matter for macro photography; and you should certainly try your hand at them. You might find these subjects challenging for your first macro photography shoot, since insects move and even the slightest breeze will sway a flower.

For your first entry into this wonderful world, you may want to experiment with the small textures and patterns of everyday objects or natural wood and rock surfaces as well as those of manmade objects: the head of a bolt or a close-up of rust or peeling paint. These don't move and you can place them where the light is just right.

NIGHTTIME PHOTOGRAPHY: CAPTURING
THE PERFECT NIGHT SHOTS

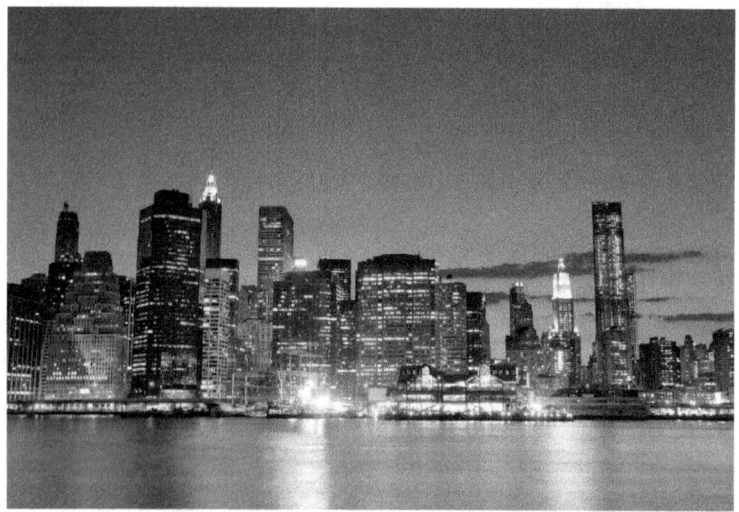

So, you think you know your city? You may be familiar with its daytime persona, especially if you commute there; but at night it's a quite different place, from a photographic perspective. Photographing a city at night can be almost as adventurous as trekking into the mountains and backcountry or a deep jungle. Plus, it's an opportunity to learn more about light and how to control and use it creatively, finding and composing interesting scenes and subjects, and operating your camera manually.

It's time to start exploring the city at night!

1. Plan Your Adventure

As with any type of photography or shooting tip, some planning will also serve you well and likely save some time. The Web is filled with information about your city, or any city, and you'll also be able to study plenty of other photographers' city images to inspire you and reveal great subject matter and the best locations to find them. You may find it useful to make a list and familiarize yourself with these locations, how to access them, etc. It may even be advantageous to scout these locations during daylight.

For a first-time, after-dark photography shoot, it's probably best to choose well-lit parts of town, either central city or restaurant, entertainment and/or arts districts. These areas will tend to have more light, more people, more interesting buildings, etc. Maybe, most importantly, these places will be safer too.

2. Plan for Safety

One of the most important reasons for making a list of your shots and their locations is so you can leave a copy with your family, roommate or a friend, so they know where you will be and when you will be there. This will help to determine the period of time you will be away and wandering the city.

An excellent safety strategy is to invite a friend to join you; he or she could be another photographer or simply someone to accompany you and provide an extra set of eyes, especially when your eye is looking through the viewfinder.

In addition, whenever it's necessary to change lenses or make other camera adjustments, you might want to step into a darker area, so people can't see you. Practice lens changes or these other adjustments in the dark first; so you can do so easily and quickly.

Another important safety consideration is to be aware of any buildings or places you are not allowed to photograph because of being possible terrorist targets or for other reasons of national security and sensitivity. You may find this information during your Web research; or you can contact the local government.

Be prepared to identify yourself to law enforcement officers quickly and without any fast movements. Don't try to hide or run from them. Stand in the light where you can be seen and explain you are photographing the city at night as an amateur photographer and private citizen.

3.   Equipped to Succeed

The camera lens or lenses you choose for your city-at-night shoot depends on the specific subject matter – more on lenses below. For many, if not most, of your compositions, you'll need a tripod and a shutter release cable or wireless remote release. Many of the best pictures require slow to very slow shutter speeds and narrow apertures (f/11 or f/16) to create plenty of depth of field, for cityscapes or architectural images. These exposure settings will also allow you to use a low ISO number, rendering your images sharp and without digital noise.

4. Lens Choices

Since many after-night city photos are actually landscapes, you want to use the same technique as shooting in the wild: a wide-angle lens or a telephoto with a wide-angle focal length, such as a 24–70mm, or similar focal length. With this range, not only can you photograph cityscapes, but also put yourself in the middle of a street carnival or other celebration and capture images with wide views. Fast lenses are also an advantage when shooting at night, anywhere. With apertures of f/1.2, f/1.4 or f/1.8, more of the limited available light can enter the camera and you won't need a flash unit. Typically, fast lenses are expensive, so consider renting such a lens for a weekend or a few days.

5. Start Early

If you wait until it is totally dark, then you'll miss the opportunity to capture the best city photos during twilight. This is the 30 to 40 minutes on either side of sundown. During the earliest part of twilight, the sun is low, diffusing the light, reflecting from the windows of a skyscraper and creating that wide contrast professionals want: a combination of brightly lit areas and deeply cast shadows. After the sun is below the horizon, there is still enough pale light to create excellent backgrounds for cityscapes and other photos. The sky will darken quickly, so you should have your camera/tripod set-up ready.

6. Why You Must Understand RAW

We explain the difference between RAW and JPEG photo files in the book; you should read it. You'll definitely want to shoot your nighttime city images in RAW. At night, there are a variety of light sources throughout the city and those lights are of different temperatures, which could confuse your camera's auto white-balance mode. With RAW files, however, you'll have all the digital information of each photo, so you can make white balance, exposure and other corrections in editing software.

7. Special Shot Tips

Cityscapes, architecture and panoramas are certainly excellent subject matter of a city at night, but the night is also filled with action and motion. Another reason you need a tripod and a remote shutter release is to shoot at very slow shutter speeds to create streaks of light with vehicles' headlights or the movement and colorful explosion of carnival or street party-lights.

Another technique that is perfect for nighttime images, especially where there are many colored lights, is to zoom the lens while you are snapping the shutter. Zoom the lens from the lowest focal length to the highest, which will create a halo or circle of light streaks moving toward the center of the image. Zoom from the highest to lowest focal length to create the opposite streaks of light.

Photographing your city at night is fun, adventurous, exciting and a great learning opportunity.

9 TIPS FOR TAKING YOUR FIRST PLUNGE INTO UNDERWATER PHOTOGRAPHY

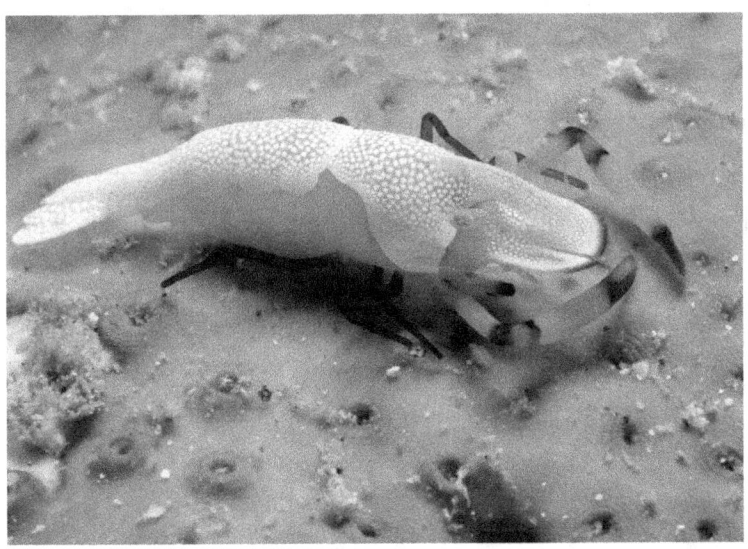

If the many underwater documentaries on TV (National Geographic Channel, Discovery Channel, etc.) have inspired you to consider trying underwater photography, then these 9 tips will help make your adventure more spectacular and keep you and your camera safe.

1. Learn with an inexpensive, single-use underwater camera.

If you're totally new to underwater photography, then you'll want to start by learning with an inexpensive waterproof, single-use underwater camera or a cheap one from eBay. Your DSLR can be used underwater with a compatible housing, but you shouldn't take this more advanced step until you have some experience.

2. Practice in a pool

Even if you're a certified and experienced scuba diver or snorkeler, but have never shot underwater photos, then it's best to practice the various underwater photography techniques in a swimming pool. This may seem too limited, especially if you're itching to dive into the ocean, but a pool is a safer environment to learn the specifics about shooting underwater. Your hands will become familiar with operating the camera underwater and if you drop it, then it's easy to retrieve. Invite your friends or family members to serve as subjects and photograph them from above the water, at the water line and underwater.

3. Adjust your shooting techniques

One of the techniques to practice in a swimming pool is to move closer to your subject because there will be less distortion in your photos when you reduce the amount of water between you and your subject. Experiment with photographing a brightly colored object at different depths, and then compare your images. What you should discover is that the color becomes duller with more depth. You can compensate this loss of color saturation by shooting during the sunniest part of the day; so more sunlight will penetrate to the deepest part of the pool. You'll also discover that you'll take better pictures if you shoot from below your subjects, which will often create interesting silhouettes. Because objects move slower underwater, it may be necessary to adjust your shutter speed. Plus, it's a good idea to bracket or shoot a number of different exposures on either side of what you think is the correct exposure.

4.   Practice in the ocean

Once you feel comfortable shooting with a disposable underwater camera in a swimming pool and you've captured some good images, then it's time to take your next practice step with a single-use underwater camera in the ocean. The characteristics of the water can be quite different than a pool and you should have some experience with it before heading for greater depths in scuba gear. Practice in the shallow waters near the beach, snapping images of friends and family members or any underwater vegetation, creatures or features you may find near shore.

5.   Protecting your DSLR

The next step is to use your DSLR in the natural environment of the ocean; but, of course, you can't submerge it without the appropriate underwater housing. There are many choices of housings for DSLR cameras, including those made exclusively for your brand, which is what you should use. DSLR housings are not cheap; so for a first-time underwater photography adventure, your best option is to rent a unit. You may even want to consider renting a camera and housing together. Take your time to research housings because some, as with all products, are better than others. You don't want to make any compromises if you've decided to dive with your DSLR.

6.   Safety is your primary consideration

For your first underwater photography experience, it may be wise to choose an underwater photography workshop that a dive club or group sponsors or may be available at the appropriate vacation spots. You'll have guidance from experienced divers and photographers; they'll know the best spots where you are likely to take some great pictures; and they will train you in all the safety protocols for underwater photography.

If you plan on scuba diving, then you'll need the appropriate lessons and certification first, which can be obtained from local dive clubs or commercial instructors or possibly community-based organizations.

7.   Research the environment and its creatures

Spend some time online researching the place/places you would like to shoot underwater or where you've selected an underwater photography vacation package or workshop. You'll score some points with your instructor that you have some working knowledge of the local underwater scene, such as reefs and wrecks, and the animals to photograph there. Pay attention to the behaviors of these creatures since you are entering their world. Most won't bother humans unless you appear or act threatening, so it's important to know the warning signs before you enter the water.

8.   The thrill of the night

As you become an experienced underwater photographer, you may want to shoot at night when different creatures are active. Again, this requires some guidance and shooting with an experienced group of divers who know the dangers and also the techniques to help you capture some truly unique images.

9.   Choose the right lighting gear

Nighttime underwater photography is impossible without photographic lighting. You actually need two light sources: either the built-in flash on your camera or a separate flash unit. This separate flash must either be a special waterproof model or be contained within the appropriate housing to keep the flash dry and operational. The second light source is what is called a modeling light. While a flash illuminates a wide area, a modeling light is a narrower beam of light that you can use to illuminate a small portion of the underwater environment. Animals are more likely to maintain a natural pose with a modeling light while the bright light of a flash unit may cause them to scatter and hide.

Underwater photography could become your favorite and it will afford you the opportunity to travel across the globe to take pictures in many of the ocean environments, each which its own unique scenes and creatures.

HOW TO CAPTURE PARTIES AND FORMAL GATHERINGS

In this world of social media and selfies, people who dress for fancy balls, cocktail and dinner parties, major family celebrations and corporate events want to do more than show everyone their style, they want photos that capture the glitziness and glamour of the event. These are opportunities for you to advance your photographic skills, record the event in photos and maybe earn a bit of money, especially if you are providing a service to your employer to take pictures for the company Website, social media pages, newsletter, press releases and annual report.

Photographing events such as these successfully requires that you understand and use specific tricks and techniques – and you'll find them here.

1. Equipped to Be Quick and Elusive

The underlying strategy of photographing formal events is to shoot quickly and unobtrusively, so leave your camera bag at home and limit your equipment to your DSLR and one lens, for example a 24–70mm, 24–105mm or 28–135mm. In most cases, you'll be photographing individuals, couples or small groups of people. You want a wide-angle focal length because you may be shooting in crowded conditions, which forces you to be close to your subject/subjects and you want a bit of telephoto focal length, so you can position yourself at a bit of a distance to snap spontaneous shots that wouldn't be possible closer. In addition, people don't want a long lens thrust toward their faces and intruding on their conversations. Remember to bring extra batteries and memory cards too.

2. Be First on the Scene

Your formal-event shoot will be easier and you're more likely to capture the photos that will please everyone if you arrive before most of the guests. Give yourself a good half hour to familiarize yourself with the layout of the event venue: the space between tables, the buffet table, where the band will be located, the dance space, a podium for announcements and presentations, etc. You can start your assignment by photographing the decorations: the entry to the event; the table settings, including a few close-ups of fancy glassware, dinnerware and flatware, guest place cards, flowers; etc. Look for a good background for portraits of women in their finery and/or standing with their spouse, significant other or escort. Finally, find a good position to photograph people as they enter the event and wait there for the evening to begin.

3.   Know the Event Schedule.

Depending on the event, there may be a schedule of presentations, speeches, entertainment, etc. with which you should be familiar before the event, including where they will take place in the venue. These are likely the photos that the event host, sponsor or coordinator and your employer will definitely want you to take.

4.   Manage Groups Professionally.

Most of your best photos of a formal event will be the interaction between individuals or within small groups. What can be frustrating is that people will form a circle and direct all their conversation and facial reactions into the circle, and without you outside the circle unable to record those reactions. If possible, make yourself part of a circle, interact a bit with the guests and ask them if you can shoot a few photographs as they mingle and talk. Let the conversation start again, so people's attention is directed toward each other, providing you with opportunities to photograph their spontaneity. You can even consider asking the group to allow you to place a chair in the center and photograph them from a sitting position. You won't be blocking their conversation and eye contact, but neither will you be shooting from an obtuse, low-angle if you crouched to the floor.

5. Study Your Quarry.

You'll also find it useful to spend a few minutes throughout the event simply to stand to the side and observe people individually and in groups. Look for people who are very extroverted or even boisterous, as they will make for excellent and interesting subjects, as well as those dressed uniquely: a hat, a colorful, glittering gown, etc.

6. Flash Not Welcomed.

You can bring a flash unit with you or use the built-in unit on your camera for portraits of individuals, couples and groups that want photographs and are prepared to gather for them as well as any "official" images that are needed. In most cases, however, you don't want to be popping a flash as you wander the event. This is another good reason to arrive at the event early, so you can test the light levels and determine where the most ambient light is present. You may have to shoot at a slightly higher ISO setting to compensate for the low light and the wider apertures and slower shutter speeds that may be required.

7. Break the Rules

Do your best to find some unusual angles to photograph the event, so your images are different than what is normally captured. Walk among the tables and the groups of people with your camera at your hip and use the continuous-shooting mode to snap a few, quick frames. Don't hesitate to stand on a chair or ask someone when you first arrive if a stepladder is handy that you can use to take high-angle, wide views of the entire hall or venue.

8. Go Social, Go Mobile.

There is no reason you can't start to upload and share your formal event photos on social media sites during the event; but, of course, check with the host or sponsor or your employer in advance. He or she may even want to announce you will be doing this on the event invitation. Weeks before the event, ask the host to invite guests to opt-in to a list with their smartphone numbers, so they can receive photos from you, the event photographer, in real-time throughout the event. This will generate more interest in the event as it is occurring, excite people that they attended and could make you a hero with them and the boss.

WHY GRAY AND RAINY DAYS MAY BE THE BEST DAYS FOR PHOTOGRAPHY

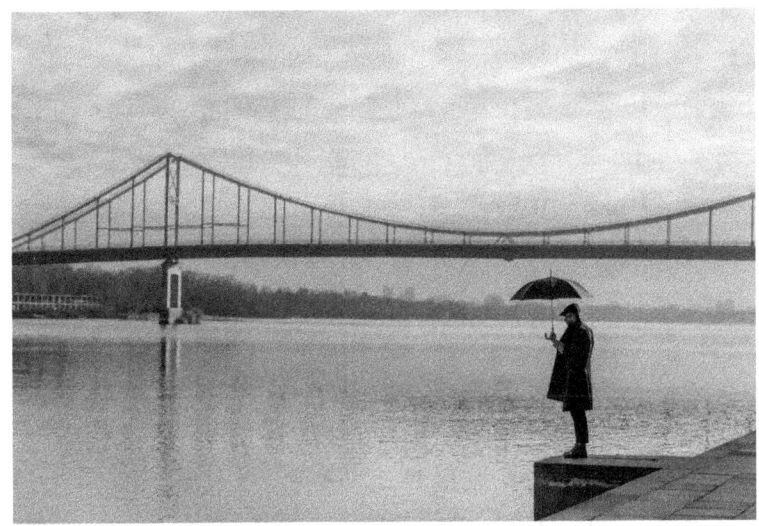

Do you find yourself waiting for the weather to be warm and sunny before you're willing to take your DSLR outdoors? Do you think full sunlight is the best light for photography? Are you bored on gray, rainy days stuck indoors?

If you answered "Yes" to these questions, then it's time to open your mind to more of the photographic possibilities that surround you – and one of the best opportunities to capture some interesting and unique images is a gray, rainy day. It will be a challenge, but accepting and learning from new photography challenges should have been one of the reasons you invested in a DSLR camera. Follow these tips to discover how much more photography is available during a gray, rainy day.

1.   Keep the gear simple

A challenge you should accept to advance your photography skills is to take as little equipment as possible with you whenever you shoot, so you must think about the shots you want to take and look for them carefully. When shooting on a cloudy day, and especially during rainy weather, you want to be able to move quickly with minimal equipment, so you can keep it protected from the elements. A 24–70mm or 28–135mm zoom lens gives you plenty of focal length choices: from wide angle for low-angle perspectives and a bit of telephoto, so you can focus tighter on distant subject matter.

2.   Working with a different light

The light of a gray or rainy day is muted and more even, causing less contrast – highlights and dark shadows. Details that may be barely visible in the harsh light of full sunlight are suddenly available to become new subjects for your camera or to enhance scenes and subjects you've shot before.

3.   Back-and-white can be beautiful

A gray day is perfect for shooting black-and-white images instead of color. Various textures and patterns will become more accentuated on wood, stone and metal surfaces. Although the light level is low, certain compositions will reveal subtle contrasts, such as the different barks on a stand of trees or pebbles in or near a stream. The sand dunes of a beach, any driftwood and even the sky will reveal elements that you never saw when viewed in color and full sunlight.

4. Better control of macros

The diffused, muted light of a gray and/or rainy day is also the best for macrophotography. There will be little or no lens flare or reflections and the brightest colors of a flower or insect can actually be more pronounced because darker or duller colors appear less saturated.

A rainy day also affords opportunities to catch little drips and the close-up patterns created when raindrops strike a small puddle or stream. Raindrops will bead on a flower petal or an insect or frog. Colors and textures can also appear differently when wet or covered by a thin sheen of water. You may need to wear raingear or use a ground cover to crawl under and through bushes to find unique macro images in a wet environment, but, like anything, the extra effort is sure to be worth it. Don't forget a rain cover for your camera too.

5. Look for the gritty in the city

For many of the same reasons cited above, a gray, overcast day can transform buildings, especially abandoned structures and operational industrial plants and factories, into interesting subject matter. Smoke can be emphasized with the use of filters. Faded signs and rundown storefronts reflect a grittiness that may not be pretty, but tell compelling stories when photographed on a gray day.

6. The right kind of rain

Keep your eyes on the weather and weather reports for the days with light, drizzly rain. Thunderstorms and downpours can create some unique photo opportunities, but you must be careful about lightning and it's more difficult to keep you and your camera dry.

7. People watching in the rain

You may be able to find covered locations throughout your city and town from where you can photograph people and traffic caught in heavy rain and windy conditions. People could be struggling with umbrellas, holding unusual objects above their heads or being splashed by passing vehicles. Someone may be wearing a brightly colored raincoat or slicker that creates a compelling contrast to all the gray and black tones.

8. Landscape enhancements

Landscapes can be more dramatic with a cloudy sky and the element of rain. A blue sky is nice, but a dark sky and the patterns of the clouds will often be better complements to your landscape compositions.

9. Wet windows

Not only will raindrops on a window serve as interesting macrophotography subject matter, but also the consistent pattern of clinging drops or running drips make for excellent portrait backgrounds, both outside and inside. Look for bright colors in a shop window and focus on the window and its drops, so the colors and any activity inside is not in focus.

10. Recognizing reflections

Although you will find them everywhere, there will probably be more reflections in the city: buildings, people, signs and traffic can be seen on wet surfaces. Lights will also cause reflections that provide images that you couldn't capture anywhere else.

11. The wet night

The effects of falling rain on surfaces and the reflections it creates can add many exciting elements to a nighttime photo shoot in the city. Cityscapes and architectural subject matter may appear clearer and sharper because the rain has washed the air clean. Conversely, fog may arise or the atmosphere may become hazy, creating innumerable images of buildings, people and objects being barely visible through the thick air.

12. After the rain

If the weather report states that skies will be clearing within a few hours, then remain outside and wait for that period of transition. The sky will be more dramatic as the sunlight starts to appear, causing streaks of light on the clouds. Reflections will become even more pronounced, as the sunlight strengthens. Slick sidewalks in the sunlight are a great contrast for city landscapes.

If you're truly passionate about DSLR photography, then don't ever let the weather keep you indoors. Be safe, but venturing into the elements with your camera is a learning opportunity not to be missed.

PHOTOGRAPHING THE FAIRYLAND OF
WATERFALLS AND MUSHROOMS

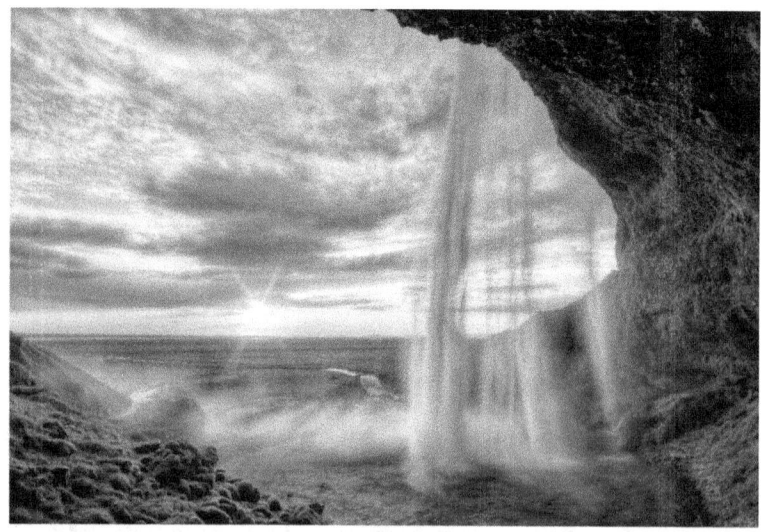

Photography is such a great hobby and art form because it can take you into worlds you've never seen and inspire you to take pictures of the wonders there that you might have overlooked without a DSLR in your hands. The fairyland of waterfalls and mushrooms is one of these worlds. Both are often found together because mushrooms and other fungi thrive in wet environments where both the ground and the air are saturated with moisture. Follow these tips and you're sure to bring home some magical images.

1. Unless you live in the desert, there are generally waterfalls everywhere, although it might take a bit of research. Some are easily accessible and attract the snapshot tourists while others are often in rugged terrain where only an intrepid photographer such as you is willing to go. As part of your research for waterfalls in your area, don't look for just the larger ones, but also try to determine where there are creeks and streams that meander and tumble down a hillside, creating mini-waterfalls that may be only a few feet or inches tall. Smaller waterfalls can be equally as interesting as large falls since you can position your camera closer.

    Spend some additional research time to determine the best locations for mushrooms. Check with the naturalist at the local municipal park or state park or a local botany club. Make sure to ask him or her if there are any waterfalls near where the mushrooms grow.

2. What photography equipment you take may be a function of the difficulty of accessing a waterfall or mushroom field. A single mid-range zoom lens may be all you need – 24–70mm, 28–135mm or even 70–200mm – should do the job, but you may want to rent a macro lens or to use a fast, fixed focal length lens, such as a wide-angle 24mm or 35mm, because of the low light levels. For complete flexibility, you'll want to include a tripod among your gear and a cable or wireless shutter release. You'll capture many of your best waterfall and mushroom images shooting at slow and very slow shutter speeds.

3. Before you start shooting waterfalls or mushrooms, you should take the time to scout the location, even during a day before your shoot. Familiarize yourself with the scene, find the best positions for your camera and carefully study the light, and its direction. Some waterfalls images can be quite dramatic shot during the brightest time of the day,

with the sunlight filtering through the overhanging trees or creating points of sparkle at the edge of the waterfall or where drops of water cling to rocks and dense vegetation immediately next to the waterfall.

Photos of waterfalls and mushrooms can be equally compelling on cloudy, rainy days, adding even more of a fairyland look. You can also plan your shoot during those early morning and late afternoon "magic hours" when the light can completely transform the environment in comparison to midday.

4.   You should also study the waterfall carefully. View it from different angles, from both sides of the watercourse as well as above and below the falls. Look at how the flowing water interacts with rocks and ledges and notice the speed of the water, which could affect the kind of photos you take.

5.   For the best waterfall photos, you won't want to use the most obvious exposure settings, although you should shoot a few of these. Although shooting at a speed fast enough to freeze the movement of the water can be interesting, what you actually want to capture is the characteristics of the waterfall and its flow, which generally requires slower shutter speeds.

The best way to approach determining exposure is to use the standard ISO sensitivity, so no grain is produced, and then select the aperture or f/stop that will render your waterfall image as sharp as possible. If there is plenty of light, this could be f/8 or f/11, but with low light levels, it could be f/5.6 or f/4. You should try to use the narrower apertures for sharpness, which will likely result in the use of slow shutter speeds. This is why a tripod and cable or remote wireless shutter release is so important.

Slow shutter speeds will allow the water to appear in motion, with a slight blur that can be much more interesting than a faster shutter speed that freezes the water's movement.

6. As you explore and scout the wider waterfall environment, keep a sharp eye for mushrooms and fungi. They may be growing on a rock wall created by the waterfall, on nearby fallen trees or stumps and hiding beneath leaf litter. If you're lucky, then you may find a mushroom in a location that allows you to place it in focus in the foreground with the waterfall as the background.

7. Wherever you find mushroom and fungi, you'll more than likely have to lay on the ground with your camera, so you're shooting at the same level as your subject matter. Because mushrooms are often in dark, covered and shaded places, a tripod that can be extended to a low level is probably a requirement. The light level will just be too low, even on a sunny day. Once again, you'll be shooting at slow shutter speeds, so you can render the sharpest images and keep the depth of field shallow. You want the background to be pleasingly defocused, so the mushroom is prominent and pops from the image.

You can also try to use your camera's pop-up flash or a separate flash to fill the dark undergrowth with sufficient light. A separate flash unit would be best, as you can position it slightly off camera, so the light is more even and you don't cast dark shadows.

8. A final word of caution about picking mushrooms to take home to eat. First, make sure you're allowed to pick them, but don't even think

about eating them unless you are absolutely sure they are edible and not poisonous or you check with someone knowledgeable about the mushrooms in the area.

9 TIPS FOR BECOMING AN ACCOMPLISHED PHOTOGRAPHER OF THE MOON

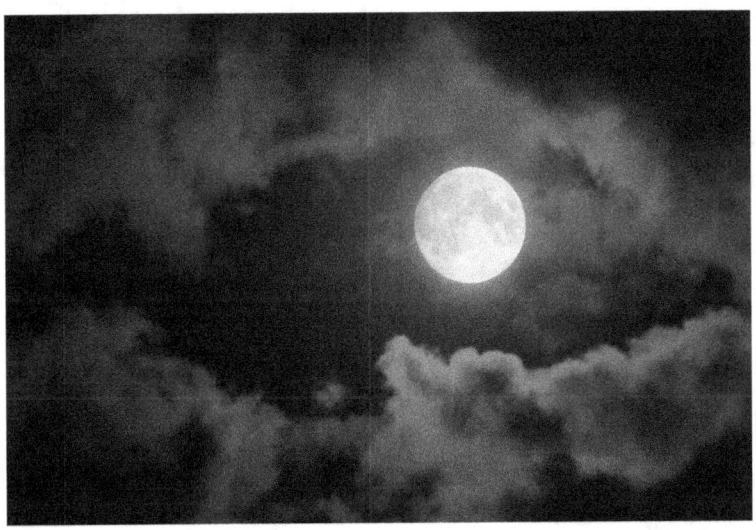

As our closest celestial neighbor, the Moon has fascinated humans since they first watched the night sky; and even though we've traveled there, it is still a mystery and a beautiful, but lifeless place. It isn't particularly difficult to capture interesting photos of the Moon, but some specific equipment and techniques are required.

1. You might think the book belabors the point, but the first step in photographing specific objects, especially celestial bodies, is to do your

research. Go online and access a moon calendar that will show you what phases the Moon will appear during the next month at your latitude. You'll certainly want to photograph it when it is full, but its crescent phases can be equally compelling. Also, take notice of different types of moon views during specific seasons: the Harvest Moon of autumn, the Hunter's Moon of November and the Lover's Moon of June.

Now that you've learned a bit about the Moon, schedule some time during a week, for instance, to watch the Moon to see how its shape and even color changes. Atmospheric conditions can render the Moon slightly blue or reddish. In most cases, these can't be predicted, but sometimes the local meteorologist will announce that an unusual Moon view will be visible during a certain night.

If you're very passionate about learning about the Moon and the many faces it presents, then try to spend an entire night under the stars, observing the Moon's progress and changes throughout the night.

2.   Do a bit of scouting to find the best location for your Moon photography session. For an unobstructed view that won't be compromised by street and city lights and any pollution in the atmosphere, it will be necessary to travel outside your city and town to a farmer's field (ask permission, of course) or broad meadow in a state park. No doubt, your backyard would be preferable for its comfort and convenience, but a natural setting will provide more opportunities to photograph the Moon above hills or mountains, reflecting off a pond or lake or accented by tree limbs.

3.   The most important equipment requirement to photograph the Moon (other than your DSLR) is a super telephoto lens. Even a 300mm focal

length isn't enough, as the Moon will only fill approximately one-eighth of your view of the sky. A 500mm or even 600mm lens is what you'll need to capture a large image of the Moon. Of course, it's impractical to purchase such a specialty lens, considering that they can cost thousands of dollars. The alternative is to rent a super telephoto from one of the many reputable companies that will ship it to you. Many Canon and Nikon super telephotos can still cost hundreds of dollars to rent for a week, but lenses from Tamron and Sigma with the correct mount for your DSLR are typically less than $100, and often as low as $50. A reasonable investment to bring home some truly incredible Moon images.

Another option is a teleconverter that multiples the original focal length of a lens by 1.4X, 1.7X or 2.0X, so your 300mm lens becomes a 420mm, 510mm or 600mm. Renting a 300mm lens and a 2X teleconverter may be less expensive than renting a 600mm super telephoto.

The downside of using a teleconverter is that the 1.4X conversion factor causes you to lose one stop of the widest aperture and the 2.0X factor loses two stops. For example, if you have a 300mm lens with the widest aperture of f/4, and you add a 1.4X teleconverter, your widest aperture is now f/5.6, or only f/8 with a 2.0X teleconverter.

This could be quite an obstacle to photograph many types of scenes and subjects, but much less so when photographing the Moon. It is so bright that many of your aperture settings will be f/8 or f/11, which the use of a teleconverter doesn't affect.

4. You'll also find it helpful to shoot all your Moon images from a tripod. Holding your DSLR with a telephoto lens and teleconverter or a super telephoto lens steady enough is essentially impossible, even at faster shutter speeds. Plus, there may be occasion when slow shutter speeds will result in very interesting Moon photos, which certainly require a tripod. You'll need a cable shutter release or, preferably, a remote wireless release, which can also be rented; most cameras nowadays also come with an app for your smartphone, so you can control the shutter release that way. Even depressing the shutter button carefully with one finger with your camera on a tripod would result in too much camera movement, blurring your images. You'll also find it very helpful to bring some sandbags or other types of weight to ground your tripod even more, so even a slight breeze can't move it.

5. You'll need complete manual control of your camera, so switch off auto exposure and auto focus. Don't rely on your camera's light meter reading of the Moon and sky because it will tend to set an exposure based on the light levels of the sky and not the Moon. This is why the Moon often appears as an undistinguishable blob of light without any features visible. The meter has adjusted the exposure, which causes the Moon to be overexposed.

6. Your exposure settings – aperture, shutter speed and ISO – may vary based on light levels and other factors; however, generally, you want the base ISO setting for your camera, typically 100, a small aperture because the Moon is very bright and a relatively fast shutter speed 1/125 to 1/250 because the Earth and the Moon are moving.

7. Shoot RAW images, which will provide you with the complete digital data of each image, so you can make crucial adjustments during post-production.

8. You'll also want to use the bracketing mode to capture images at more than one exposure combination, since determining the exact exposure for your Moon photos isn't easy.

9. Since you are likely to commit a number of hours for your Moon photography – and being exposed to the elements in an open field – you'll want to be as comfortable as possible. Dress for the weather, knowing that even summer nights can be cool outside the city. Make sure you have raingear for yourself and a rain cover for your equipment setup. Maybe, most importantly, tell others where you will be, especially if you will be shooting during the wee hours of the morning in an isolated field or park. When you first arrive, check that you can receive cell phone service, so you can call in case of an emergency.

EXPLORING THE WORLD OF VIDEO
WITH YOUR DSLR

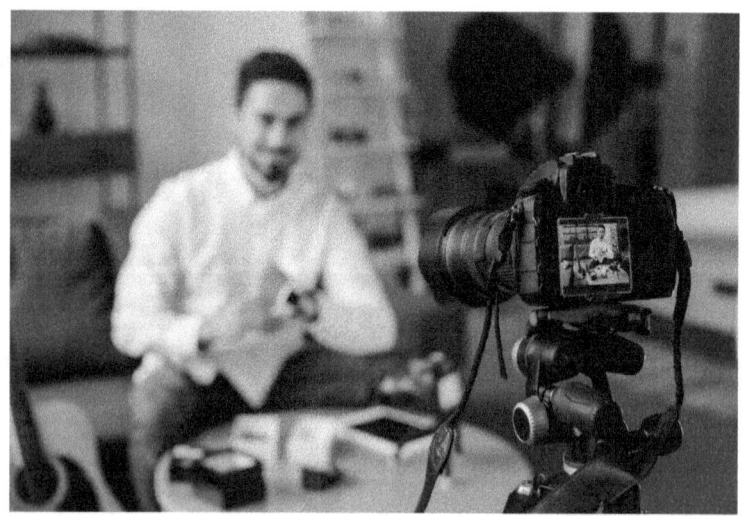

Digital photography technology is so amazing, but so commonplace, it's easy to take it for granted that the DSLR camera you purchased for hundreds or even a thousand dollars or more is actually two cameras in one. The video capabilities of early DSLR models were quite limited and almost an afterthought on the part of manufacturers. Every new DSLR available today, however, records full 1080 HD video, and most record stereo sound.

Another trend that has brought video to the forefront is that professional photographers take it more seriously than they did originally. Those with long careers as still photographers are recognizing the value of being a videographer as well. In fact, a number of major motion pictures have been recorded with professional-level DSLRs, including the first DSLR capable of shooting in the 4K-format, the Canon EOS-1D-C.

Video has also become the darling of social media and is being used by more major brands and retailers as an integral part of their online content marketing their products and businesses. To have you own YouTube channel is a sign of prestige.

For all these reasons and many others, you simply can't overlook your DSLR's video capabilities and learning how to use them. Although you may have shot video with a compact camera and shoot it with your smartphone, the video functionality of your DSLR is a completely different beast and the following tips will help you add videography to your skills.

1.　More versatility to tell a story

Of course, you can shoot random video clips of your family and friends just as you take still pictures; however, video is most powerful when you use it to tell a story. The same principles and techniques apply as presented in the section, "Be a Storyteller, and Not Just a Picture Taker." With the addition of motion and sound, however, you have more tools, more versatility, to tell, even create, a story with video.

2.   Storyboard your story

Although it's not necessary to write a script or create the elaborate storyboards Spielberg or Eastwood require to shoot a major motion picture, it is a good idea to sketch a brief plan for your video story. At the very least, develop a beginning, middle and end for your video, so you are showing how someone overcomes a problem or takes on a challenge. It could be as simple as a beginning of your children planting a vegetable garden, a middle portion of them tending the garden as it grows, and then the ending of them harvesting and eating the vegetables they grew (as if).

3.   Editing is an essential element of a story told in video

In the movie business, the editor is often considered as important as the cinematographer, as much as what makes a story compelling is dependent on how the editor assembles the raw footage of the action. It's no different for your simple little story of your children growing vegetables. As you shoot the story, you'll want to record many of the same scenes and action from different angles and distances: a close-up of a child's hand picking a vegetable, a mid-range shot of two children working together and a wide shot of the garden as part of your backyard.

With these raw pieces of video footage, you'll create your story as a finished product, intermixing the footage in interesting ways to hold viewers' attention and win a bit of praise for your efforts. Of course, this requires learning how to use video editing software, but it is not as difficult as you might think and there are many online tutorials and workshops you can attend to develop this entirely new set of visual skills.

4. The element of sound

Not only can your DSLR record full 1080 HD video, but also sound, in either monaural or stereo. This element greatly enhances your story. You can record your children's spontaneous sounds and words as they work in their garden, interview them as to why they have a vegetable garden and add music either as a sound bed behind their words or as the only audio to emphasize emotional moments.

5. Equipped to excel

The lens or lenses and their focal lengths that you choose to shoot video are no different than still photography. A 24–70mm or 28–135mm will be sufficient for most of the family, party and vacation videos you'll record; however, shooting wildlife, sports and other action from a distance will require a lens with a longer focal length.

Although you can shoot video handheld, you'll find you have more control with the use of a tripod and a video ball head or gimbal. It doesn't take much body or camera movement to cause shaky, disorienting video.

You should also use high quality, high performance memory cards since they have faster buffer rates than inexpensive cards.

The built-in stereo microphone on your DSLR is a great feature, but it can record sounds of the camera operating and your movement, or even breath, with your face close to the back of the camera. You may find an external stereo microphone a better option since you can place it off-camera. Most DSLRs also have a port to connect a separate external microphone. You may need an assistant to hold the separate microphone or mount it on a tripod or light stand.

When you need artificial lighting to record video, you must use continuous light sources and not a flash. In addition, you need enough light to illuminate the entire area through which your subject will be moving. At least initially, try to limit your video projects to the outdoors, so you don't need artificial lighting, since you'll need multiple lights and you must learn how to balance the lighting of any space.

6. Set your camera for video

Camera settings for video are different than shooting still images.

- The auto-exposure, auto-white balance and auto-focus functions of newer DSLRs for video recording have improved significantly, and you should certainly use them, but you'll become a better videographer if you go totally manual.

- The standard exposure values for video are a shutter speed of 1/50th of a second (another good reason for a tripod) and an ISO of 200. Shutter speed and ISO will dictate the aperture setting as well as your subject and the available light. To create enough depth of field, however, you'll want to use mid-range f/stops, f/5.6 or f/8.

7. Shoot like a pro

- It's best to record raw video segment of at least 15 seconds.

- Always shoot in horizontal, or landscape, orientation. Vertical, or portrait, orientation should be reserved for still photography.

- Practice panning shots with your camera on a tripod. It's likely you'll discover that you pan too fast, a common beginner's mistake.

- Because you'll be focusing manually, you'll also want to practice the skill of follow-focus, which often requires a change of focus as a subject moves towards or away from your camera position.

You spent the money – so realize the full value of your investment by learning how to use the video capabilities of your DSLR. It's an entirely new and different world of creativity and you just might discover you're good at it.

HOW TO MAKE THE MOST OF THE
MAGICAL HOUR OF TWILIGHT

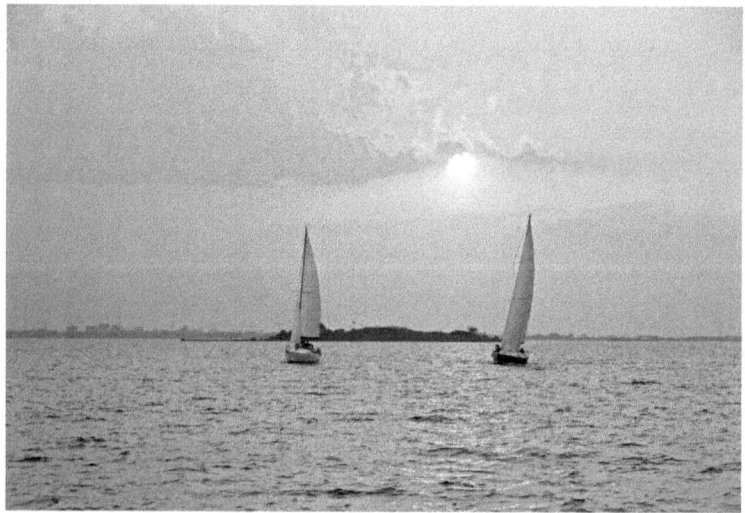

An early lesson that every photographer should learn is that the best pictures are typically not taken during the brightest time of the day. Although the sun is bright and provides plenty of light, it's actually too much light for great photography. The light is harsh, creating deep, dark shadows and often rendering skin tones too pale or without definition.

The quality and creativity of your images are virtually guaranteed to improve if you shoot during the two magic hours of the day, sunrise and sunset. Twilight is particularly magical because light is disappearing from the sky. By definition, twilight is the period of time from when the sun is still visible, although low in the sky, and total darkness.

One of the reasons the noonday sun is so harsh is that the light rays must travel the shortest distance through the atmosphere. At twilight, however, the rays of the sun are at an obtuse angle to the curvature of the Earth, so they must pass through much more of the atmosphere. This results in softer, very diffuse light that creates more even light and muted shadows.

It's important, as a photographer, to study twilight, and learn how to distinguish the three distinctive periods of twilight, as each lends itself to different kinds of photos.

1. Early Twilight

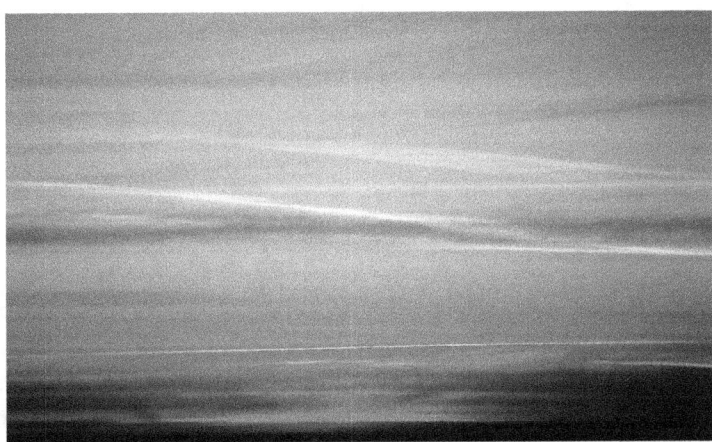

Early twilight is usually the 30 minutes following a total sunset. There is enough light for most photos, although some may require a tripod, especially during winter. The horizon line is still visible and you will start to see the brightest stars and the planets that reflect much light from the Sun.

Because the Sun is just below the horizon, the sky may appear golden or even pink. This is also the period when clouds can be their most dramatic, backlit by the Sun, and in many hues of gray, charcoal and dark blue against the pastel-colored sky. This is also when the temperature of the light changes quickly from orange/red at the hot end of the spectrum to blue at the cooler end.

Early twilight is also the period of time to be creative with a combination of ambient light and a flash. The process is a bit counter-intuitive. Although there is still a good amount of sunlight, you choose an exposure combination according to the light from the flash. You don't change that exposure since it is sufficient to light your subject, even when there is no ambient light. As the amount of ambient light changes, you can try various combinations of apertures and shutter speeds to create different balances of light and some very interesting images.

2.   Middle Twilight

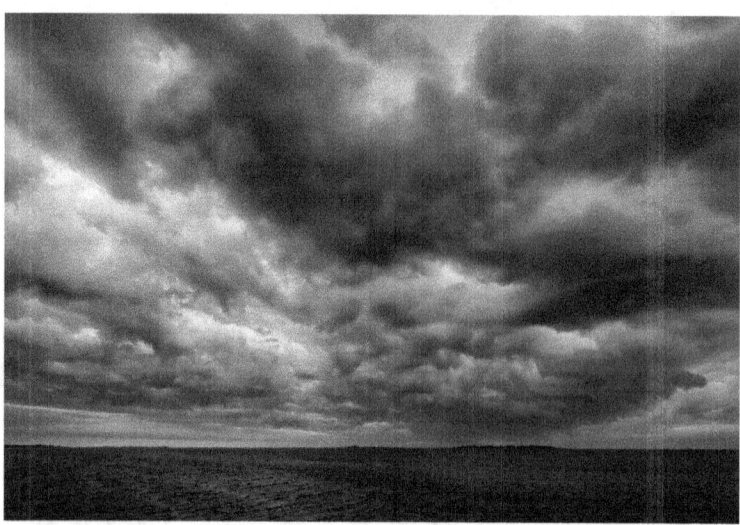

The next 30-minute period is middle twilight and is defined by a sky that is deep blue to black. Although the sun is much farther below the horizon line, there may still be patches of the sky with some gold and reddish light, creating a nice contrast with the darkening sections. Don't expect to handhold your camera during middle twilight; a tripod will be necessary unless you're using flash. This is also the period of twilight when streetlights and colored signs appear brighter than the sky. Look for boulevards and parks with a series of lights, which can illuminate someone walking or sitting or other activity just enough to contrast with the slightly lit sky.

3. Late Twilight

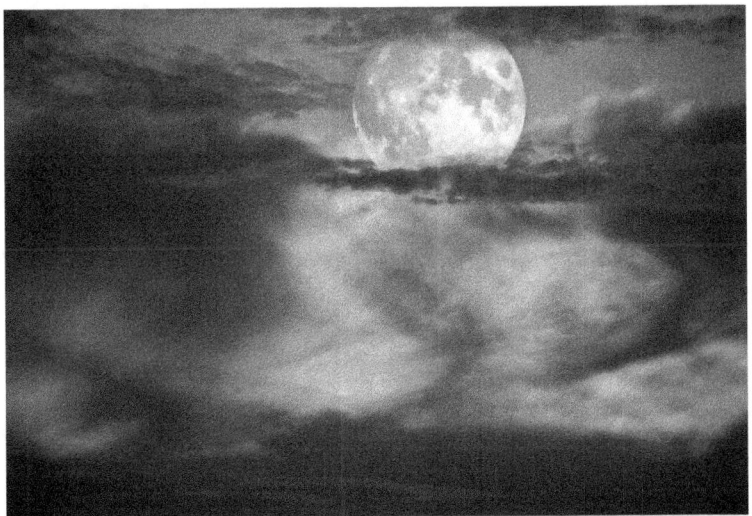

During this final 30-minute period, there is almost no sunlight remaining, as the night sky becomes totally dark and black. This can be a good time to start a Moon photography or astrophotography session, with the bright Moon against a not-yet, all-black background. Shoot photos during late twilight at long exposures, causing moving lights on cars, for example, to streak or a gathering of people around a campfire in the wild with the dancing flames creating a blurred orange/red light reflected off the faces. Architectural photography can also be very interesting during late twilight, with the exterior lights of a building defining its shape and silhouetted against the last remaining sunlight.

MORE ABOUT USING A FLASH DURING TWILIGHT

As mentioned above, middle twilight is when you'll want to use a flash to create either a balance with the remaining ambient light and/or to create some compelling and dramatic images. To learn this technique, however, requires a bit of practice.

- Ask someone to be your test subject and find a location, such as a beach or large open field without any distant obstructions, so he or she is backlit by the light from the west.

- Take a light-meter reading of the sky and match it to the sync speed of your flash, which will likely be $1/250^{th}$, f/5.6 and an ISO setting in the range of 200 to 400. You'll only have a few minutes to shoot at this exposure because the light level will decrease rapidly; so be prepared to lengthen the shutter speed to $1/125^{th}$ and $1/60^{th}$.

- Once you've reached a shutter speed of $1/60^{th}$ and captured a few frames, purposely increase the shutter speed back to $1/125^{th}$ to overexpose the scene, which will underexpose the background by one stop. Then, try the even faster shutter speed of $1/250^{th}$, which will underexpose the background by two stops. The flash will provide adequate light to illuminate your subject, but by using the "wrong" shutter speeds, you are able to take control of the ambient light to give your images more contrast or a more dramatic atmosphere.

- You can continue to create interesting images by manipulating the exposure of the ambient light as the sunlight becomes even dimmer. Eventually, you'll need to lengthen the shutter speed to $1/30^{th}$, but instead of increasing the shutter speed, back off one stop on your flash. You can keep the shutter speed at $1/60^{th}$, but instead of an aperture of f/5.6, select f/4. The balance of light is the same. It may be evident that this formula continues when the ambient light becomes so low that you now need $1/15^{th}$ of a second, but simply shoot at $1/60^{th}$ at f/2.8 as you stop down another stop on your flash.

HOW TO REVEAL AN UNSEEN WORLD
WITH HDR PHOTOGRAPHY

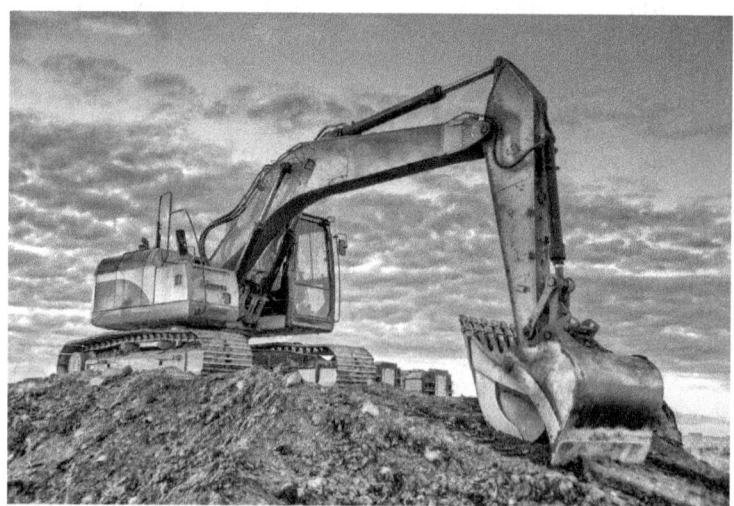

One of the greatest rewards of advancing your photography skills is learning how to combine relatively basic concepts and simple techniques and using the right equipment and editing tools to create new visions of the everyday world. That is the reward, the challenge, of HDR photography.

The first basic concept is dynamic range. If you viewed a color photograph as a black-and-white image, then the range of tones would be the whitest part of the image, or the area that reflects the most light, to the darkest or blackest part that reflects little or no light. Beginner DSLR photographers and even hobbyists and enthusiasts with some experience don't tend to look at their photos in this manner, but they – and you – should. You may want to read the section about histograms to help you understand this concept better.

Any scene or subject you photograph has a limited dynamic range. In mathematical terms, the range for a camera is 1:1,024 while the range for the human eye is 1:65,500. Obviously, your camera can't come close to reproducing the dynamic range of the human eye. Eventually, the lightest and darkest areas of a photo lose all of their detail because they're beyond the limit. This is when the lightest areas are described as "bloomed" or "washed out" and the darkest areas are like black holes: nothing is there; it's just a distracting black shape. HDR photography allows you capture more of a scene's dynamic range and make it visible, which is why HDR is an acronym for High Dynamic Range.

If you've never seen HDR photos, then the Web is full of them. What you'll notice is that a common view is somehow enhanced; the colors are more vibrant, the edges of the objects seem to almost vibrate and you might think you are viewing the everyday world you know so well through the eyes of an alien from another planet. Take the time to research the masters of HDR photography, so your images are not gimmicky, as too many amateur HDR images are.

How the HDR look is achieved requires a number of specific steps that are not particularly difficult, but must be followed precisely. If you're ready for the challenge, then continue reading.

1. An HDR photo is a compilation of multiple images of the same scene or subject, each with a slightly different exposure value. All the images are then combined using HDR software. Because each image is shot at a different shutter speed and aperture setting, each will have a slightly different depth of field and luminosity, or level of brightness.

2. The equipment required for HDR photography is also quite basic. First, you want to shoot with a DSLR camera with Auto Exposure Bracketing (AEB). Having the camera automatically change the exposure for each of the single images you'll capture for your final HDR photo ensures they will blend together better. You can manually change the exposure for each image, but you might move the camera and the time it takes to make manual adjustments means the scene may change or the subject move. A very experienced photographer may be able to shoot the set of images handheld, but the better choice, regardless of your experience, is to use a tripod. It's much more likely that all the images will align very precisely, which results in a better HDR image. You'll also want a remote, wireless shutter release (preferably) or a cable release, at the very least, so you don't have to touch the camera.

3. As you begin to look for scenes or subjects to shoot for your HDR photography, keep these tips in mind.

   ▪ Static subjects are best for HDR photos. Any motion makes the combination of images almost impossible. You should also be careful to choose scenes or subjects that won't change much for approximately 5 to 10 seconds.

   ▪ Look for scene or subjects with a wide dynamic range. You'll be able to recognize them easier once you learn how to look at any photo according to its lightest and darkest areas.

- Shoot all your images in RAW, so you capture all the data, which will result in a maximum amount of detail and the widest possible dynamic range.

4. Once you've shot a number of single images to combine into an HDR image, you need HDR software to complete the process. There are many HDR software products available and the two that seem to be the best reviewed and that most HDR photographers recommend are Photomatix Pro and HDR Efex Pro. It's also possible to create HDR photos using Lightroom and Photoshop in combination. Part of your decision of which software to buy and use depends on how much HDR photography you plan to do. If you just want to try HDR photography, then one of these free programs may be a better choice.

- Fusion F 1
- Luminance HDR
- Picturenaut
- FDR Tools Basic

In addition to Photomatix Pro and HDR Efex Pro, here are another 15 HDR software products that are also widely recommended.

- Canon Digital Photo Professional
- Dynamic-Photo HDR 5
- Easy HDR
- Essential HDR
- Full Dynamic Range Tool
- HDR Darkroom 3 Pro

- HDR Expose 3

- HDR Projects 2

- LR Enfuse for Lightroom

- Machinery HDDR

- Oloneo HDR

- Paintshop Pro X6 Ultimate

- Photoshop CC – Merge to HDR Pro

- PhotoStudio

- SNS-HDR

HDR photography is specialty that can be fun and rewarding, and is also an important learning experience about exposure bracketing and using editing software.

AERIAL PHOTOGRAPHY TIPS AND TRICKS

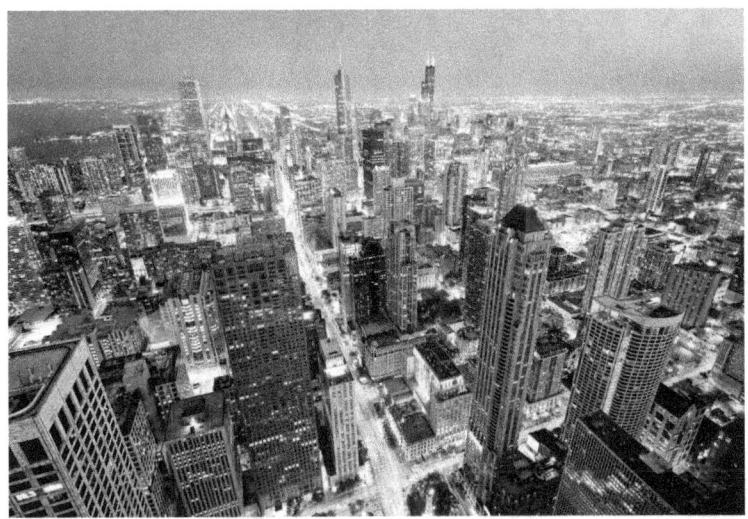

Much of becoming a better photographer is about finding new and unusual angles, perspectives and points of view – well, at least new to you, as most professionals already know how to use angle, perspective and point of view to achieve more creative results. The aerial point of view is not one available to you on a regular basis, but when you do have the opportunity, you want to be prepared to capture the best images possible from a lofty height.

FROM YOUR SEAT IN AN AIRPLANE

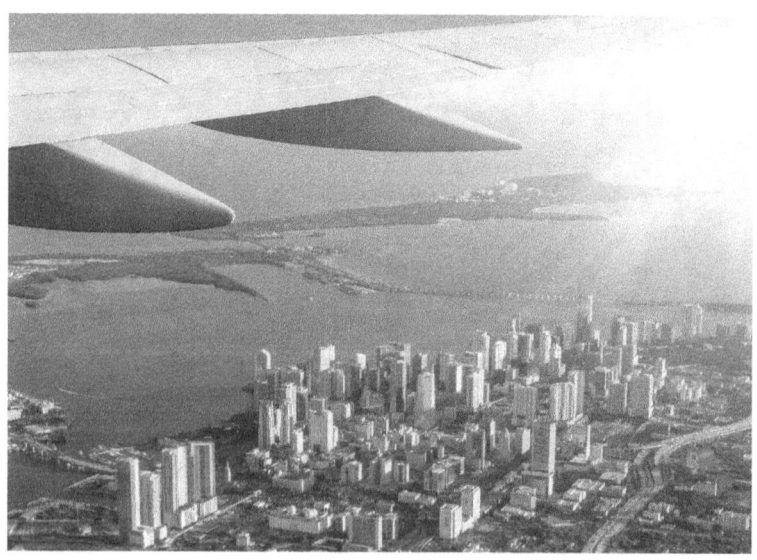

It's likely that whenever you're defying the laws of gravity, you are a passenger traveling in a commercial airplane. Although not as good as hiring a pilot and his or her small plane or helicopter, you can capture some interesting images from your seat. Of course, you must be in a window seat. If not, then ask the person in your row if he or she would switch for a period of time. What you don't want to do is to make yourself a nuisance or worse, a hazard, by roaming the aisles, leaning into rows and trying to shoot over other passengers' heads. Given the security concerns on airlines today, you may not like the consequences. Assuming that you have an opportunity to sit in a window seat, these tips should help you capture the best photos possible.

- You'll want a range of focal lengths available, from wide-angle to telephoto and, given the tight quarters, you don't want to be fumbling with multiple lenses, so a moderate zoom is a good choice: 24–70mm, 28–135 or even 18–200mm.

- Make sure to attach the lens hood to reduce or eliminate any flare or reflections.

- Don't rely on the autofocus system in your camera, as it has to read the scene through the multiple panes of glass in the airplane window and can also be fooled by nearby clouds. Use manual focus exclusively.

- It may seem like a good idea to place the lens against the window, but because it is part of the structure of the plane, the lens and camera will be more susceptible to vibrations and movements. It's better to hold the lens close, but off the window, and use your body to help dampen the vibrations.

- The best aerial photography period in a commercial airplane is during takeoff and landing. First, you're closer to the ground and even some of the smaller objects in view, people and vehicles, will be recognizable. Second, this is when the plane often banks and, if you're on the "down" side of the bank, you'll have almost a complete view of the ground below. Once you've reached the typical cruising altitude of approximately 35,000 feet, most anything below will be too small to make for an interesting photo.

- As with almost all photography outdoors, it's those magic hours of sunrise and sunset that provide the best kind of light for photos from a plane. The low light adds distinctive shadows to photos during takeoff and landing as well as interior pictures when the sun is low in the sky, shining directly into the passenger compartment.

IN A SMALL PLANE, HELICOPTER OR HOT-AIR BALLOON

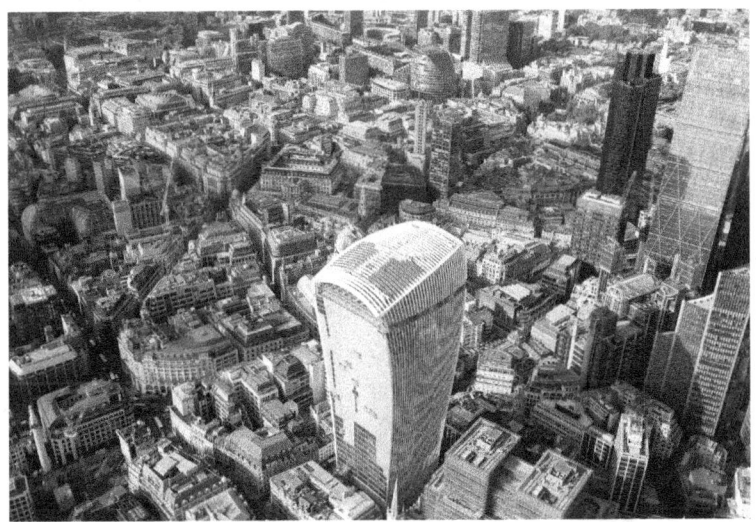

If you're truly serious about capturing exciting images of your city, attractions or natural wonders from the aerial perspective, then you'll have to pay for the services of a pilot and a small plane, helicopter or hot-air balloon. If you've hired someone to take you aloft, then you obviously have more control about where you go and at what altitude you'll fly than as a passenger on a commercial airplane. Many of the same tips above apply, but there are a few that are unique to these aerial platforms.

▪ Since you are paying for the ride and it's limited by what you're willing to spend, create a plan in advance with the pilot when you contract him or her for hire. Let the pilot know what you would like to photograph, so he or she can check if those locations are possible. Remember, there are many buildings and installations that are off-limits and the government will not be very forgiving even if you accidentally include these places in your aerial photos.

▪ Again, sunrise and sunset are the best lighting conditions, but the even light of cloudy days is also an excellent shooting environment. When in the air, request that the pilot try to keep the sun behind you.

▪ Since you're hiring an aerial service, you can bring and use more than one lens, but the fewer the better. Again, a zoom with a wide-angle and telephoto focal length is likely your best choice.

▪ Also, consider bringing a tripod, as smaller planes and helicopters will produce more vibrations than a commercial airplane. A smaller tripod is more likely to fit, or a monopod is another good option. Some planes and helicopters may have camera-stabilizing systems that professional aerial photographers use, although there may be an extra charge for such equipment.

▪ When you're planning your aerial photography trip, remember a plane will be able to take you to the highest altitude. Consider a helicopter instead if you want images from a moderate height or even hovering a short distance from the ground.

▪ A fun option is a hot-air balloon. You travel only as fast as the movement of the air, the ride is quiet and relatively steady and you can shoot 360 degrees. A hot-air balloon is a good choice if you want to create a panorama with a number of images stitched together either by your camera or with editing software.

- Of course, you want a UV filter on the front of your lens, but also bring your lens kit, as a polarizing filter and/or neutral density filter can allow you to manipulate the light from the sky for dramatic or spectacular cloud formations, sunrises and sunsets.

Aerial photography is certainly an exciting adventure since the average photographers has so few opportunities to shoot from this perspective. Of course, be aware of motion sickness, even if it you never suffer from it during a commercial flight, as a small plane or helicopter will be making more abrupt movements.

8 TIPS FOR FINDING THE UNIQUE PHOTOS BETWEEN WINTER AND SPRING

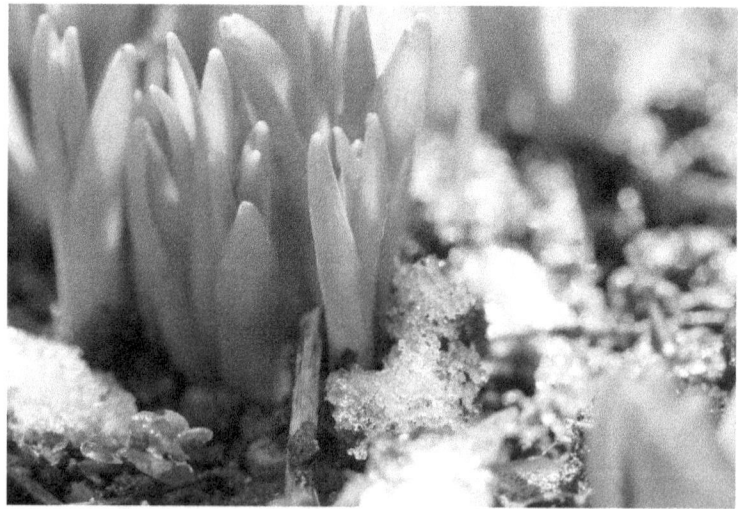

It's easy to wait until the snow and ice have melted, the sun is warm, the trees are green and the flowers are fully opened before leaving the house with your camera after winter hibernation. Photography is supposed to challenge you to be more creative, however; and the short transition period between winter and spring offers a number of unique, but fleeting images, but you must put in the effort to find them.

1.   Melting snow and ice

As the land and objects shed their mantle of snow and ice, you're presented with numerous interesting images that can only be captured during a few days. Check your local weather report to know when a cold morning is expected to become a warmer day and step into a pair of rubber or waterproof boots because you'll be walking where it's wet. Make sure you're outside early with your camera on a clear morning to find reflections and other plays of light as the sun rises. Cold nights and warming days is when icicles often form and then begin to drip. Thin lines of snow or ice may cling to horizontal surfaces, such as tree branches, fences, etc.

2.   Misty mornings

As the early morning sun warms the air above the cold ground, mist and fog can appear, which is a creative element that can turn otherwise everyday images into something special. Look for those eerie, often magical, scenes as mist rises through a stand of trees or off a lake. If you live near a working harbor, then head to a strategic shooting location where you can frame boats moving through a fog. On occasion, the fog may remain close to the ground while the bright, early morning sun strongly reflects off a skyline.

3.   Big water

Although many people don't particularly welcome the melt waters of winter, especially if they cause flooding, you can anticipate that local streams and rivers will be filled with rapidly moving, even raging, waters. Waterfalls are typically at their peak capacity and low ground or swamps are inundated with excessive runoff. Of course, you shouldn't put yourself in danger, but you may even be able to capture some photos of flood conditions and damage.

4.   Rare sun angles

The transition from winter to spring and fall to winter is when the tilt of the Earth changes; and as springtime approaches, the Northern Hemisphere is tilting toward the sun. These are the days when you can shoot with the light of the sun at angles that only happen during these brief periods. Your portrait work can assume unique qualities with the early morning and late afternoon sun that is brighter than a few weeks ago, but still near its lowest point in the sky. This same brighter, but lower-angled light gives landscape, cityscape and seascape images an interesting quality that you won't be able to capture within a few weeks.

5.   Tree buds

Of course, spring is when the natural world wakes from its winter slumber and starts to show bursts of greenery and color. As with any natural subject matter during early spring, you'll find it helpful to do a bit of advanced research to determine which species of trees first begin to bud. Although certainly not as spectacular, tree buds can present some interesting and unique shapes and textures. Plus, you can even schedule a regular return to a certain species and record its progress from bud to flower to leaves. Make note of trees that have bright, colorful flowers as well as those that produce nuts.

6. Early spring flowers

Flowers are often the most-photographed subject matter during early spring. Again, do your research, so you know which are the early and late bloomers, so you have multiple opportunities to record as many species as possible. Position your camera low with a wide-angle lens to frame that first lonely colorful wildflower against a dark stand of bare trees, with maybe a bit of mist. If you're lucky, then a narrow shaft of early morning sunlight might illuminate just the flower. Your research may also reveal which species of wildflowers typically create a carpet-like effect in an open field, in a forest glade, beside a lake or surrounding a small stream or waterfall.

7. Early critters

Just as the trees and flowers begin to come alive during early spring, so do many animals. Again, research will reveal which are the hibernators in your vicinity and when they begin to emerge. In the right location during dawn, you may find a group of deer munching on wildflowers or strolling through a misty landscape. Learn about which bird species return to or migrate through your part of the world during early spring. This is also the time when you may have a better opportunity to capture nest building. Don't forget about insect life, as various species will emerge ready to feed on flowers, leaves and other insects. Early spring can be a great time to rent a macro lens to photograph insects.

8. Black-and-white mood

Although too many photographers, especially amateurs, are prone to overdo black-and-white photography, early spring is one of the rare periods when it can create the perfect effect. Look for the broad contrast of melting snow and ice reflecting the sunlight as well as hiding in dark corners refusing to give into spring. At this time of the year, snow and ice appear in dirty streaks and partially melted piles along city streets and sidewalks making for some interesting gritty photos. Any of the images suggested above also lend themselves to the black-and-white mode when there is mist and/or fog. Again, you're apt to capture a high contrast image, which indicates you're developing more of a professional's eye.

Although the conditions may not be ideal, early spring presents an interesting portfolio of images, so dress for the weather and put yourself in the action.

5 REASONS YOU SHOULD MASTER BLACK-AND-WHITE PHOTOGRAPHY

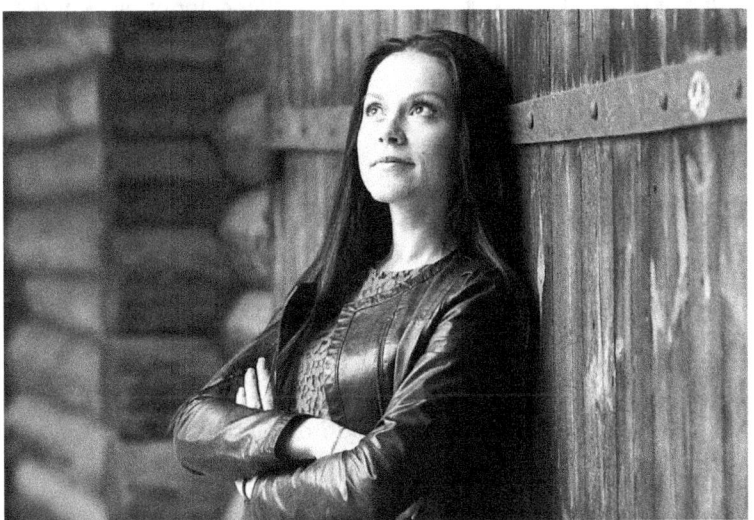

You put your camera to your eye and what often captures your attention before all other elements in the frame is color. Seeing and distinguishing colors is an important human attribute that has served the species well during the millennia of its evolution and survival. The movie studios and the TV networks understand how much humans are attracted to color, which is why it's almost impossible to sell them on the production of a black-and-white film or TV show.

An important step in your advancement as a photographer, however, is to discover the world behind the color, a world of just black, white and the many shades of gray between them. Black-and-white photography is not only a creative palette all its own, but also an excellent training ground to see, learn and use the fundamental qualities of any photograph: shapes, textures, light, shadows, contrast and perspective.

1.   Shapes

One of the qualities of the best photos, either color or black and white, is the relationship of the shapes within the composition. Learning how to recognize shapes instead of relying on the everyday definition of the objects you see in the frame is an important skill to master in the development of the photographer's eye. The elongated shadows of a wrought iron fence that the sun casts during the late afternoon is not a fence, but a series of diagonal, thin shapes that add interest to your image and, if placed properly within the frame, leads the viewer into the depth of your photo.

Shapes also relate to an important technique that the best photography instructors always teach: the fewer shapes, the simpler shapes result in better photos. A helpful exercise is to shoot photos of a person and a tall building from a low angle, so most of the background is sky, and during a cloudy day. Place the person on one side of the frame and the building in the other. Then, instruct the person to strike various poses that may show the curves or straight lines of the human body in contrast to the straight lines of the building. Maybe, he or she bends backwards and thrusts an arm in the air, with the index finger of that hand pointed skyward next to the building from the camera's perspective.

2. Textures

Let's say you're photographing old wooden boats painted in various bright colors in a harbor or pulled onto a sandy beach in a neat row. Initially the colors attract your photographic eye and you discover an interesting close-up of a coil of rope and other nautical items on a colorfully painted deck. Certainly an interesting image; however, see it and shot it in black and white, and suddenly the color isn't the attracting element, but the texture in the rope and how the sun's direction helps to define the texture. The textures in the sea-worn wooden planks of the boat deck are also more dominant because they are no longer competing with color. Textures like these are everywhere and you'll acquire a better sense of how to use them in color images when you first photograph them in black and white. Plus, you're apt to shoot some excellent black-and-white keepers.

3. Light and Shadows

Light and shadows are inseparable since shadows don't occur without the sun striking one side of an object or subject and creating what seems like another dimension where the object or subject also exists. Shadows are also shapes in your photos, which you must recognize and use to create a balanced composition.

Schedule some time with your camera during early morning, high noon and late afternoon. Then, look for objects and their shadows, exclusively, and shoot black-and-white photos of the same objects during each period of the day. By studying your set of images, you'll not only learn more about the direction of light, but also understand the shapes of shadows and how you can use them to add emotion and drama to your photos.

The next time you watch a major motion picture, notice how often the light strikes just one side of an actor's face, leaving the other side in total shadow, or maybe just enough light leaks over the nose to light just the eye. Ask a friend to pose for you and use this technique to shoot a series of black-and-white images. Position the light at various angles and distances from one side of your subject to create a deep shadow and various lighter shadows and partial light on the other half of his or her face. You'll then be able to use this technique for future color portraits, making them much more interesting.

4.   Contrast

Contrast is a companion to light and shadows. Learning how to compose images that juxtaposition the lightest areas with the darkest images may be the most important step forward for your photography skills. This quality or balance is one of the fundamental elements that can be seen in the top professionals' photos. By experimenting with black-and-white photography, you not only see the direction of the light and the shapes of the shadows clearer, but also you can consciously position yourself and your camera to compose contrast. Once you have acquired this skill, your color images will significantly improve.

5.   Perspective

The concept of perspective was one of the most important results of the Renaissance period when the artists of that era refined its use for their paintings. Without going too deep into the science, perspective helps the eye to realize the three-dimensional world on a two-dimensional surface, such as a canvas or a photograph. Simply put, perspective is achieved with a horizon line, which defines the furthest point, or vanishing point, of the background. All lines within the composition converge on this point.

Understanding perspective is critical to becoming a better photographer and shooting in black and white will help you see the perspective in any scene, and then use it to compose a more interesting image. The easiest example is railroad tracks receding towards a distant horizon line. Although we know the tracks remain parallel in the real world, both tracks appear to merge in the distance. Schedule some time to look for other receding lines in the real world and record them as black-and-white images for study. Then, the next time you shoot any kind of photo, black and white or color, consciously position yourself and your camera to create a horizon line to which all imaginary lines from the foreground would converge on a distant vanishing point. Acquire this skill and you've taken another step forward.

9 OF THE VERY BEST TIPS TO BRING HOME STUNNING SUNSET PHOTOS

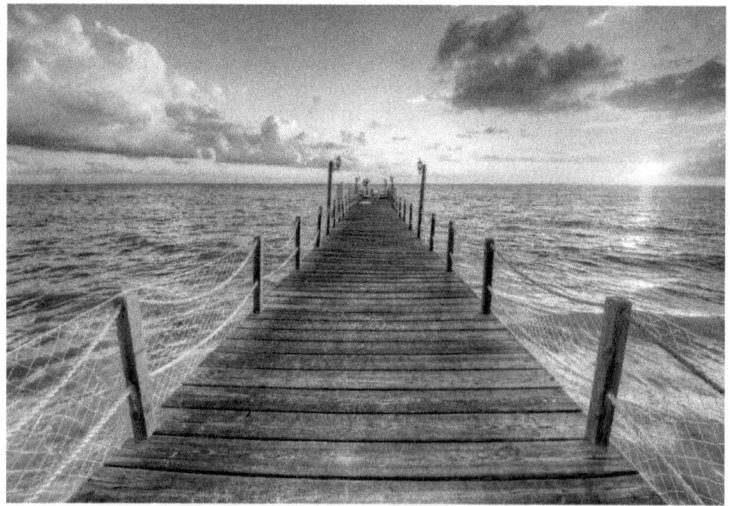

It should be no surprise that the sun constantly fascinates humans. It defines the day, controls are biological clocks and is directly responsible for the food and its nutritional value that is required for all of life. As a photographer, the sun is the single source of natural light for all your images. The sun has such a powerful influence on the Earth and all its inhabitants that has been a primary subject for photography since its beginning. As serene and warming a morning sunrise can be, it's a sunset that reveals our star's power and light and the beauty, emotion, excitement and drama it evokes at the end of day.

Granted, millions of photographers have probably taken billions of photographs of sunsets, but that doesn't mean you can't capture something special and even unique, especially if you apply the following concepts and techniques.

1.   Scout for the best locations.

Yes, you might be lucky and stumble upon a great sunset and have your camera, the right lens and the other necessary accessories with you, but don't count on it. Spectacular sunset photos begin by spending some time looking for the best locations. From a ground perspective, it may be nearly impossible to find a clear horizon line if you live in a city, unless you shoot from a high position, such as the roof of a tall building (Of course, you must ask permission).

There may be hills or mountains outside your city, which would provide an excellent position for sunset photos and would allow you to include the city skyline as a complementary element. If you live near the sea, then it should be quite easy to find many shooting locations: on a high bluff overlooking the beach and from the beach perspective as well. The other alternative is driving some distance from your city to open countryside where you can see a horizon line.

2.   Access sunset time data.

The period of sunset is brief and the light changes minute-by-minute, so you must know the exact time of sunset in your part of the world and during whatever season you want to photograph sunsets. You'll find this information on the Internet and there is also an app you can download to your phone. In addition, the best days for sunset pictures is when it rains during the day, but has cleared by late afternoon, with the last storm clouds still moving across the sky.

Make sure you arrive at your shooting location at least a half-hour before official sunset, so you have time to set up your gear. Then, you'll be able to photograph the progression of sunset until the sun has disappeared over the horizon. As they say in those annoying TV commercials, "But, Wait There's More!" Approximately 25 minutes after the sun is no longer visible, there is what is called the "second sunset," which can offer some equally and even more spectacular images.

3.   Pack your gear

Capturing beautiful sunsets require more than a camera and a lens; you'll also need a tripod, a remote trigger to release the shutter and a neutral density filter. Make sure you've cleaned your camera and lens. Since a sunset is essentially a landscape photo, your primary lens choice is wide-angle. This will, of course, make the sun appear smaller than reality in your image. You may also want to bring a telephoto lens, which will enlarge the sun in your photos.

4.   Rule of Thirds

Keep in mind the Rule of Thirds (there is a whole section devoted to this topic in the book). Compose your sunset images, so the horizon line separates the frame into one-third and two-thirds, top or bottom, and not across the center. From a high location, you may be able to place the horizon line near the top of the frame, so the sun is present, but doesn't dominate your composition.

5. Foreground framing

As with the best landscape images, look for a foreground or a small foreground object of interest and position your camera low with a wide-angle lens to include it in the frame. This helps to create depth. On a beach, it could be a piece of driftwood, the silhouette of a boat pulled onto the sand or a line of old pier supports in the surf. In a field, it could be a fence rail or an old piece of farm equipment. Use a neutral density filter, with the darker side matched with the sky to help emphasize the colors. With the lighter half of the filter matched with the darker foreground, the objects there will be better defined and recognizable.

In terms of the sky, you want some clouds, and the last of storm clouds, if possible, as mentioned above. With the clouds streaking from or to the horizon, the sun will give them more dimension, contrast and drama.

6. Exposure control

While the sun is still visible, you can shoot in aperture priority mode with exposure compensation, which will adjust the exposure as the light changes throughout the progression of the sunset. Once the sun has disappeared, however, it's best to determine exposures manually, since your camera's meter is likely to be confused with the much lower light levels. In most cases, you'll want to underexposure your sunset images slightly, which makes the colors more vivid and intensifies the depth and dimensionality of objects.

7.   White balance

The auto white balance function of your camera is also unlikely to react accurately to the low light and contrasts. Try the "shade" mode or manually set white balance.

8.   Raw is right

Shoot all your sunsets as Raw files because you'll need the complete data to accentuate all the delicate lines, tones and colors during post-production.

9.   Look behind you!

As part of your scouting, take notice not just of the sun, but also the view behind your possible camera locations. Often, there are just as spectacular images in the other direction, as the low and redder light of the sun will uniquely illuminate a building, field of flowers, a mountain range, a lake, etc., providing you with a two-for-one shooting opportunity.

6 WEDDING PHOTOGRAPHY TIPS FOR BEGINNERS

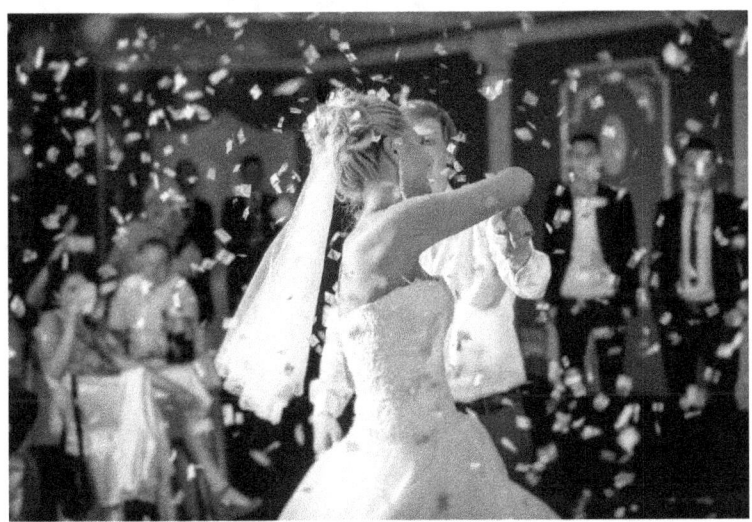

Don't be surprised if one day a friend asks you to photograph his or her wedding. Maybe, he or she simply can't afford an experienced professional or the wedding is so small and brief that a professional is unnecessary. You may also be asked because your friend sees you with what he or she considers a high-quality camera and assumes you know how to use it to shoot wedding photos. To give your friend the photos that he or she is expecting, you'll need more than that DSLR in your hands; you'll also need the following 6 tips well planted in your head.

1. Planning is the most important factor.

To be a good wedding photographer, you must think and act like a photojournalist because a wedding is a live event and many of the events of the day will only occur once, so you better be prepared to capture them. You'll be more confident that you'll deliver acceptable images, if you spend some time talking with the bride and groom and providing them a checklist of photos they are more likely to want. Start with this list:

- Groom with the best man and groomsman prior to the wedding.

- Bride in the last stages of dressing, with her mother adjusting her veil.

- The bride and her father walking up the aisle of the church.

- A wide-angle photo of the entire church from the back of the aisle or a rear choir/organ balcony.

- Photos of the ceremony if the clergy allows it.

- The bride and groom walking down the aisle.

- The guests throwing rice outside the church.

- Formal group portraits as explained below.

- Newlywed photos, preferably in a natural, outdoor setting.

- The bride and groom in the back of the limousine.

- A series of candid shots of guests at the reception: in the buffet line, sitting at tables, dancing, talking with the bride and groom, etc.

- The bride and groom dancing.

- The bride dancing with her father.

- The bride and groom cutting the cake.

- The groom tossing the garter.
- The bride tossing her bouquet.

With this list or one the bride and groom and you create, you'll know where and when you need to be during the day to take these photos. Typically, you should arrive at the church 30 to 45 minutes before the ceremony, so you have time to shoot the pre-ceremony photos above.

2. Equipment Redundancy

Part of your careful planning is being sure all your equipment is working properly and thoroughly cleaned, all power units fully charged and, most importantly, having at least one backup for virtually every piece of equipment. At a minimum, you need two cameras, in case the first becomes non-operable. Two cameras also allow you to mount a fast, wide-angle lens on one, such as a 28mm or 35mm f/1.8 or at least f/2.8, and a mid-range telephoto zoom, 28–105mm. With two cameras, you won't have to switch lenses, which could result in you missing a "live" shot, plus, professional wedding photographers try to shoot weddings with available light instead of a flash, so a fast, wide-angle lens is a must.

Of course, you should have extras of all cables, battery packs, batteries, memory cards and any other accessories. Include a tripod also for the formal group portraits.

If you need to rent extra equipment for the day, then tell the couple during the planning stage and ask that they pay for the rental.

3. Capturing the Moment

One of the most difficult skills for beginner wedding photographers to learn is to be in the center of the activity, but unobtrusive. Your function or task is the same as the staff serving food and beverages and the band: to provide a service. Unlike them, however, you must be up-close-and-personal with the bride and groom and members of their families, capturing the candid moments, but not being a burden or an obstruction to them enjoying this joyous occasion.

Many couples also want loving, often quite intimate photos of just the two of them in an indoor or outdoor setting away from the guests. Now, you must utilize skills similar to a movie director, helping the couple pose, personally and naturally, and still show their love and passion for each other.

4. Composing and Lighting Formal Groups

Whenever a wedding is large enough to have a wedding party of maid of honor, bridesmaid, best man and groomsmen, most couples will want formal group portraits. These may include the following:

- The bride alone.
- The bride and groom.
- The bride and groom and the clergy.
- The bride and groom and maid of honor and best man.
- The bride and groom and the maid of honor and bridesmaids.
- The bride and groom and the best man and the groomsmen.
- The entire wedding party.
- The bride and groom with her parents.

- The bride and groom with his parents.

- The bride and groom with both sets of parents.

- The bride and groom with grandparents and other family members.

Obviously, you must take all these photos in the shortest amount of time as possible because you don't want to be a cause of a delay in the wedding's schedule. To accomplish this, it's important that all these people are gathered together, waiting outside of camera range and ready to step into the appropriate photos quickly. You might want to ask one of the groomsmen to serve as a "people manager" to make sure everyone is gathered, so you can concentrate on your setup and the photos.

Traditionally, these pictures are often shot at the altar of the church since many have a series of steps that will allow you to create better groupings. It may also be advantageous to scout the church and the reception area to find a large enough area and background to shoot these group shots. Because some of these photos could include many people, a single source of light won't be sufficient. You may need two or more flash units on light stands that fire from a remote controller. You'll find it very helpful to ask the bride and groom for a few minutes during a rehearsal when the entire wedding party will be there to practice the staging of these group portraits, so everyone knows in which photos they are expected to be. Shoot some test images to determine that you will have sufficient lighting.

5. Post-Production Skills

In today's digital environment, shooting the wedding photos is only the first step in the process. You'll want to shoot all images in RAW, so you have the complete data set of each photo. Then, you'll need to review each image (especially those the couple expect from the list) and perform whatever editing and manipulation is necessary to make them their best.

There are also many software products and apps that allow you to create a slideshow presentation of the photos for the couples review and Websites to which you can upload the images and provide the couple with a unique username and password to their secured page of the photos.

6.   A High Patience Quotient

Maybe, the most important tip and skill you must develop to shoot a wedding as a beginner or professional is plenty of patience. Because it is a live event, there will be moments of stress: You just barely positioned yourself in time to shoot an important photo, the available light is not being cooperative, a member of the wedding party is not present for a group portrait, etc. The exciting part of a wedding is that spontaneous actions and behaviors will occur and you must also have the patience to look for them, spot them quickly and be ready to capture the memories that will thrill the bride and groom and their families and friends.

SCOUT PHOTOGRAPHY LOCATIONS FOR BETTER RESULTS

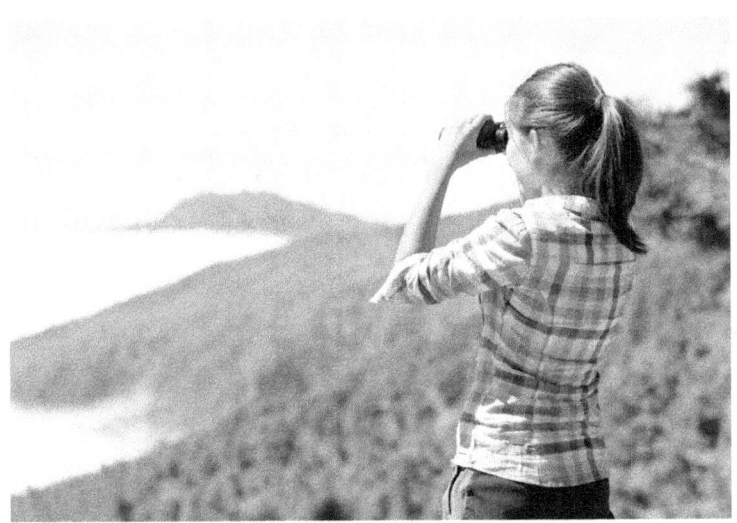

Among the many important techniques that amateur photographers can learn from the professionals is to scout shooting locations in advance. Not all high-level portrait, fashion, food and product photography occur in a studio, although many professionals love and prefer this controlled environment. To push the boundaries of creativity, professionals must often shoot these and similar types of assignments outside the studio. Real-world settings add context to a clothing style or to show a product in the actual environment in which it will be used.

To choose the right locations, professionals will add time to the front end of a shooting schedule for one or more scouting trips. With assistants, equipment and maybe models in tow, no true professional photographer would just hope to find a good location. He or she must know not only where they will be shooting in advance, but also detailed information about the lighting, background and the exact equipment and crew he or she will need. Other issues must also be addressed in advance, such as obtaining permission to shoot on public or private property, having adequate insurance coverage, parking, a secure equipment vehicle or temporary structure, catering, etc.

As a photography hobbyist or enthusiast, there is nothing wrong with wandering through the streets of your city or a nearby park or forest and finding good locations, serendipitously. It's an excellent challenge to your photography skills and a learning experience, but you should also plan an occasional shoot in more detail and, like the professional, do some scouting first.

1. Scouting preparation

Before starting your photography scouting trip, spend some time online researching your area. You may have lived there your entire life, but there will be many excellent shooting locations of which you are not aware. Look for both familiar and unfamiliar locations that relate to the type of photos you want to take. If you're shooting casual outdoor portraits, then don't automatically head to the nearest city park. Purposely look for locations across town and even outside your town that will give your portraits of family members, friends or even a paying client a more unique setting than the nearby locations where most of your neighbors have been photographed.

Designate these locations on a maps app that you can save on your smartphone.

2. Prime locations

To use your scouting time wisely, look for locations that you can use more than once and for more than one type of photo. Again, if it is portrait locations you need, then try to find places where you could turn the camera at various angles for quite different backgrounds. Widen your search from what appears to be a good location to find other excellent shooting spots that might be within a few hundred feet of your initial location.

3. Scouting specifics

When you do find useful locations, take detailed notes in the notebook or the Notes app on your smartphone, relating to lighting, backgrounds, etc. You may even want to take your camera to snap a few reference photos of these detailed features of the locations to help you plan your shoot. A smartphone GPS is also a handy device to record exact camera positions and directions. You can't actually understand the value of a location or if it is even the right location unless you visit it during different times of the day. Of course, sunrise and sunset are those magic hours when many of the best photographs are taken, so definitely plan to scout then. At sunset, remain at the location throughout twilight, or the period after the sun has disappeared over the horizon. You may discover even more magical lighting conditions.

Also, take note of the larger environment. Will the headlights of cars on a nearby road during twilight or night cast ugly shadows on your location? Is there any nearby construction that might fill the air with dust? Do great numbers of birds perch in the trees above, making your location a target for their droppings or could they suddenly fill the background on the wing, spoiling the light and the ambiance?

4.   Complements and contrasts

Looking for a location that complements the primary object or subject of your photo shoot is an obvious goal, but also think outside the box. Often, a location that creates a contrast with the object or subject can be more creative and dramatic. A gritty city street or abandoned industrial property can bring a rather startling ambiance to photos of an elegantly dressed couple, either as a fashion shoot or a wedding. Want to photograph an haute cuisine seafood dish? Instead of a fancy, upscale restaurant with beautiful people, show two burly, sweaty members of a construction crew eating the dish for lunch on a makeshift table made from two sawhorses and a few raw planks of wood.

5.   Safety first

Keep in mind any safety issues that may relate to the locations you've scouted. Abandoned buildings can be creative shooting environments, but they can also be dangerous. Be sure you have cellphone connection wherever you're shooting, so you can call for emergency services if needed. Safety also relates to obtaining permission to shoot on private property, which also includes a farmer's field, even it contains no crops or livestock. In addition, check with local law enforcement about any restrictions as it relates to sensitive communications, government or military buildings or installations.

6.   Market your local information

As a longtime resident of your greater community and after having scouted many locations for your own photography, you could become a valuable resource for professional photographers, documentary filmmakers and even movie companies that want to shoot in your town. You can share your detailed notes about various areas and possibly serve as a special assistant during a shoot for a nice fee.

WHAT YOU CAN LEARN AS
A PHOTOGRAPHER'S ASSISTANT

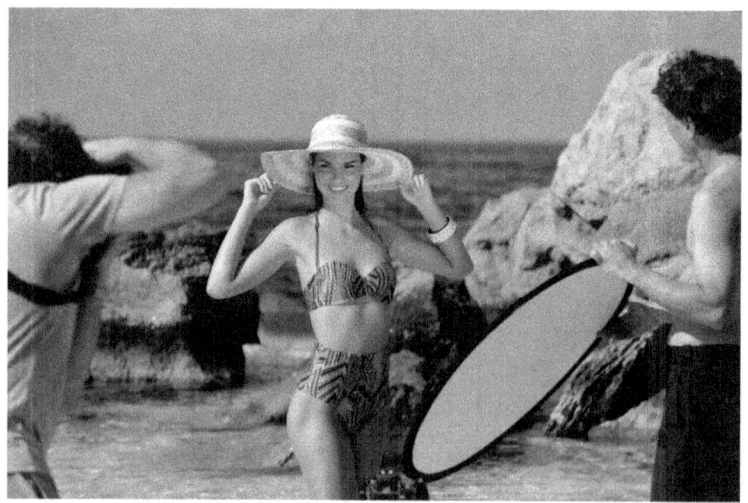

As an amateur photographer, being a photographer's assistant is a great opportunity to improve your skills, take the first steps on a path to becoming a professional with your own photography business, as a supplement to a formal photography education and simply to earn some extra money. This section highlights what you can learn as a photographer's assistant.

1. Planning a shoot

Regardless of what type of photography the professional shoots, your first lesson will be observing and participating in the planning of his or her assignments. Except in very rare instances, every photographer starts an assignment with a plan. Not only must he or she carefully create a schedule and a budget, but also manage all the logistics of a shoot: scout locations; make travel arrangements; select, clean and pack equipment; screen and hire models; etc. It's likely that, as an assistant, much of this work will be assigned to you.

2. Operating a photography business

Photography may be a creative profession, but it is also a business, with much the same requirements as any other. Professional photographers, in particular, need a well-managed business, so they can concentrate on bringing home the images their clients or editors demand. Even if you never have your own photography business, you can learn much about business management in general and what skills are necessary to be a successful entrepreneur.

3. Developing the qualities of a professional

The definition of a professional doesn't just include technical skills; a professional is considered such and respected because of his or her character, or the intangible qualities that inspire others and attracts clients. The 8 that you may observe as a photographer's assistant are integrity, discipline, perseverance, confidence, entrepreneurship, learning, audaciousness and giving.

4. Learning and succeeding from failing

Professional photography is a precarious profession since failure is always lurking in the shadows. Many of the most successful people will tell you that they learned much more and achieve much greater goals because they failed – and often more than once. As a photographer's assistant, therefore, you are likely to benefit much more from observing what the photographer does when faced with failure than the high points of his or her success. It may be as subtle as a piece of equipment that breaks at a critical point in a shoot or a major failure, such as losing a client.

5. Composition

For professionals, photographic composition doesn't just take place when their eye goes to the viewfinder. During their preparation for a shoot and with the description of the assignment, they are already beginning to envision what and how, and maybe even where, they will photograph.

Although much of your time as an assistant will include hauling and assembling and disassembling equipment and serving as a gofer, many professionals are committed to mentoring their assistant. Without being a pest, take the initiative to ask the photographer questions about how they compose an image to satisfy an assignment; however, you never want to be disrupting him or her will their working. Often, however, he or she will be happy to spend time after a shoot to explain how they were able to create their vision in the images they shot.

6. Equipment Technique

A photographer will expect you to have some experience with cameras, lights, etc.; however, he or she also knows that there is much more for you to learn to be a "professional" assistant. Most photographers will like their cameras, tripods, lights, etc. set up in a specific way and for very good reasons. At the appropriate times (never during a shoot), you can ask questions about why they used certain equipment a specific way. You should also try to be very observant during a shoot about how they using equipment, although a good assistant is always busy doing something.

7. Equipment

Just as you're likely to learn much about photography equipment technique as a photographer's assistant, it's also an excellent opportunity to learn about the latest equipment and many of the accessories and peripheral pieces of equipment that make the photographer's job easier and enhances his or her work product. With this knowledge, you'll make better choices about what equipment to buy for yourself and how to use it for maximum value.

8. Working with...

You'll quickly learn that a professional photographer's job is more than creating images that fulfill assignments and generate income. He or she must also be a pro when it comes to working with clients, editors, models and anyone else who is involved with a shoot. Although the quality of the work product is very important, often, the best and most successful photographers are those who have a skill for managing clients and editors. These photographers have excellent people skills, knowing the difference between

317

delivering what the client wants and expects and subtly "maneuvering" and "manipulating" their thinking, so they want the photographer's vision more than their own and so the photographer exceeds their expectations.

You can also learn much about working with models, as they are professionals too and also have their own ideas of how they should be posed and photographed. You'll have the opportunity to observe when and how the photographer listens and tries to incorporate the model's point of view and when and how the photographer insists on the model acquiescing to the photographer's vision.

9.   Production Workflow and Editing

In the professional's world, capturing images in the camera is only half of the process; post-production is often where as much creativity occurs as behind the camera. The typical professional must have a rather elaborate production workflow process in place and all the computer equipment and software required to finalize the client's images. Observing how a photographer takes a RAW file and edits it into a great photo and asking questions is a priceless learning opportunity for any assistant. In addition, many photography assistants, once they've proven their editing skills, are often assigned many of the post-production tasks, making them invaluable to the photographer.

10. A vision

Finally, maybe the greatest benefit of being a photographer's assistant is learning how to develop your inner vision of what it means to be a professional and how to transfer the vision in your head for a photo to the camera.

FOOD PHOTOGRAPHY TIPS FOR
THE BEGINNER

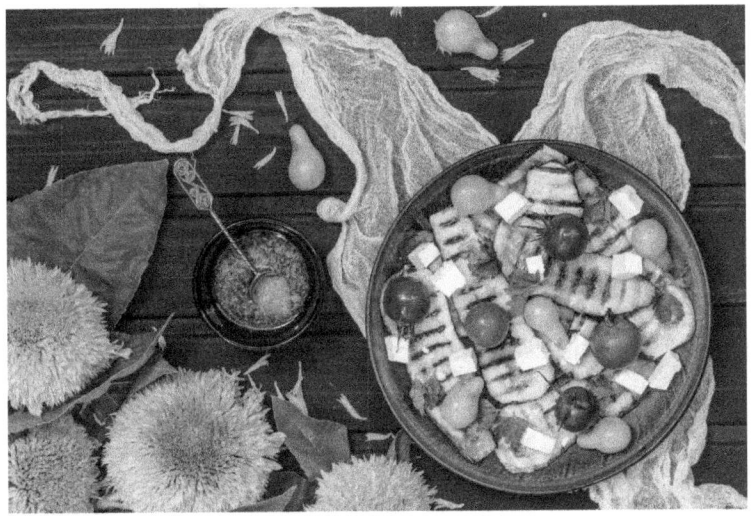

With the improvements in smartphone cameras, the popularity of social media and the increasing number of food bloggers, food photography is no longer just for the professional who specializes in this genre. As a hobbyist or enthusiast, food photography can be an excellent exercise, or learning laboratory, to improve your lighting, camera and post-production skills, even if food photography doesn't particularly interest you.

1. Planning, Preparation and Styling

Before you concern yourself with how to light and photograph food, you must first focus on what food you want to shoot, its preparation and creating, or styling, the setting in which it will be photographed. Essentially, every form and type of food can become a great photo, from a single fresh vegetable or fruit to food preparation techniques to a mouthwatering finished dish that seems to beg to be consumed.

Fresh vegetables and fruit and cheeses can be staged on a well-used wooden cutting board or a slab of stone, easily acquired at a home improvement or stone retailer. These raw food products can also be photographed outdoors on weathered and natural surfaces to emphasize their natural quality and appeal.

Prepared or finished dishes generally require a carefully selected plate that complements, enhances or even contrasts the food. It's best to avoid square or rectangular plates, although they are stylish, because they can look odd in your photos. Depending on the size of the prepared dish you're photographing, it's better to use a salad plate than a larger dinner plate, so it's easy to fill the plate. Try plates with patterns and bright colors, but make sure they don't clash with the color of the food or overwhelm the food.

If you are photographing a meal, then you probably want to create a table setting that includes glassware, flatware, a tablecloth or placemats and napkins. The style of these should match the food. The table setting for haute cuisine for a formal dinner party should be elegant; a Thanksgiving turkey and the trimmings need a family-oriented look; and the accessories for photographs of casual or party food should be equally casual, fun and festive.

2. Lighting

Probably, no element is more critical to the quality of food photography than lighting. As a beginner, you may not want to invest in artificial lighting equipment to photograph food, although it's not as expensive as you might think and not difficult to learn how to use. For the purpose of this section, however, there are just two rules to follow: don't use your flash and photograph food with natural light.

Although the flash will illuminate the food, it will also create harsh shadows and, because the flash is so close to the food, the light of the flash will reflect off the food item, creating a rather flat and unappealing image. The better alternative is to find a window in your home and use the natural light penetrating the room. There's no reason to photograph food only in your kitchen; it's more important to find the right window, even if it is a bathroom. This may take a bit of experimentation because natural light can be different during the various seasons of the year and whether the window has a north, south, east or west exposure.

You'll quickly learn that direct sunlight is too bright and essentially creates the same unappealing image as a flash. Look for a window that has a thin, diaphanous curtain that acts similarly to a diffuser you'd attach to a flash. There will be enough light, but it will be slighted muted, helping to reproduce the true colors of the food item and making it more appetizing. The angle of the light from the window is also important. The best is typically in the short range around 45 degrees.

3. Food Composition

As a starting point, following the Rule of Thirds will place the food item or collection of items in the best location within the frame for an interesting composition. Don't necessarily restrict your composition to a complete view of the food item. Often, a close up of a few drips of melting ice cream on the outside of the bowl sparks viewers' imagination more than seeing the entire bowl.

Some food items look best from different angles. For instance, photograph a pizza or any flat item from directly above. Photograph a sandwich or burger from eye level, so the various layers of ingredients are visible. Other items, such as a basket of rolls or a loaf of fresh-baked bread, require a 45-degree angle, so their three-dimensionality is emphasized.

Composing food photos is an experimental, trial-and-error exercise that can be the most appealing challenge and learning opportunity for the beginner food photographer.

4. Equipment

You'll definitely need a tripod and a remote shutter trigger because illuminating your food item with natural light may require a slow shutter speed, and to create enough depth of field. Photographing food is similar to portrait work, so you'll likely shoot with a slight telephoto focal length. Wide-angle lenses can create interesting images, but they could also include too much of the background. In addition, add a simple reflector to your equipment, using either a white post board from an art supply store or covering a piece of board with aluminum foil. Reflecting the window light at an additional angle onto the food will illuminate it more evenly and give it more three-dimensionality.

5.   Image Making

Generally, when photographing food, you'll have the best results by going totally manual. It's likely there will be elements in your composition, either the color of the food, setting and accessories or the light that will confuse the light meter in your camera. This is when food photography provides an excellent opportunity to learn how to use a separate, handheld meter. An accurate white balance is also critical, so the color of the food is true. You can certainly try the auto white balance feature of your camera, but it's likely you'll find the custom white balance setting is better.

Your exposure equation depends on many variables: the amount of light, how much depth of field you want, etc. As mentioned above, the natural light levels may be low enough to require slow shutter speeds and if you want more depth of field, you'll need a narrower aperture. You can hike the ISO a bit to compensate, but keeping it in the "normal" range will avoid any digital noise that would be a distraction. The Av, or aperture priority mode, is one automatic camera function that will help select the right shutter speed in relation to the aperture you want.

PRACTICALITIES AND CONTINGENCIES

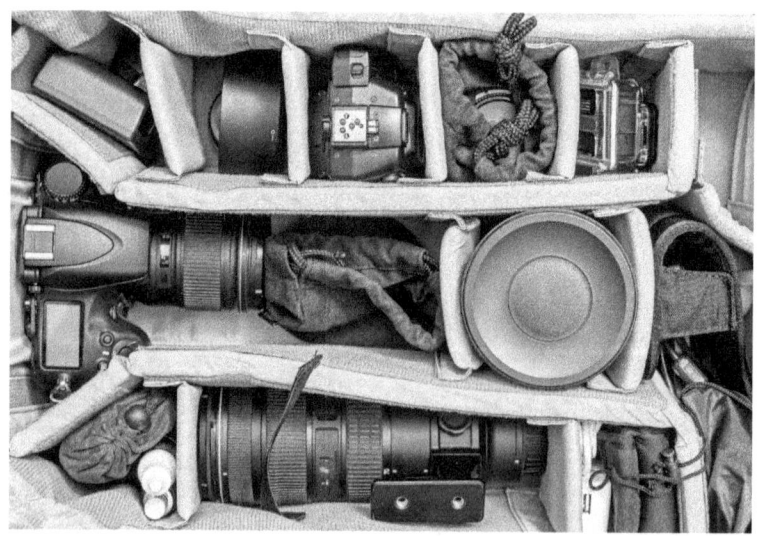

This section may be the most important section of the book. Up until now we have covered digital photography almost in its entirety. Choosing a camera and lenses was the first step. Next came the hard part, learning the science of photography, how the camera works, proper exposure, choosing subject matter, and all of the other knowledge that is required for the final outcome, a picture that says more than words, something that you can be proud of.

You might think that you have achieved everything necessary to take the perfect pictures. You have your camera, your lenses and the ability to use them. Now you must deal with issues that, from a practical point of view, are far more important than just taking pictures.

What are you going to do if there is an equipment malfunction? How are you going to diagnose the problem and make the necessary corrections? Things break, things fail, and these failures, which will eventually happen to everybody in this business, require as much training to deal with as is required to take great pictures.

The chapters in the section will deal with things as simple as remembering to take spare batteries and memory cards with you. Accessories such as choosing the right tripod, the right camera strap, and other things not covered very well in the manual that came with your camera.

Do you have a camera bag? How accommodating is it? Does it have compartments for accessories? What other portable containers exist to protect and transport your equipment? There's advice on where and how to buy and not to buy equipment. But not to worry, these things and more you will learn as you read on.

Contingency plans will come into play and will be explained here. Properly packing your equipment so that it isn't damaged during transport, whether by air, land or sea. Learn to protect your camera from rain and snow, freezing temperatures, heat and humidity. Understand what effects the weather will have on it and how the damage can be prevented.

Don't forget about yourself either. There are safety concerns, be it lifting heavy equipment, or standing or walking across hazardous surfaces. How will seasonal changes affect your equipment? The proper gear is important, all the way down to socks and shoes, insect repellent, sunscreen, first aid, water and food for those photographic expeditions that you are planning. Just using the wrong camera strap can be as bad as wearing the wrong shoes. Your shoulder and neck can get as sore as your feet.

You have to think about theft, either theft of equipment from your car, person or home, or even a temporary home away from home, a hotel. Does your insurance cover theft? What can you do to deter theft? Read on to find the answers.

Let's get started with an assortment of things you might not always think about, but must when going out and taking pictures.

7 ESSENTIAL FEATURES OF YOUR FIRST TRIPOD

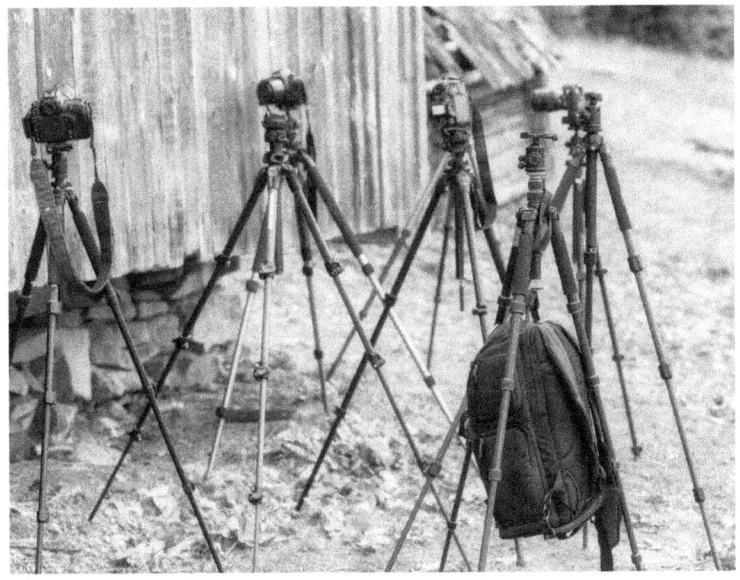

Although you don't need every little accessory to experience and enjoy fully the world of DSLR photography, the first piece of non-camera equipment you should consider buying is a tripod. The biggest reason is a tripod (3 legs, remember?) is more stable than you (just 2 legs). As your skills advance, you'll eventually want to try some types of photography or shots that require a slow to very slow shutter speed, and you'll take good ones with a tripod. As equally as important for many DSLR beginners is the desire to be included in a family photo, and also shoot the picture. By attaching your camera to a tripod and using the camera's timer, you'll have a few seconds to place yourself in a family portrait before the shutter releases.

As with any photography (or other) product, there are many manufacturers of tripods, made with different materials, of different sizes and other variables to take into consideration when choosing your first.

1. Stability capability

The fundamental purpose of a tripod is to provide a stable platform for your camera – and the more stable the better. Of course, the practical element of price must be a factor also. You don't want to buy the lowest-cost tripod, nor do you need the kind of tripod a professional would purchase and buy, costing hundreds of dollars. There are a number of features of a tripod to take into account to determine its stability measured against cost.

- Construction materials – Most of your tripod choices will have aluminum legs, which is a good material for this purpose. It's the thickness of the aluminum legs that is the most important stability factor. Generally, aluminum tripod legs that are thin and lightweight won't provide enough stability; however, thicker aluminum legs will be heavier. This becomes an important consideration if you plan to use your tripod to shoot landscapes, nature, wildlife, sports, etc., which will require that you carry it with you.

If you will be using a tripod to shoot in locations where you must carry it, then you may want to choose a tripod with carbon fiber legs instead of aluminum. When comparing the two, carbon fiber reduces the total weight of the tripod by as much as one-third, and is more rigid. The tradeoff, however, is in price, as a carbon fiber tripod costs significantly more than an equivalent tripod with aluminum legs. It's likely that once you carry an aluminum tripod during a few long hikes, you will realize that you should have spent the extra money for carbon fiber. A less-expensive aluminum tripod will probably not last as long as a good carbon fiber tripod either, which is another reason to spend the extra money for your first tripod.

- Leg sections – The second feature of a tripod that comes into play when deciding which to buy is the leg sections, which are typically either 3 or 4 on most tripods. There is another tradeoff here, too. You'll spend less time locking and unlocking 3 sections, but tripod legs with 4 sections are usually smaller when the legs are totally collapsed. Again, if you plan to walk great distances carrying your tripod or take it with you when traveling and packing it in luggage, then 4-section legs are a better choice.

- Leg locks – You also have 2 choices of leg locks. The first is called quick release, which is typically a small lever that you snap into place to hold the leg's extended length and snap in the opposite direction to release the leg. The other type is a twist mechanism, much like you'd twist a light bulb into a lamp socket. The downsides of the twist type are that they take more time to operate, they are more likely to slip and you can't actually tell if they are locked without testing them. The quick release is your best option; however, keep in mind that the levers protrude from the legs and they cause the tripod to weigh more – another tradeoff.

2. Leg angle versatility

Another feature to check on any tripod you are considering purchasing is how far the legs will splay from 90 degrees to bring the camera to a low level. Some have a limit and others will allow the bottom of the tripod platform almost to touch the ground. A major reason tripod legs are sectioned is so you can set each leg at a different length if you're shooting where you can't set all three legs on a level surface. You want to be sure that the tripod will be just as stable with the legs at different lengths.

3. Load limit

Another important specification of any tripod is the maximum weight it can hold and still remain stable and functional. Make sure you know the weight of your camera and the lens you will use most of the time, and then choose a tripod that has a load limit that is significantly more. You don't want to buy a tripod with a load limit the same as the weight of the gear you plan to attach to it. Conversely, you don't want to spend money on a tripod that is meant to hold the much heavier DSLR camera and large telephoto lens of a professional wildlife or sports photographer since you are unlikely ever to have a camera and lens that will weight that much.

4. The feet factor

The bottom of most tripod legs have a rubber foot, which helps to cushion the tripod as well as not mar any floors if the ends were metal. Some tripod companies offer options, such as spiked feet, so they can be pushed into the ground for added stability. Whenever you're shooting outdoors, there could be enough wind to cause a tripod with rubber legs to move ever so slightly, resulting in blurry images.

5.   The center column

A tripod's center column can be extended to raise the height of your camera. The primary reason is to allow you to look through the viewfinder without having to bend your neck at an odd and tiring angle. You must also be careful because the higher you extend the center column, the less stable the tripod and the easier it could tip with your camera being the first thing that hits the ground. Extending the center column also allows you to shoot over an obstacle or photograph any subject or object from a higher angle for a more interesting photo. Some center columns have a mechanism, so they can be adjusted to become a boom arm. Others can be removed and inserted upside down, so you can position your camera close to the ground. You may also want a tripod with a center column that includes a hook at the bottom, which allows you to hang a weight from it. Again, if you're shooting outdoors and there is a strong wind, the weight will provide additional stability.

6.   Tripod head

Most of the tripods you would choose as your first will come with what is called a pan-and-tilt head. The camera attaches to the flat platform at the top of the tripod. A handle and a set of adjustments allow you to position and lock the camera at various angles or rotate it 360 degrees.

Although it's not possible to present even a sampling of the many tripod manufacturers and their products here, some of the names you may want to research are Vanguard, Manfrotto, Sirui, 3-Legged Thing, Gizmo and Really Right Stuff.

FIRST AID FOR YOUR BROKEN, DAMAGED OR WATERLOGGED CAMERA

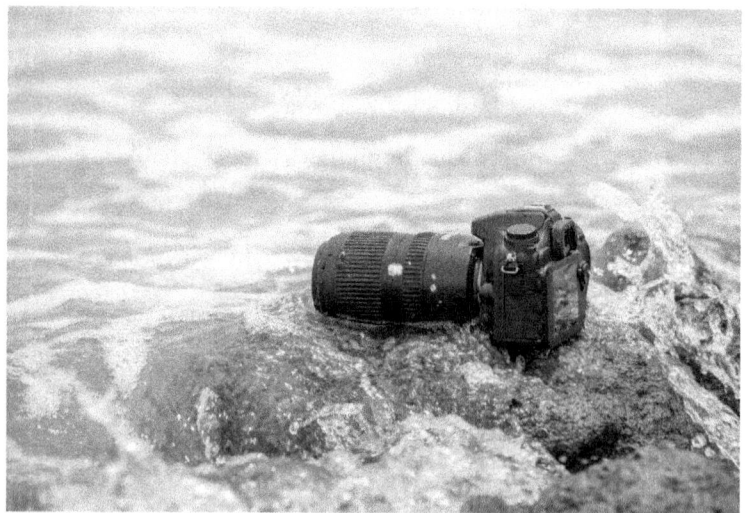

Camera manufacturers know amateur and professional photographers carry their camera with them most of the time, transport them great distances and expose them to the weather, the vagaries of the wild and the nasty, unforgiving world in general. This means most DSLRs are designed and built to withstand a certain amount of rugged use. Many even come with seals throughout the body to help retard moisture from entering the camera, but typically in the form of humidity or dew.

Of course, you bear most of the responsibility for protecting your camera and using it in a manner that doesn't put it in harm's way. These protective measures include a good, wide camera strap and carrying the camera around your neck or diagonally across your body; transporting your camera in a camera bag when not in use; a rain cover for your camera if you're caught in the rain; and camera insurance.

Despite the manufacturers' efforts to build protection into their DSLRs and your best intentions to keep your camera safe from harm, accidents or simple foolishness can happen; so you should know how to administer first aid to your broken, damaged or waterlogged camera.

THE DROP SHOT

Dropping a camera, especially onto a hard surface, is a typical cause of damage. If your camera has broken into pieces, then the damage may be fatal, but severe internal damage can also occur although the camera remains in one piece.

- In this case, first aid begins by examining the inside of the camera to determine if any parts have become loose inside the body. Look for any dents or cracked surfaces.

- Next, examine the lens, for external dents and cracks and the condition of the glass elements. Try to operate the focus ring or zoom mechanism if it is a zoom lens. You may also want to detach it from the camera body to determine if it does so normally and whether the camera and/or lens mounts have been damaged. A broken glass element is usually the worst-case scenario, as that will mean either repairs from the manufacturer's authorized service centers or, sadly, a replacement lens.

- You can also try to turn the camera on if it was off or determine whether it is still on. If you receive no response, then "hospitalization" may be necessary.

- If the camera does seem to turn on correctly and the lens appears to be undamaged or only has a slight dent, then try to operate the camera by taking a few pictures. Check the various auto-functions, such as exposure, focus, white balance as well as the viewfinder, the LCD display, menu, shutter button, built-in flash, etc.

RETRIEVING THE PIECES

If your camera has dropped very hard, then it may be in pieces. You may stare in disbelief for a few moments when you see the debris field, but try to overcome your panic and concentrate on finding all the pieces. There are many tiny parts in a DSLR, so look carefully. If possible, you may want to place major pieces in separate Ziploc bags and any tiny pieces in another bag. This will save any other small pieces that are about to disengage from the body or lens.

DSLRS AND WATER DON'T MIX

Placing your camera on a moist surface after a rain, such as a park bench or a stone wall, is unlikely to cause any damage; however, if that surface has a puddle of water, even less than an inch, or you drop your camera into a body of water, then it could be an immediate goner.

When it's obvious water has entered your camera and/or lens, there are a few first aid steps you can try.

- Remove the camera and/or lens from the water immediately and hold them so any water on the inside can drain off.

- Remove the memory card and batteries first. Dry them both. It's likely any images on the card can be retrieved intact.

- Next, dry the outside of the lens and camera. Detach the lens from the camera and inspect the inside of the camera to make sure no parts have come loose. Don't try to dry the inside of the camera or lens yourself since there are too many delicate parts. You can try to use a hairdryer at a warm-temperature setting, but be gentle. If possible, place the camera or lens in a container with silica bags for a few days to absorb any remaining moisture.

- These first-aid applications may help the recovery, but DSLRs typically suffer from major internal damage when immersed in water, so don't count on any of these techniques to revive your camera. If you drop it in water, then you will have to send it to the manufacturer's authorized dealer for a professional inspection and possible repair; however, the technician is more apt to confirm that your camera is dead.

AFTER THE FALL OR DUNK

You're typically facing one of two scenarios: either your camera and/or lens can be repaired or they're goners and you must buy replacements. If you must have a camera for a planned vacation or a schedule assignment, then you can rent a camera at affordable rates while yours is being repaired. Even if the technician hasn't told you your camera can't be repaired, then it's probably a good idea to consider it non-repairable and start to think how you can replace it. If buying a new camera is not financially feasible, then you may want to buy a reconditioned model at a lower cost until you can afford a new DSLR again. Regardless of the final verdict, what's left of your camera can be sold as usable parts to a local camera repair shop; or you can offer it online as a source of parts. You can recoup some of your loss and apply it to a new or used camera.

The potential damage to your camera and lens, either by dropping it or immersing it in water, is a good reason you should be fully aware of the warranty details when you buy your camera and any lens. Typically, warranties consider accidents as human error and, therefore, do not cover the cost of repairs or replacement parts. If you have insurance coverage, specifically for your camera, lens and other photography gear, then, again, know the details when you buy the insurance. Ask the agent to explain if the coverage covers accidents, such as described here. You may find the deductible, however, is more than the cost of repairs or even to replace your camera.

HOW TO CHOOSE A CAMERA BAG FOR
YOUR TYPE OF PHOTOGRAPHY

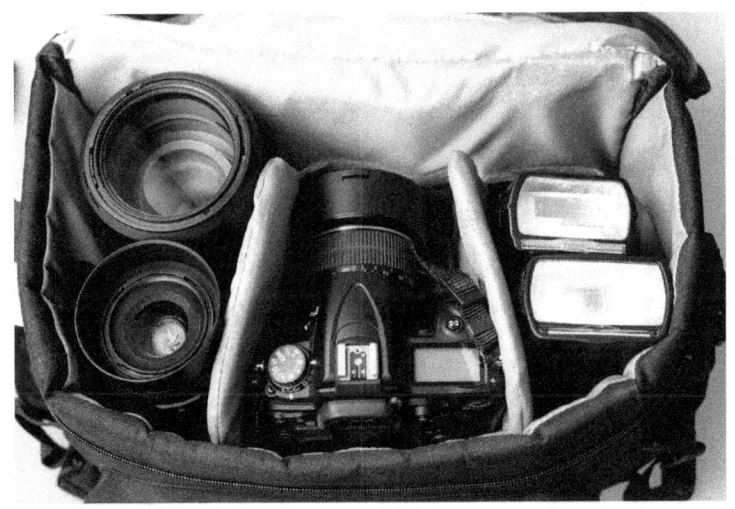

What piece of photography gear should you buy after a camera and lens? Some would argue a tripod, a flash or a set of filters; but before you acquire all of these, plus additional lenses and other paraphernalia, the priority is typical a camera bag. Although there are many features to consider when choosing a camera bag, two are probably the most important:

Matching the bag to your type of photography

Choosing a slightly bigger bag to accommodate future gear purchases

There are 6 basic categories of camera bags, although there are also a number of variations and a few niche bag categories too. The examples are from manufacturers known for their quality construction, products with years of use in the real world of photography and well respected and even endorsed by many professionals. These brands and products are a good start when shopping for a bag, but there are many others that deserve your consideration.

1. Shoulder Bag

As its name implies, the shoulder bag is a general-purpose camera bag that may be the best choice if you're a new DSLR photographer. These are typically well-padded bags with a wide, comfortable shoulder strap and will hold a DSLR with a smaller zoom attached, such as a 24–70mm, 1 to 2 other lenses and even a flash unit. Most will have an interior pocket or two for small items, such as batteries and memory cards, and maybe an exterior pocket for a cellphone or with enough space for a folded rain cover or raincoat. The better shoulder bags are good choices for event and wedding photographers.

The Naneu Correspondent Series of shoulder bags comes in various sizes from extra small to large. This series of bags is also designed for the MOLLE system, or Modular Lightweight Load-Carrying Equipment, so you can attach two or more Correspondent bags together as you add more equipment.

2. Messenger Bag

The messenger bag is also carried on the shoulder, but many are designed to look less like a camera bag and more like a standard bag you might see anyone carrying to work. This is meant to make this type of bag less conspicuous to thieves, plus the flap completely covers the top and the front of the bag, so no one can easily access the interior. This kind of bags is often called an urban bag because they are ideal for street and travel photography.

The Lowpro Event Messenger 250 is a good example, as it is also designed with a well-padded pocket for a tablet or laptop as large as 13 inches. The dividers in the main compartment can be adjusted for your specific set of gear. The Event Messenger 250 has room for 3 to 4 lenses, with one as large as 70–200mm f/2.8, or a combination of a flash and 3 lenses.

3. The Backpack

A backpack-type camera bag is your best choice if your photographic passions are landscapes, wildlife and nature – whenever and wherever you must hike into the backcountry to find the best visions of the natural world. Obviously, backpacks are manufactured with tough, durable materials that can withstand most any weather conditions and they include enough room for all your photography gear as well as personal gear. They are also designed with the most comfortable strap systems since you will likely be carrying it for hours and days.

Photobackpacker is very serious about the comfort of this type of bag, as it studied and conferred with alpine hikers and mountain climbers to create the RPT P3 Camera Backpack with what is known as a technical suspension system. This makes the backpack seem lighter than it is, even when fully loaded. Plus, Photobackpacker provides you with a custom fit by configuring 8 different belts, 3 different shoulder straps and 2 different torso frame sheets. Photobackpacker even offers backpacks for medium-format and large-format cameras.

4.   Travel Camera Bag

You can certainly travel with most every kind of camera bag, but some are designed specifically for the photographer, especially professionals, who are always traveling. The best of these bags satisfy the regulations for carry-on luggage and fit into an airplane's overhead compartment. They also have a wheel-and-trolley system, so they're easy to roll through an airport or on most hard surfaces during a long day of shooting.

An excellent example of the travel camera bag is the Vanguard Xcenior 62T. This full-size bag has plenty of customizable space for 2 to 3 full-frame DSLRs with grips and 7 to 11 lenses, flash units, all the necessary accessories and a laptop as large as 17 inches. Plus, you can attach a tripod to the front or side of the Xcenior 62T. This Vanguard bag and most of its type are also designed with added security features, such as locks and heavy-duty zippers.

5.   The Hard Case

For the ultimate protection of precious photography gear, there is no substitute for a hard case. Many are injected molded, using advanced plastics of military grade, waterproof, even submersible, and withstand a considerably amount of impact and rough handling without damaging any of your gear. They also have highly secure latching systems.

SKB has a long history of manufacturing hard cases for professional musicians for their instruments and audio equipment. The company has applied its experience and knowledge to create the iSeries of hard cases for photographers. The interior of the 1914 Pro DSLR Case is filled with high quality PE foam that has sculpted compartments for 2 DSLR cameras, four lens slots and additional space for a flash and all the accessories.

6.   Harness and Holster

Harness and holster products are not camera bags with the capacity for cameras, lenses and accessories. Their primary benefits are allowing you to carry your camera in a comfortable position and being able to grab it quickly and bring it to your eye. Instead of carrying your camera on a strap over a shoulder or around your neck, a harness or holster system makes it easy to carry your camera for hours with little or no fatigue. Plus, both of your hands are free for other tasks.

The Cotton Carrier Camera Vest comes in two variations, one for a single camera and the Vest System 2 that has the flexibility to carry a second camera. The Spider Holster is a belt and quick-release, but totally secure, system, so your camera can hang on your hip. Because many of its parts are interchangeable, the Spider Holster belt can accommodate a second camera on your other hip.

WHY YOU NEED CAMERA INSURANCE

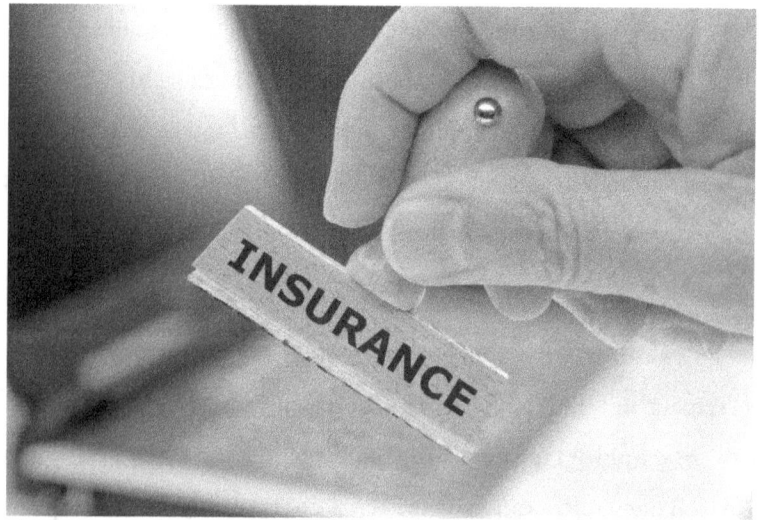

If you're spending hundreds, or even thousands, on a new DSLR or mirrorless interchangeable lens camera and anticipate buying additional lenses and other gear, then you definitely need camera insurance. Here are some of the major reasons it should be your second purchase after a camera – and researched and shopped before you buy.

1. **Can you afford to replace any equipment that is stolen or damaged?**

Many photographers save for a long time to afford a new DSLR or lens and you don't have to buy much of a tripod, flash unit, camera bag, filter kit and other accessories before these total additional hundreds of dollars. A policy may have a deductible like any insurance, but that is a much softer hit on your wallet than having to replace everything.

2. **Thieves would love to steal your camera.**

According to Lenstag, which makes anti-theft devices, these are the 11 places where your camera is likely to be stolen, and listed from most likely to least likely.

Place	Percent
Automobile	27%
Burglary	24%
Public transportation	9%
Robbery	9%
Lost	7%
Event	7%
Airport/Airplane	5%
Bar/Restaurant	5%
Package theft	3%
Hotel	3%
eBay/PayPal Fraud	1%

With the automobile and home are the top 2 places where your equipment is likely to be stolen and they probably spend the most time in these 2 locations, camera insurance is essential.

3. **"Doesn't my homeowner's policy cover my camera equipment, as it does all my other personal property?"**

It might, but often it doesn't. The best plan is to check with your insurance agent before you buy the first expensive photography item, most likely a DSLR camera. A good option to consider is an all-risk floater that is added to your homeowner or renter's policy. For all-risk insurance, you'll have to provide your agent with a list that specifies what equipment is covered and its market value/replacement cost. This is the value of your equipment today, as used, so any claim payment you receive won't be enough to replace used equipment with new. You should seriously consider an all-risk floater if you have equipment valued in the thousands of dollars; however, it's important to remember that an all-risk floater won't cover your equipment if you start to use it to generate income. That classifies you as a professional with the insurance industry, which requires a different kind of policy.

4. **Know your responsibilities before renting equipment.**

The standard homeowner's policy usually doesn't cover any equipment you rent. You may need the all-risk floater for rented equipment, but, again, it's best to check with your agent. Photo equipment rental companies may offer optional coverage similar to an auto rental. Either way, make sure you ask the rental company before finalizing your transaction.

5.   Earn any money with your camera and the ball game changes.

It's not unusual for amateurs with a DSLR to be offered and paid for occasional photo assignments, such as baby portraits, pets, an event for an employer, at your kids' school, business headshots, etc. This is also how many amateurs evolve into full-time professionals and quit their day jobs. Before accepting any paying gig and certainly before shooting any photos, check with your insurance agent because there are other types of policies you may need.

- Equipment insurance now takes the form of what is called a commercial inland marine policy. Your equipment will be fully covered for theft, damage and all other situations when you're using it professionally.

- Protect you, your home and other personal assets with liability insurance. Even if you're only being paid $100 to photograph a neighbor or friend's baby in his or her home, then you must absolutely have General or Business Liability insurance. If you damaged the home or any of your neighbor or friend's furniture or other possessions or if the baby was injured during the shoot, you could be liable for an enormous judgment in court and lose most everything of value. The same circumstances apply if you're shooting for your boss in the building where the business is located or a church, reception hall or similar venues. In fact, many times you must prove you have Business Liability insurance before you're allowed to shoot in these locations.

- Another type of liability insurance your agent may strongly recommend is Errors & Omissions. Let's say someone is paying you to shoot some photos that can only be shot once, but then the memory cards are damaged or lost and all the photos with them. If the other party can prove that it had a dollar loss because of your negligence, even if it was an accident and not intentional, then, again, you could be liable for reimbursing he or she for that loss. Errors & Omissions will protect you from such an incident.

Rent commercial space as a studio, even permanent or temporary, or decide to use part of your home or a separate structure, such as a garage, for a studio and you'll have to address some other insurance considerations. You're almost guaranteed that you won't be able to rent any commercial space from any property owner without a Proof-of-Insurance certificate for business liability, equipment and maybe even additional fire coverage. A standard homeowner or renter's policy won't cover the use of your home or other property as a business location. Again, before you take this step, you'll want to have an in-depth discussion with your insurance agent, describing your photography business plans, exactly what kind of photography will be generating income, where you will be shooting it and how much your vehicle will be used. You must also prepare a complete list of equipment with values and make sure to update it whenever you acquire new items.

Do your research and shopping, as the insurance company that covers your home or apartment and your car may not offer specific policies for camera equipment, either for amateur or professional use. You can also look for insurance companies that specialize in policies for photography equipment and businesses.

THE WHYS AND WHEREFORES OF ENTERING, AND EVEN WINNING, A PHOTO CONTEST

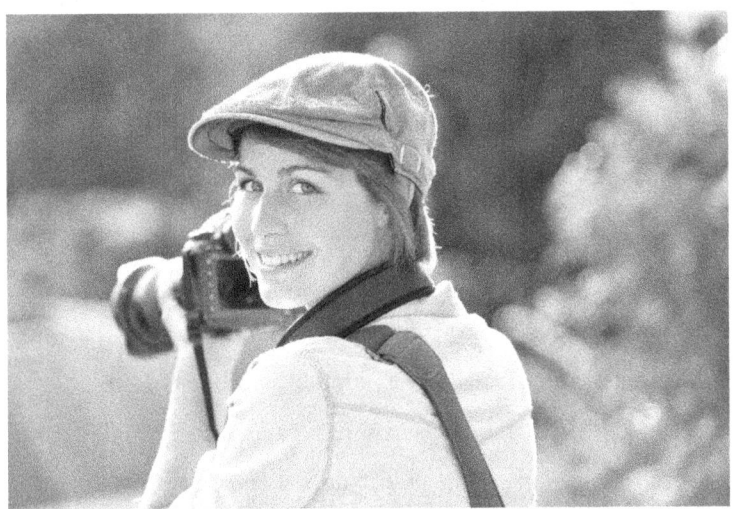

Although a photo contest may award cash prizes and being a winner would likely boost your ego, the best reason for entering is to discover more about the kind of person and photographer you are. Do you have the patience, perseverance and organizational skills to work towards a goal? Can you be ambitious without being arrogant? Are you learning photographic skills and, more importantly, consciously applying them? Are you able to learn from defeat or victory?

From a purely photographic perspective, entering a photo contest is an opportunity to take on the challenge of an assignment and see how your work compares to the other contestants. If you truly want to become a better photographer, then you can't be afraid to have your photos judged, and even rejected. With all due respect to your mother, other family members and friends, they are not the best judges of the quality of your images. Putting your work in the hands of strangers, albeit experienced professional photographers and/or photo editors, will provide you with much better feedback about what you do well and don't do well with a camera.

Follow these pointers about entering photo contests: They won't guarantee that you'll win, but they will likely put you in a better position to be noticed by the judges.

1.   Enter Today!

There are photo contests you can enter today, tomorrow, next week for every skill level and for virtually every kind of photographic genre: portraits, landscapes, babies, pets, flowers, animals, architecture and maybe even decorative doorknobs. Surf the Web and do your research. Contact your local photography club, museums of arts and similar organizations that may host/sponsor photo contests. The point is there is no reason to wait until you have a better camera or more education or experience.

2.   Follow the Rules

You may (or may not) be surprised how many photographers' entries don't quality for photo contests simply because they couldn't follow the rules. If they state you must submit 8 x 10 prints, then don't send another size. If each entry must include your full name, address, phone number and email address, then double-check that you've done so before sending your entries. You may still be one of hundreds or thousands of entries, but many judges take notice of those that were able to follow the rules.

3.   Be the First Judge…and the Most Brutal

Ultimately, the best judge of your work is you. You're more likely to increase your odds of winning if you're brutally honest with yourself about the images you are considering for entry. Much like an athlete, the only person against whom you are competing is you. In fact, if entering a photo contest gives you an opportunity to be better today than you were yesterday, (in other words, beating yourself), then you may have won much more than whatever the contest prize is worth.

- Look for the obvious flaws in your images, such as poor exposure, non-parallel lines, disregarding the rules of thirds or not using depth of field properly.

- Next, study your photos to determine how you shot them. Are you always shooting from a standing position? Are all your shots during the brightest time of the day and none during the magic hours of sunrise and sunset? Did you try to control or manipulate the light source or add lighting or did you just rely on the available light and hoped for the best?

- Make sure each of the photos you are thinking of submitting to a contest tell a story. Judges look for and are more attracted to the story of a photograph as well as how you composed the image to tell the story. Because judges must review so many entries, they don't spend much time on each, especially during the first pass, so your message must be bold and obvious.

4.   Plan a Shoot

The photos you submit to a contest don't have to be any that are already in your portfolio, although you should certainly do a thorough search to determine if any are worthy of submission. You may already enjoy taking pictures of pets or babies or flowers, so you should certainly look for contests that match your photographic interests. A more challenging approach is to enter photos of a genre that you've never photographed, so you are required to plan a photo shoot in terms of location, time of day, props, lighting, etc.; the kind and composition of the images you'll shoot; the right equipment you'll need; and even a vision of how you'll edit those images as you compose and shoot them.

5.   Don't Over Create.

Many elements in a photo reveal the creative thinking of the photographer, but usually the creativity that catches the eye of a photo contest judge is simple, natural and not contrived. Trying to be too creative can be one of the biggest mistakes you can make when entering a photo contest. Avoid composing your contest images based on a current photographic trend or fad that you discovered while researching on the Web. Don't even think that you are somehow more creative because you've transformed color images into black and white or one object in the image remains in color. P-l-e-a-s-e! If you want to submit black-and-white photos, and they're allowed, then compose and shoot images in black and white because the scene or subject is somehow rendered better without color or the story of the photo is more dramatically conveyed in black and white.

350

6. Ultimately, It's Subjective.

You may not know the names of the judges; and even if their names are listed in the contest announcement and you research them on the Internet, you'd be making a mistake to try to outthink them, based on what you've discovered about them. Regardless of the judges' professionalism and experience, they are human and will approach the contest subjectively, with prejudices and pre-conceived notions about what makes a good and winning photo. One set of judges could select your image as a finalist and another set not give it a second glance. Don't stop entering contests just because an image you thought was good was quickly rejected. Enter it in other contests and think about how you could shoot it again and make it better.

11 MISTAKES TO AVOID WHEN PURCHASING USED EQUIPMENT ONLINE

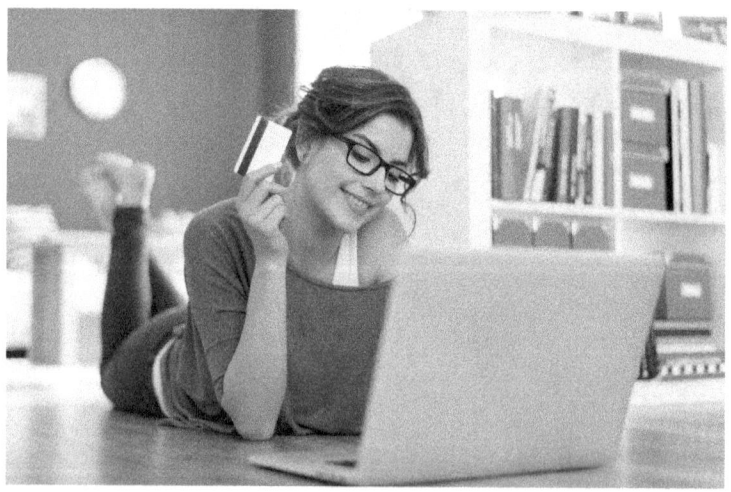

Your first reaction may be, "Why would I want to buy any used photography gear online? It doesn't seem like a wise move. I'm more likely to be scammed." Yes, that is a real possibility, but the benefits typically outweigh the problems if you are careful. The purpose here is to show you how to avoid making a bad purchase; but let's start with why it might be a good decision.

- For whatever reason, you simply may not be able to afford a new camera, lens, etc. You're a student or specifically a photography student. You may not be sure if you'll like photography, as a hobby, or a lifelong interest, so buying used equipment will help to determine your level of interest without draining your bank account.

- As you've advanced from the beginner to intermediate level, you've discovered some specific photography genres that truly stir your passions, such as macrophotography, astrophotography, etc. You want to explore these new genres, but without making a major commitment of money for a new lens or other necessary equipment.

- Maybe, you've been shooting with a digital camera for many years. Your older model still works just fine and produces quality images; however, the manufacturer has discontinued a lens or other piece of equipment that you need or would like to acquire.

- The photography bug may have bitten you so hard that you'd like to see what you could do with a film camera and learn classic darkroom techniques.

- As a longtime photographer, you have quite a collection of old, vintage cameras that you proudly display at home – and you're always on the hunt for a rare model that someone may find when cleaning the garage or attic.

ONLINE BUYING STEPS

1. Ask the seller when and from whom he or she bought the piece of equipment. Don't hesitate to ask for a copy of the receipt.

2. Ask him or her to describe in as much detail as possible how the gear has been used, i.e., by a part-time hobbyist, a serious amateur or a semi-professional or professional photographer. For example, the shutter

system on most cameras has a limited lifetime and a professional's camera may have reached that limit, compared to a hobbyist's camera.

3. Whether the seller has used the piece of equipment recently or it's been sitting in a closet, ask him or her to put the equipment through its paces: Look inside the camera body for any loose connections and inside the lens with a strong light to be sure there are no cracked glass elements.

4. What kind of photography has been shot with the equipment? A camera or lens from a part-timer may have been barely used while equipment from a professional may have had heavy use and plenty of exposure to the elements, especially if he or she has been shooting landscapes, nature, wildlife, sports and other outdoors subject matter. Not only ask that he or she fires a flash unit, but also determine if it is taking a full charge and recharges as quickly as the specifications state.

5. Then, ask the seller to take a series of photos with the camera or lens inside and outside, under different lighting conditions, at various exposures and of a variety of subjects. Request that he or she send you the photo files, unedited, for your inspection.

6. Obviously, buying online is not like shopping at a used camera shop where you can put your hands on the equipment, so request the seller take a comprehensive set of photos of the piece for sale. You want to see photos of the entire camera, lens, etc. as well as close-ups of the exterior and interior, so you can inspect it carefully. If the seller hasn't previously volunteered information about scratches, dents and any parts being replaced, but they are evident in the photos, then you may not want to buy from this person.

7. Request the equipment's serial number, which is typically found in the EXIF (Exchangeable Image File Format) data embedded in each photo. Then, use an online service, such as Stolen Camera Finder, to determine the validity of the seller's ownership.

8. If you're planning to buy a piece of used photo gear that you've never used and/or with which you are not familiar, then download the manual and look for photos online to familiarize yourself with its configuration. You can't truthfully know if a piece of equipment is what the seller says it is without knowing in advance what it should look like. This step will help you identify any non-OEM replacement or jerry-rigged parts you may see in the seller's photos.

9. If you've spotted a listing on Craigslist for used photo equipment, then you may have the opportunity to travel to the seller's location and actually inspect the gear. It may be a bit of a hassle, but it's worth the effort to know you are buying accurately represented equipment. You want to ask the seller the same set of questions above and take the time to shoot a variety of images with a camera or lens and use other equipment. Make sure the seller knows that you will be taking these steps before you arrange a meeting. If he or she is reluctant about allowing you to inspect it in person and shoot images with it, then it's very likely a situation to avoid.

10. As soon as you acquire a new piece of used equipment, contact your insurance agent/company to add it to the list of equipment the policy covers. This is an absolute must for collectors.

11. Finally, if you're still unsure about buying used photo equipment from private parties or used equipment at all, then look for reputable used

photo equipment companies online, such as KEH, Adorama, etc. There are also many others. Most of them have a rating system, so you know the relative condition of the equipment. Some have used equipment they acquire refurbished by the manufacturer or by their experienced service technicians. All of them provide some kind of warranty and return policy to protect you and your purchase. In addition, they will usually buy back the gear you bought from them.

WHY AND HOW TO CREATE A PHOTOGRAPHY PORTFOLIO TODAY

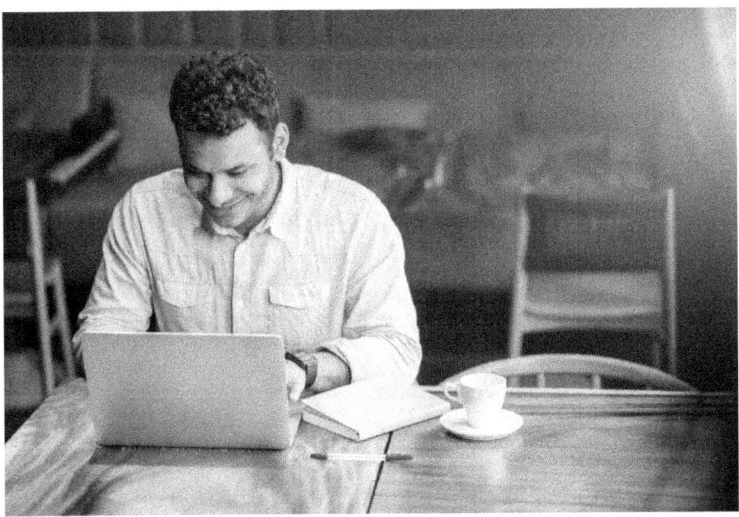

Becoming a semi-professional or full-time professional photographer may not be a goal of your photography experience. There are innumerable stories, however, of people who had successful careers in other fields and became so passionate about photography as a beginner that they chucked it all to pursue their passion and found themselves earning a living as a photographer.

Family members, friends or neighbors may ask a hobbyist they know to photograph their baby, pet or family, revealing to the photographer that he or she has a unique ability to take these kinds of images. The photographer's reputation spreads and, within a year, he or she is inundated with similar requests. Someone sees a landscape or nature image you've shot and wants it for a calendar. An editor of a magazine or Website sees the image and wants to buy more like it. Suddenly, you need a portfolio to present to open a whole new world of photographic opportunities – and for money.

Even if you're perfectly satisfied with being a weekend, travel and/or vacation photographer, then creating a portfolio is an excellent method to help you recognize your best work and to share your images with others, either friends or other photographers, to obtain meaningful critiques.

You may be planning a career in photography, or already a student. The photography school probably includes creating a portfolio as part of the curriculum, but if you're seeking admittance at a photography school, then a portfolio may be required as part of the process or creating one voluntarily could make a strong impression and show your eagerness to learn.

Whatever the reason, learning how to create a portfolio should be part of your early development as a photographer.

FOR THE AMATEUR

For amateur photographers – be they beginners, hobbyists, enthusiasts or serious amateurs – the best kind of portfolio is typical digital, on a Website that is accessible from a tablet or a smartphone, and even in a mobile-friendly version. You can, of course, build your own Website, but there are many companies, such as Zenfolio, SmugMug and Squarespace, that specialize in online photo portfolios, providing easy-to-use templates and hosting services, if you don't want to manage your own. You can also create slideshows and galleries of your photos with the online tools of Photodex, Roxio, Slidely and others. Ubookoo and Sticky Albums will help you create a mobile marketing Website for quick, clean viewing of your photos on a smartphone.

You might also consider having photo books printed, each displaying a specific photography genre: portraits, landscapes, etc. Good resources are Viovio and Nations Photo Lab, among others.

PORTFOLIO TIPS

1. Be honest – be brutal.

The hardest part of choosing images to include in a portfolio is being as objective as possible. Even as an amateur, you want to follow a fundamental rule of portfolios: less is more. It's better to show everyone your 5 very best images instead of them and various lesser images that will only dilute the power of your portfolio.

2. Constructive critiques and careful comparisons

Undoubtedly, you THINK you know which photos are your very best, but are they? Some may exhibit excellent composition or the use of color or a nice balance of contrast, but if the focus is not absolutely sharp, it shouldn't be used. Probably, the best process is to choose your best 20 images, and then ask others to review them and provide critiques. Here is another excellent reason to be a member of the local photography club, even if you're a novice. Its members, especially those with considerable experience, will be happy to help and give your constructive criticism. You may learn a few tips and techniques that make it worthwhile to reshoot a photo to transform it from very good to WOW. With all this feedback, you'll have solid reasoning for determining the 5 truly best of those 20 for your portfolio.

It can also be helpful to compare these initial 20 to similar photos on the best professionals' Websites. Study his or hers and yours carefully and ask yourself honest questions about what makes his or her landscape of a mountain lake, for example, better than yours. Even if your images have only a few of the outstanding elements or techniques of the pros, then they are probably excellent choices for a portfolio.

3. Narrowly focus the subject matter

It's particularly important if you aspire to be hired for a photography assignment that your portfolio specializes in a narrowly focused genre or type. There are so many photographers competing in the commercial photography world that you want your portfolio to say, "I am the specialist of macro images of butterflies" or reflect your long-term study of a less-photographed desert, mountain or river.

This kind of narrow focus can be equally helpful to the beginner and hobbyist who are committed to becoming a better photographer. You have the freedom to try many kinds of photography genre and find the one that excites you the most and will drive you to excel at that genre despite the weather, the location or the time required.

4. The portfolio story

Generally, the first image of a portfolio should be your very best, so anyone viewing it is hungry to see more. The last photo should also be a big winner because people tend to remember the last image they saw. Again, this is particular important for the professional or aspiring professional.

If possible, pick 2 or 3 images that when viewed in succession or on facing pages tell a story. You can also create surprise, which will maximize the remembrance of your portfolio, by presenting 3 images on succeeding pages. The first causes the viewer to anticipate what the next image may be. The second fulfills that expectation, so the viewer is even surer about the third image. It, however, doesn't follow the "logical" pattern the viewer's brain expects, thus shocking the viewer and leaving him or her with a feeling of wonder. If you can create this kind of reaction, then you know your portfolio is excellent.

DON'T LEAVE THE COUNTRY WITH YOUR DSLR CAMERA WITHOUT PROTECTING IT FIRST

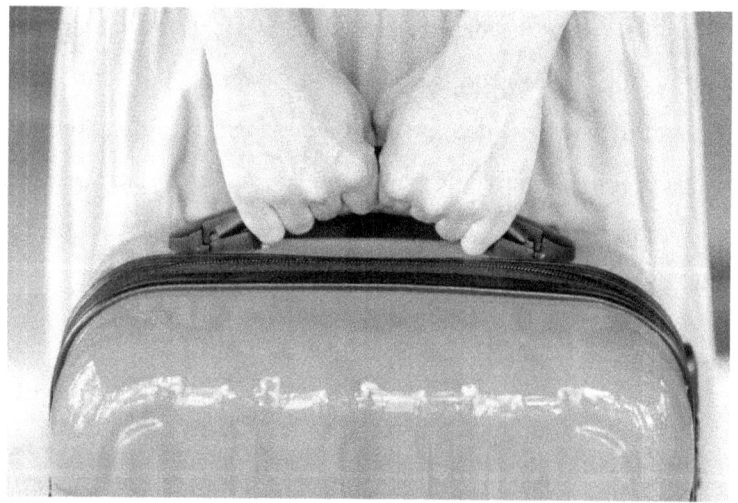

Taking your DSLR camera with you when traveling may seem like a no-brainer – and it is – but there are some practical and important steps you must take before you leave to protect your camera, especially during international travel.

1. Don't step over the line.

Previously we emphasized the importance of understanding as much as possible about your destination in advance, so you have an idea of what you want to photograph and the best times of the day to avoid crowds and for the best lighting conditions. Make sure part of your research includes government regulations of where and what you are not allowed to photograph as well as cultural prohibitions about photographing children, women, etc. You may think that you've made an honest or innocent mistake, but the local authorities may not agree, and you could be arrested, your camera confiscated and/or be fined.

2.   Maybe you should leave your camera at home.

You may find it wise to consider renting a camera and whatever other equipment, so your camera won't be vulnerable to damage or theft. During your destination research, look for reputable companies in the countries where you're traveling that rent photography equipment. As mentioned in the travel photography section, some of the better equipment rental companies in the United States will ship the equipment to your hotel. It won't take space in your luggage and the rental company will insure the equipment (although they might charge a small fee for use outside the US).

3.   Tag it.

Your camera and EVERY piece of gear that you are taking with you should be clearly identified with your name and contact information, such as a phone number and/or email address. Remember, lenses, lens hoods and filters are separate pieces as well as cables, battery chargers, memory cards, etc. Check with your local police department, as many have an identification program that engraves this information into the body of your camera or lens, so it is easier to identify and retrieve in case of theft.

Another identification tactic is to attach a piece of glaringly colored tape to all the pieces of equipment, so it's obvious they are part of the same group.

4. Create a list.

There are a number of good reasons for also creating a list of all the equipment that you will be taking. The first reason is so you can provide a copy to your insurance agent. We will explain why you must have insurance for your DSLR camera – and specifically camera insurance – but your agent may tell you that your homeowner's policy doesn't cover a more expensive camera, such as a DSLR, or when you take it outside the US. He or she may be able to provide a rider to your existing policy for your travel plans and this is another reason to consider renting equipment.

5. Bag it.

As mentioned previously, it's best to pack your camera and accompanying equipment in a separate bag that airlines' regulations allow you to take on board as carry-on luggage. Although camera bags are obviously designed for this purpose, you may want to choose a bag that looks less like a camera bag, so thieves can't easily notice it. Make sure you attach a tag to the outside of the bag with your name and contact information and also include some kind of identification inside the bag too. Wrap a piece or two of the same colored tape you used to identify the various pieces of equipment around the handle or grip of the bag.

6. US Customs is your ally.

Cameras and other photographic equipment are often purchased overseas in duty-free zones or because the prices are lower in some companies. To prove that the camera and equipment you are bringing back from your travels is the same you took when you left, you'll want to register your equipment with US Customs.

Since citizens from the US and other countries need a passport to travel internationally, it is critical that part of your travel planning is becoming thoroughly familiar with the regulations of your country as well as the country or countries you are visiting.

In the US, you will need US Customs form 4577, and one for each piece of equipment, completed and submitted to US Customs. You'll find that this process will require some time, so do it well in advance. Carnet may be a better option, which many professional photographers use. It is a single form for all of your equipment and more than 75 countries, the US included, consider it a legal document that establishes your ownership of the equipment in your possession.

7. Travel securely.

During your travels, follow some common sense tips to protect your camera and equipment.

- Keep your camera in your bag until you're ready to shoot with it.
- When carrying your camera bag or camera, never place the strap just on your shoulder; it's too easily stolen. Always place it over your head and on the opposite shoulder, so the strap is across your body.

- When you prepare and pack your camera, consider buying a thicker strap than the one that came with your camera. Look for one with strong camera-attachment points, so a thief can't grab the camera body and rip it from the strap.

- If you don't plan to carry your camera with you on certain days, visiting specific locations or eating at restaurants, then NEVER leave it in your room. Check with your hotel in advance that it has a safe or other secure, locked facility where you can leave your camera.

Although thoroughly protecting your camera and other photography equipment for international travel and destinations can be a bit time-consuming, it's worth it and will make your travel more pleasurable, less of a hassle and maximize the opportunity to bring home the best photos.

www.ingramcontent.com/pod-product-compliance
Lightning Source LLC
Chambersburg PA
CBHW072011230526
45468CB00021B/1189